ADDISON WESLEY

Math
Makes Sense

4

Author Team

Peggy Morrow

Bryn Keyes

Steve Thomas

Angela D'Alessandro

Don Jones

Linden Gray

Trevor Brown

Ralph Connelly

Jason Johnston

Jeananne Thomas

Maggie Martin Connell

Michael Davis

Sharon Jeroski

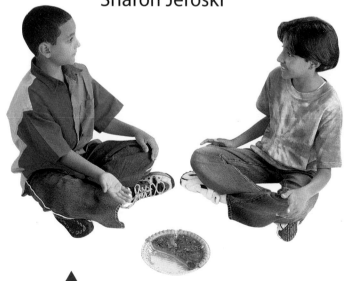

PEARSON
Addison
Wesley

Publishing Team
Lesley Haynes
Enid Haley
Mei Lin Cheung
Lynne Gulliver
Ingrid D'Silva
Susan Lishman
Kirsten Vanstone
Kathleen ffolliott
Stephanie Cox
Denise Wake
Judy Wilson

Publisher
Claire Burnett

Product Manager
Anne-Marie Scullion

Photo Research
Karen Hunter

Design
Word & Image Design Studio Inc.

ISBN 0-321-11819-7

This book contains recycled product and
is acid free.

Printed and bound in Canada.

4 5 6 -- TCP -- 07 06 05 04

The information and activities presented in this
book have been carefully edited and reviewed.
However, the publisher shall not be liable for any
damages resulting, in whole or in part, from the
reader's use of this material.

Brand names that appear in photographs of
products in this textbook are intended to provide
students with a sense of the real-world applications
of mathematics and are in no way intended to
endorse specific products.

The publisher has taken every care to meet or
exceed industry specifications for the
manufacturing of textbooks. The spine and the
endpapers of this sewn book have been reinforced
with special fabric for extra binding strength. The
cover is a premium, polymer-reinforced material
designed to provide long life and withstand rugged
use. Mylar gloss lamination has been applied for
further durability.

PEARSON

Addison
Wesley

Program Consultants and Advisers

Program Consultants

Craig Featherstone
Maggie Martin Connell
Trevor Brown

Assessment Consultant
Sharon Jeroski

Elementary Mathematics Adviser
John A. Van de Walle

Program Advisers

Pearson Education thanks its Program Advisers, who helped shape the vision for *Addison Wesley Mathematics Makes Sense* through discussions and reviews of prototype materials and manuscript.

Anthony Azzopardi	Peggy Hill
Sandra Ball	Auriana Kowalchuk
Bob Belcher	Gordon Li
Judy Blake	Werner Liedtke
Steve Cairns	Jodi Mackie
Daryl Chichak	Lois Marchand
Lynda Colgan	Cathy Molinski
Marg Craig	Bill Nimigon
Ruth Dawson	Eileen Phillips
Jennifer Gardner	Evelyn Sawicki
Lorelei Gibeau	Leyton Schnellert
Florence Glanfield	Shannon Sharp
Pamela Hagen	Martha Stewart
Dennis Hamaguchi	Lynn Strangway
Angie Harding	Mignonne Wood

Program Reviewers

Field Testers

Pearson Education would like to thank the teachers and students who field-tested *Addison Wesley Math Makes Sense 4* prior to publication. Their feedback and constructive recommendations have been most valuable in helping us to develop a quality mathematics program.

Aboriginal Content Reviewers

Early Childhood and School Services Division,
Department of Education, Culture, and Employment
Government of Northwest Territories:

Steven Daniel, Coordinator, Mathematics, Science, and Secondary Education
Liz Fowler, Coordinator, Culture Based Education
Margaret Erasmus, Coordinator, Aboriginal Languages

Grade 4 Reviewers

Holly Barabash
Estevan Rural School Division 62,
SK

Brent Carbery
School District 63 (Saanich), BC

Michelle H. Chizick
Toronto District School Board, ON

Gwyneth Davidson
Ottawa-Carleton District School
Board, ON

Catherine Dudley
Limestone District School Board,
ON

Linda Edwards
Toronto District School Board, ON

Cheryl Felgate
Estevan Rural School Division 62,
SK

Jamie Fraser
Kanata, ON

Wendy Gallant
Algonquin and Lakeshore Catholic
District School Board, ON

Mary Gervais
Durham Catholic District School
Board, ON

Gloria Gustafson
School District 43
(Coquitlam), BC

Deb Kirkland
Lambton-Kent District School
Board, ON

Georgia Koniditsiotis-Chatzis
Peel District School Board, ON

Chester Makischuk
York Catholic District School
Board, ON

Elvira Masur
Thames Valley District School
Board, ON

Richard McKinnon
Halifax, NS

Denise Milne
School District 91 (Nechako
Lakes), BC

Barbara Nicolson
York Region District School Board,
ON

Peter O'Donnell
London Catholic District School
Board, ON

Terry Pavely
Swift Current School Division 94,
SK

Susan Perry
Durham Catholic District School
Board, ON

Leta Potter
Toronto, ON

Peter Rasmussen
Lakehead Public Schools, ON

Nancy Reid
School District 57 (Prince George),
BC

Shelley Ridgeway
Toronto District School Board, ON

Barb Scott
St. Albert School District No. 6, AB

Deb Scott
St. Vital School Division 6,
MB

Gay Sul
Frontier School Division, MB

Kyme Wegrich
School District 43 (Coquitlam), BC

Katherine J. Willson
University of Alberta, AB

Table of Contents

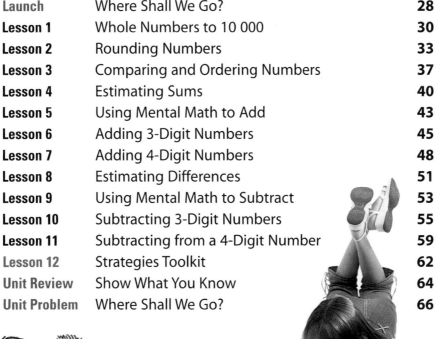

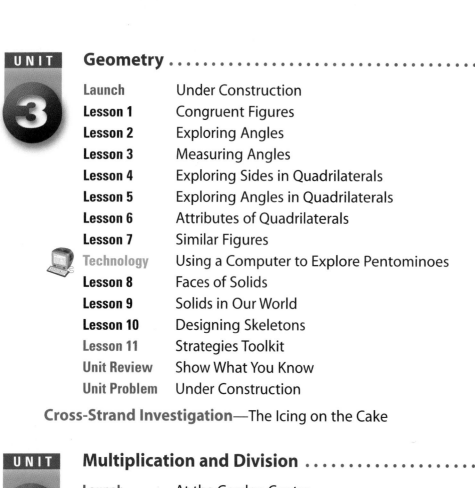

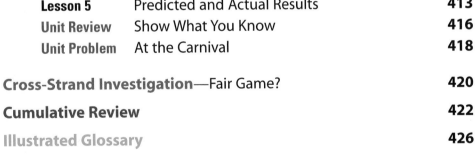

ix

Welcome to
Addison Wesley Math Makes Sense 4

Math helps you understand what you see and do every day.

You will use this book to learn about the math around you. Here's how.

In each Unit:

- A scene from the world around you reminds you of some of the math you already know.

Find out what you will learn in the **Learning Goals** and important **Key Words**.

In each Lesson:

You **Explore** an idea or problem, usually with a partner. You often use materials.

Then you **Show and Share** your results with other students.

Practice questions help you to use and remember the math.

reminds you to use pictures, words, or numbers in your answers.

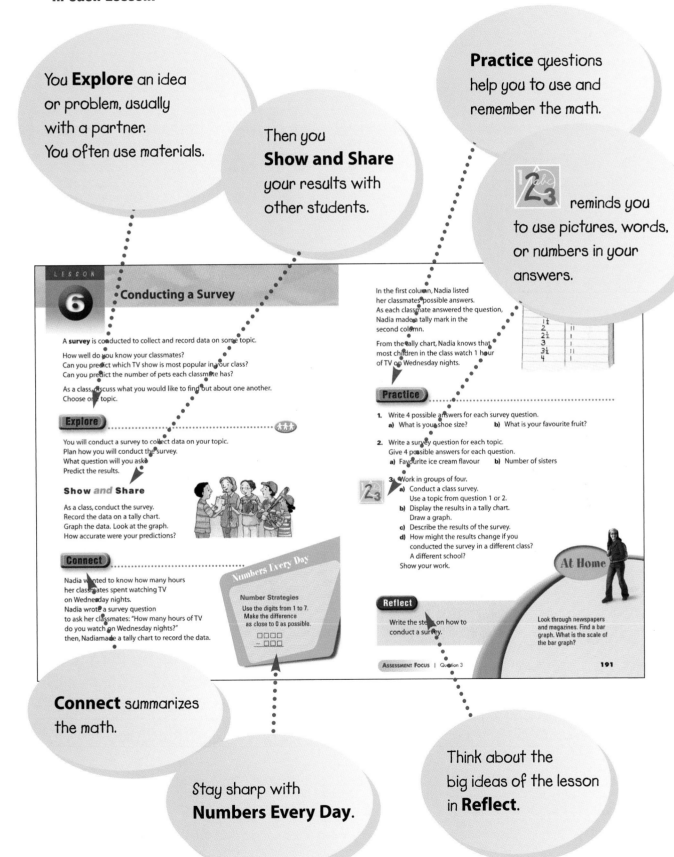

LESSON

6

Conducting a Survey

A **survey** is conducted to collect and record data on some topic.

How well do you know your classmates?
Can you predict which TV show is most popular in your class?
Can you predict the number of pets each classmate has?

As a class, discuss what you would like to find out about one another.
Choose one topic.

Explore

You will conduct a survey to collect data on your topic.
Plan how you will conduct the survey.
What question will you ask?
Predict the results.

Show and Share

As a class, conduct the survey.
Record the data on a tally chart.
Graph the data. Look at the graph.
How accurate were your predictions?

Connect

Nadia wanted to know how many hours her classmates spent watching TV on Wednesday nights.
Nadia wrote a survey question to ask her classmates: "How many hours of TV do you watch on Wednesday nights?"
then, Nadia made a tally chart to record the data.

Numbers Every Day

Number Strategies
Use the digits from 1 to 7.
Make the difference as close to 0 as possible.
□□□□
− □□□

In the first column, Nadia listed her classmates' possible answers.
As each classmate answered the question, Nadia made a tally mark in the second column.

From the tally chart, Nadia knows that most children in the class watch 1 hour of TV on Wednesday nights.

1½	
2	II
2½	
3	II
3½	
4	II

Practice

1. Write 4 possible answers for each survey question.
   a) What is your shoe size?   b) What is your favourite fruit?

2. Write a survey question for each topic.
   Give 4 possible answers for each question.
   a) Favourite ice cream flavour   b) Number of sisters

3. Work in groups of four.
   a) Conduct a class survey.
      Use a topic from question 1 or 2.
   b) Display the results in a tally chart.
      Draw a graph.
   c) Describe the results of the survey.
   d) How might the results change if you conducted the survey in a different class?
      A different school?
   Show your work.

Reflect

Write the steps on how to conduct a survey.

At Home

Look through newspapers and magazines. Find a bar graph. What is the scale of the bar graph?

ASSESSMENT FOCUS | Question 3

191

Connect summarizes the math.

Stay sharp with **Numbers Every Day**.

Think about the big ideas of the lesson in **Reflect**.

- Learn about strategies to help you solve problems in each **Strategies Toolkit** lesson.

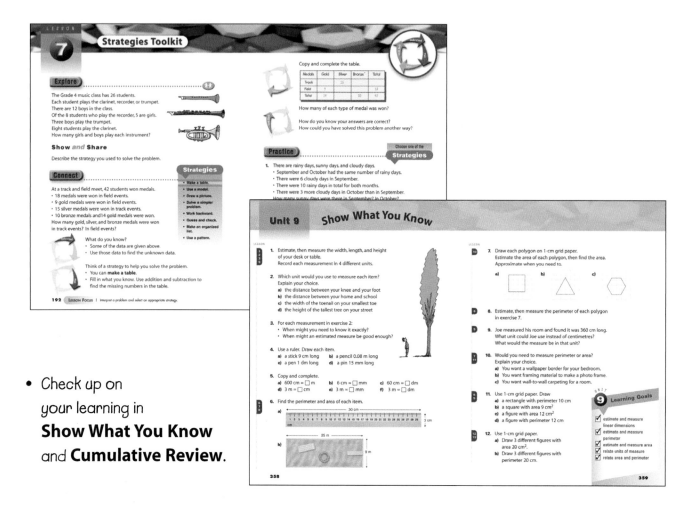

- Check up on your learning in **Show What You Know** and **Cumulative Review**.

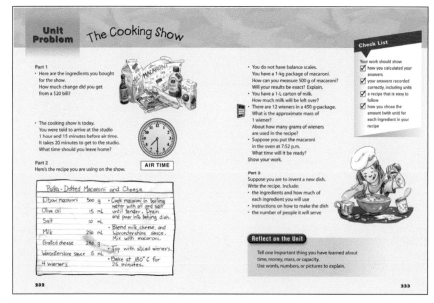

- The **Unit Problem** returns to the opening scene. It presents a problem to solve or a project to do using the math of the unit.

Explore some interesting math when you do the **Investigations**.

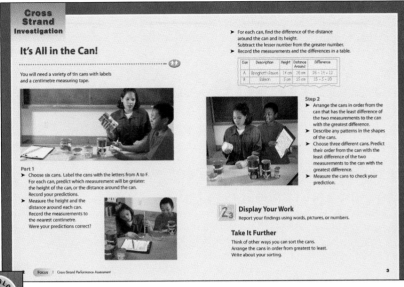

Use **Technology**.

Follow the step-by-step instructions for using a calculator or computer to do math.

Look for  and .

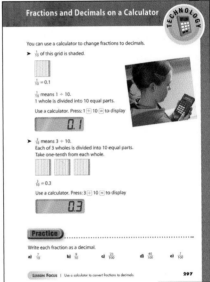

You will see **The World of Work** and **Games** pages.

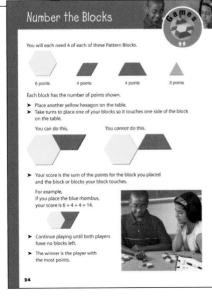

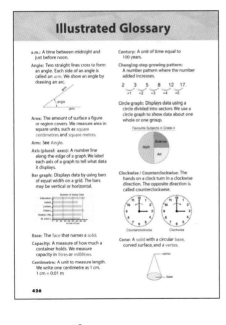

The **Glossary** is an illustrated dictionary of important math words.

It's All in the Can!

You will need a variety of tin cans with labels
and a centimetre measuring tape.

Part 1

➤ Choose six cans. Label the cans with the letters from A to F.
  For each can, predict which measurement will be greater:
  the height of the can, or the distance around the can.
  Record your predictions.

➤ Measure the height and the
  distance around each can.
  Record the measurements to
  the nearest centimetre.
  Were your predictions correct?

➤ For each can, find the difference of the distance around the can and its height.
  Subtract the lesser number from the greater number.
➤ Record the measurements and the differences in a table.

Can	Description	Height	Distance Around	Difference
A	Spaghetti Sauce	14 cm	26 cm	26 − 14 = 12
B	Salmon	5 cm	25 cm	25 − 5 = 20

Part 2
➤ Arrange the cans in order from the can that has the least difference of the two measurements to the can with the greatest difference.
➤ Describe any patterns in the shapes of the cans.
➤ Choose three different cans. Predict their order from the can with the least difference of the two measurements to the can with the greatest difference.
➤ Measure the cans to check your prediction.

Display Your Work
Report your findings using words, pictures, or numbers.

Take It Further
Think of other ways you can sort the cans.
Arrange the cans in order from greatest to least.
Write about your sorting.

1

Number Patterns

Calendar Patterns

ski	**January**	crossed paddles

Sunday	Monday	Tuesday	Wednesday	Thursday	Friday	Saturday
	1	2	3	4	5	6
7	8	9	10	11	12	13
14	15	16	17	18	19	20
21	22	23	24	25	26	27
28	29	30	31			

Learning Goals

- use charts to display patterns
- identify the rule for a number pattern
- extend number patterns
- create number patterns
- use patterns to solve problems
- investigate equations

April

Sunday	Monday	Tuesday	Wednesday	Thursday	Friday	Saturday
1	2	3	4	5	6	7
8	9	10	11	12	13	14
15	16	17	18	19	20	21
22	23	24	25	26	27	28
29	30					

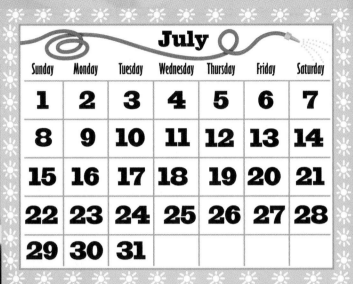

July						
Sunday	Monday	Tuesday	Wednesday	Thursday	Friday	Saturday
1	2	3	4	5	6	7
8	9	10	11	12	13	14
15	16	17	18	19	20	21
22	23	24	25	26	27	28
29	30	31				

Key Words

pattern rule

repeating pattern

term

core

growing pattern

shrinking pattern

equation

October						
Sunday	Monday	Tuesday	Wednesday	Thursday	Friday	Saturday
	1	2	3	4	5	6
7	8	9	10	11	12	13
14	15	16	17	18	19	20
21	22	23	24	25	26	27
28	29	30	31			

- What patterns do you see in these calendar pages?

- How do the patterns change when the first day of the month is on Monday instead of Sunday? Explain.

Patterns in Charts

1	2	3	4	5	6	7	8	9	10
11	12	13	14	15	16	17	18	19	20
21	22	23	24	25	26	27	28	29	30
31	32	33	34	35	36	37	38	39	40
41	42	43	44	45	46	47	48	49	50
51	52	53	54	55	56	57	58	59	60
61	62	63	64	65	66	67	68	69	70
71	72	73	74	75	76	77	78	79	80
81	82	83	84	85	86	87	88	89	90
91	92	93	94	95	96	97	98	99	100

Look at this hundred chart.
There is a pattern in the numbers.
There is a pattern in the positions
of the coloured squares.

Describe the number pattern.
Describe the position pattern.

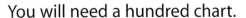

Explore

You will need a hundred chart.
➤ Decide on a number pattern
for a hundred chart.
Keep it secret.
Colour the first ten numbers in your
pattern on a hundred chart.

➤ Trade patterns with your partner.
Describe the patterns in your
partner's chart.
Write the numbers in the pattern.
Extend the pattern.

Show *and* Share

Talk with your partner.
How did you know how to extend
your partner's pattern?
How are the number pattern and
the position pattern related?

Numbers Every Day

Number Strategies

Order the numbers from least
to greatest.

- 142, 132, 213, 143
- 600, 620, 602, 260
- 927, 879, 792, 287

Connect

Here is the start of a pattern
on a hundred chart.

You can describe the pattern
in different ways.
These are **pattern rules.**

1	2	3	4	5	6	7	8	9	10
11	12	13	14	15	16	17	18	19	20
21	22	23	24	25	26	27	28	29	30
31	32	33	34	35	36	37	38	39	40
41	42	43	44	45	46	47	48	49	50
51	52	53	54	55	56	57	58	59	60
61	62	63	64	65	66	67	68	69	70
71	72	73	74	75	76	77	78	79	80
81	82	83	84	85	86	87	88	89	90
91	92	93	94	95	96	97	98	99	100

➤ Look at the positions of the
coloured squares.
Starting at 2, every third square
is coloured.

One pattern rule is:

Use 2 as the start diagonal.
The coloured squares lie along every third diagonal.
The diagonals go 1 down, 1 left.

➤ Look at the numbers in the coloured squares.
The first 10 numbers in the pattern are:
2, 5, 8, 11, 14, 17, 20, 23, 26, 29

*What did I do
to get from 2 to 5?*

Another pattern rule is:

Start at 2. Count on by 3.

You can complete the pattern
using either rule above.

1	2	3	4	5	6	7	8	9	10
11	12	13	14	15	16	17	18	19	20
21	22	23	24	25	26	27	28	29	30
31	32	33	34	35	36	37	38	39	40
41	42	43	44	45	46	47	48	49	50
51	52	53	54	55	56	57	58	59	60
61	62	63	64	65	66	67	68	69	70
71	72	73	74	75	76	77	78	79	80
81	82	83	84	85	86	87	88	89	90
91	92	93	94	95	96	97	98	99	100

➤ Continue to colour the numbers
that lie along the diagonals
that go 1 down, 1 left.
Colour new diagonals
to continue the pattern.

➤ Continue to add 3.
…, 29, 32, 35, 38, 41, 44, 47, 50, …

7

1. On the same hundred chart:
   - Start at 3. Count on by 3s to 100.
     Shade these numbers with one colour.
   - Start at 4. Count on by 4s to 100.
     Shade these numbers with another colour.
   a) Look at the numbers that are shaded in both colours.
      Describe the pattern in these numbers.
   b) What is a rule for this new pattern?

2. Anthony has guitar lessons every
   Wednesday in April.
   His sister has piano lessons
   every third day, starting April 2nd.
   a) On what date do both Anthony
      and his sister have a lesson?
   b) How did you solve the problem?

April						
S	M	T	W	T	F	S
	1	2	3	4	5	6
7	8	9	10	11	12	13
14	15	16	17	18	19	20
21	22	23	24	25	26	27
28	29	30				

3. Look at the coloured squares
   on this hundred chart.
   a) Describe the position pattern.
   b) Describe the number pattern.
   c) Write a pattern rule for each pattern.

101	102	103	104	105	106	107	108	109	110
111	112	113	114	115	116	117	118	119	120
121	122	123	124	125	126	127	128	129	130
131	132	133	134	135	136	137	138	139	140
141	142	143	144	145	146	147	148	149	150
151	152	153	154	155	156	157	158	159	160
161	162	163	164	165	166	167	168	169	170
171	172	173	174	175	176	177	178	179	180
181	182	183	184	185	186	187	188	189	190
191	192	193	194	195	196	197	198	199	200

4. On 1-cm grid paper,
   make a 5-wide hundred chart with
   5 columns and 20 rows.
   a) Find five different patterns in
      the 5-wide hundred chart.
      Record the patterns.
   b) How do the patterns in a
      5-wide hundred chart
      compare to the patterns in a
      10-wide hundred chart?
   Show your work.

5-Wide Hundred Chart

1	2	3	4	5
6	7	8	9	10
11	12	13	14	15

5. Explain how these two patterns are related.

×	1	2	3	4	5	6	7
1	1	2	3	4	5	6	7
2	2	4	6	8	10	12	14
3	3	6	9	12	15	18	21
4	4	8	12	16	20	24	28
5	5	10	15	20	25	30	35
6	6	12	18	24	30	36	42
7	7	14	21	28	35	42	49

1	2	3	4	5	6	7	8	9	10
11	12	13	14	15	16	17	18	19	20
21	22	23	24	25	26	27	28	29	30
31	32	33	34	35	36	37	38	39	40
41	42	43	44	45	46	47	48	49	50

6. Look at the coloured squares in this addition chart.
   a) Describe the position pattern.
   b) Describe the number pattern.
   c) Write a pattern rule for the number pattern.

+	10	11	12	13	14	15
10	20	21	22	23	24	25
11	21	22	23	24	25	26
12	22	23	24	25	26	27
13	23	24	25	26	27	28
14	24	25	26	27	28	29
15	25	26	27	28	29	30

Math Link

Your World

There are number patterns in the rows of this train schedule.

Train Schedule / Saturdays						
Oakville	07 30	08 30	09 30	10 30	11 30	12 30
Clarkson	07 38	08 38	09 38	10 38	11 38	12 38
Port Credit	07 44	08 44	09 44	10 44	11 44	12 44
Long Branch	07 49	08 49	09 49	10 49	11 49	12 49
Mimico	07 54	08 54	09 54	10 54	11 54	12 54
Exhibition	08 00	09 00	10 00	11 00	12 00	13 00
Union	08 07	09 07	10 07	11 07	12 07	13 07

Reflect

How can you use a position pattern on a hundred chart to check for mistakes in a number pattern?
Use words and pictures to explain.

Exploring Number Patterns

Explore

➤ How are these patterns the same?
How are they different?

| 1 | 1 | 2 | 2 | 1 | 1 | 2 | 2 |

| 1 | 3 | 5 | 7 | 9 | 11 |

| 1 | 2 | 4 | 7 | 11 | 16 |

| 91 | 87 | 83 | 79 | 75 |

Write a pattern rule for each pattern.
Write the next four numbers in each pattern.

➤ Create three different number patterns.

Show and Share

Trade patterns with a classmate.
Write the next four numbers in each of your classmate's patterns.

Connect

There are different types of number patterns.

➤ This is a **repeating pattern**.

2   5   2   3   2   5   2   3   2   5   2   3 ...

The first four **terms** are 2, 5, 2, 3.
These terms are the **core** of this pattern.
The core of a pattern is the smallest part that repeats.

➤ In a **growing pattern**, the numbers get bigger in a predictable way.
You can make a growing pattern by adding a number.

1   4   7   10   13   16   19
  +3 +3 +3 +3 +3 +3

 The pattern rule is:

Start at 1. Add 3 each time.

Another way to make a growing pattern is to multiply by a number.

1   2   4   8
  x2 x2 x2

 The pattern rule is:

Start at 1. Multiply by 2 each time.

You can also make a growing pattern by adding numbers that follow a pattern.

2   4   8   14   22   32
  +2 +4 +6 +8 +10

 The pattern rule is:

Start at 2. Add 2. Increase the number you add by 2 each time.

➤ In a **shrinking pattern**, the numbers get smaller in a predictable way.
You can make a shrinking pattern by subtracting a number.

71   66   61   56   51   46
  -5   -5   -5   -5   -5

 The pattern rule is:

Start at 71. Subtract 5 each time.

Numbers Every Day

Mental Math

Estimate each sum.
What strategies did you use?

31 + 48
28 + 53
63 + 17
99 + 88

11

1. Start at 3. Add 7 each time.
   Write the first six terms of the pattern.

2. How are these patterns alike?
   How they are different?

   a)
   | 5 | 10 | 15 | 20 | 25 |

   b)
   | 50 | 100 | 150 | 200 | 250 |

   Write each pattern rule.

3. Describe each pattern. What is the pattern rule?
   Write the next three terms for each pattern.
   Which patterns have a core? Write each core.
   a) 2, 4, 6, 8, …   **b)** 8, 7, 6, 8, 7, 6, 8, 7, 6, …
   c) 85, 76, 67, 58, …   **d)** 6, 13, 20, 27, 34, …

4. Use 5 as a start number.
   Write three different growing patterns.
   Write a pattern rule for each pattern. Show your work.

5. **a)** Why is this a growing pattern? What comes next?
      2, 2, 4, 4, 4, 4, 6, 6, 6, 6, 6, 6
   b) Create a new pattern that is like this one.
      Trade patterns with a classmate.
      Write the rule for your classmate's pattern.

6. Copy, then complete each pattern.
   Which patterns have a core? Write each core.
   a) 15, 26, 37, 48, ☐, 70, 81
   b) 40, 34, ☐, 22, 16, 10, 4
   c) 2, 9, 1, 2, ☐, 1, 2, 9, 1
   d) 5, 6, 8, 11, ☐, 20, 26, 33, 41
   e) 28, 26, 24, 22, ☐, 18, 16
   f) 13, 26, ☐, 52, 65, 78, 91

… AND THEN 7, 6, 7, 9, 4, 2 ….

7. Joe made a design with 8 strips of coloured tape .
The first strip is 1 cm long. The second strip is 2 cm long.
The third strip is 4 cm long. The fourth strip is 7 cm long.

Strip	Length
1	
2	

a) Copy and complete the table.
Look at the lengths of the strips.
What is the pattern rule?

b) Suppose this pattern continues.
How long is the 8th strip?

c) What is the total length of tape Joe used?
How do you know?

8. Paige built a racetrack for her younger sister's toy cars.
The track had 7 loops.
The first loop used 90 cm of track.
The second loop used 95 cm of track.
The third loop used 100 cm of track.

a) Record the pattern in a table.

b) Suppose this pattern continues.
What length of track did Paige use to build
the 7th loop?

c) How much track did Paige need for all 7 loops?
What pattern in the lengths makes it easy
to add mentally?

9. Write a story problem that can be solved using a number pattern.
Trade problems with a classmate. Solve your classmate's problem.

Reflect

You have learned about three different types of patterns.
Use words and numbers to explain the patterns.

Number Patterns with a Calculator

You can use a 4-function calculator
to explore number patterns.
These keystrokes are for the TI-108.
Key in your favourite 1-digit number.
Press: [+] [=]
What do you notice?
Press [=] again several times.
Record the numbers.
Describe the number pattern.

Explore

You will need a 4-function calculator.

➤ Key in a start number between 10 and 20.
   Press: [+]
   Enter a different number greater than 10.
   Press [=] repeatedly.
   Record the numbers.
   What patterns do you see in the ones digits?
   The tens digits?

➤ Use your calculator to make a number pattern by multiplying.
   How are the keystrokes different?

Show and Share

Show your patterns to a classmate.
Ask your classmate to:
• find a rule for each pattern
• write the next three terms in each pattern

➤ Sunil made this pattern with his calculator.
He chose 10 as the start number and counted by 25s.

Press 10 $+$ 25
$=$ $=$ $=$

10, 35, 60, 85, 110, 135, 160, 185, ...

This is a growing pattern.
- There is a repeating pattern in the ones digits:
  0, 5, 0, 5, 0, 5, 0, 5, ...
  Its core is 0, 5.
- There is also a repeating pattern in the tens digits:
  1, 3, 6, 8, 1, 3, 6, 8, ...
  Its core is 1, 3, 6, 8.

➤ Tamara made a number pattern with this pattern rule:
Start at 1. Multiply by 3 repeatedly.
She pressed 3 $\times$ 1, then she pressed $=$ repeatedly.

The pattern is: 1, 3, 9, 27, 81, 243, 729, 2187, ...

This is a growing pattern.
- There is a repeating pattern in the ones digits:
  1, 3, 9, 7, 1, 3, 9, 7, ...
  Its core is 1, 3, 9, 7.

1. Start with 3. Multiply by 2 repeatedly.
   Record the first nine terms.
   Describe any patterns in the tens digits
   and ones digits.
   What is the core of each pattern?

2. Start with 101. Subtract 9 repeatedly.
   Record the first eight terms.
   Describe any patterns in the tens digits and
   ones digits.

Numbers Every Day

Calculator Skills

Find two odd numbers
with a product of 57.

Find three odd
numbers with
a sum of 111.

3. Mr. Jones rewards students with stickers. He has 1000 stickers.
Every week Mr. Jones gives out 12 stickers.
After 16 weeks, how many stickers will Mr. Jones have left?

4. Describe the rule for each pattern.
How did you find the rule?
a) 44, 55, 66, 77, 88, 99, 110, 121, 132
b) 898, 794, 690, 586, 482, 378
c) 688, 776, 864, 952, 1040, 1128, 1216
Write the next three numbers in each pattern.

5. Add.
12 + 21
13 + 31
14 + 41
Continue the pattern. Find each sum.
Find a rule. Does this rule always work? Explain.
Show your work.

6. Write any 3-digit number, with all digits different.
Write the number you get when you reverse the digits.
Subtract the lesser number from the greater number.
Reverse the digits of your answer.
Add your answer and the reverse of your answer.
Repeat for three different 3-digit numbers.
What do you notice?

The reverse of 389 is 983.

7. Priya has a calculator. The ⊗ key is broken.
How can Priya use the calculator to find 256 × 4?
Explain.

Math Link

Music

There are many patterns in music. A melodic ostinato is a short pattern in the melody. It repeats throughout a song.

Reflect

How does using a calculator make it easier to explore number patterns?
Use words and numbers to explain.

Equations Involving Addition

An addition fact for the number 6 is:

$4 + 2 = 6$

You can model this with counters.

+	0	1	2	3	4	5	6
0	0	1	2	3	4	5	6
1	1	2	3	4	5	6	7
2	2	3	4	5	6	7	8
3	3	4	5	6	7	8	9
4	4	5	6	7	8	9	10
5	5	6	7	8	9	10	11
6	6	7	8	9	10	11	12

Use the addition chart.
How many different addition facts can you find for the number 6?

Explore

You will need 30 counters and 2 squares of paper.

➤ Write $+$ on one square.
Write $=$ on the other square.

➤ Choose a number from 10 to 15.
Use as many counters as you need
and your paper squares.
Model, then write, all the
addition facts for your number.
How do you know when you have
all the facts?

Show and Share

Show your addition facts to another
pair of classmates.
What patterns do you see in the addition facts?

Connect

Steve chose the number 9.
He took 18 counters.
He wrote these addition facts.

$0 + 9 = 9$	$5 + 4 = 9$
$1 + 8 = 9$	$6 + 3 = 9$
$2 + 7 = 9$	$7 + 2 = 9$
$3 + 6 = 9$	$8 + 1 = 9$
$4 + 5 = 9$	$9 + 0 = 9$

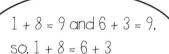

Numbers Every Day

Mental Math

Estimate each difference.
What strategies did you use?

$59 - 38$
$61 - 27$
$75 - 49$
$80 - 65$

There is a pattern in the numbers that are added.
The first number in each fact increases by 1: 0, 1, 2, 3, …
The second number in each fact decreases by 1: 9, 8, 7, 6, …

An **equation** is a statement that two things are equal.
An addition fact is an equation.

$3 + 8 = 11$ This is an equation.

You can make an equation using
any pair of addition facts for a number.

$3 + 8 = 6 + 5$ This is an equation.

$1 + 8 = 9$ and $6 + 3 = 9$,
so, $1 + 8 = 6 + 3$

Practice

Use counters to complete the questions.

1. Copy and complete the pattern.
   How do you know when you have completed the pattern?
   $1 + 19 = 20$
   $2 + 18 = 20$
   $3 + 17 = 20$

2. Are the sums in each pair equal? How do you know?
   If the sums are equal, write an equation.
   a) 2 + 6 and 3 + 5   b) 4 + 3 and 6 + 2
   c) 7 + 3 and 8 + 4   d) 11 + 11 and 10 + 12

3. Find each missing number.
   a) □ + 3 = 7   b) 10 = 5 + □
   c) 9 = 9 + □   d) 12 + □ = 22

4. Find the number that makes each statement an equation.
   a) 5 + 7 = 3 + □   b) 6 + 8 = □ + 5
   c) □ + 12 = 10 + 6   d) 4 + □ = 5 + 7

5. Find two numbers that make each statement an equation.
   How many different ways can you do this?
   How do you know you have found all the ways?
   Show your work.
   a) 5 + 4 = □ + □   b) □ + □ = 8 + 7
   c) 10 + 3 = □ + □   d) □ + □ = 16 + 2

6. Find the number that makes each statement an equation.
   What strategies did you use?
   a) 112 + 48 = 82 + □   b) 412 + □ = 563 + 621

7. Write 10 as a sum of three numbers.
   □ + □ + □ = 10
   How many different ways can you do this?

Reflect

How can you use patterns in addition facts to help you find a missing number? Use words and numbers to explain.

At Home

Use pennies and nickels. How many different ways can you show 20¢? Write each way as an equation.

Equations Involving Subtraction

Explore

There are 10 counters altogether.

You will need 12 counters.

➤ Choose a number from 8 to 12.
   Use that number of counters.
➤ Arrange the counters into two groups.
   Hide one group under a piece of paper.
   Ask your partner to write the subtraction fact.
➤ Take turns.
   Keep playing until you have written all the
   subtraction facts you can for your number.
   How do you know when you have all the facts?

Show and Share

Show your subtraction facts to another pair
of students.
What patterns are there in your subtraction facts?

Connect

Suppose you have 5 counters.
You can write these subtraction facts:

$$5 - 5 = 0 \qquad 5 - 2 = 3$$
$$5 - 4 = 1 \qquad 5 - 1 = 4$$
$$5 - 3 = 2 \qquad 5 - 0 = 5$$

There is a pattern in the numbers.
The number that is subtracted decreases by 1: 5, 4, 3, 2, 1, 0
The difference increases by 1: 0, 1, 2, 3, 4, 5

LESSON FOCUS I Explore patterns in equations involving subtraction.

You can make equations using subtraction facts.
The differences must be the same.

$10 - 6 = 4$
$12 - 8 = 4$
$10 - 6 = 12 - 8$

Each of these is an equation.

$7 - 5 = 2$ and $8 - 6 = 2$
so, $7 - 5 = 8 - 6$

Practice

1. Copy and complete this pattern:
   How do you know when the pattern is complete?

   $14 - 1 = 13$
   $14 - 2 = 12$
   $14 - 3 = 11$

2. Are the differences in each pair equal?
   If the differences are equal, write an equation.
   a) $20 - 4$ and $19 - 5$ **b)** $15 - 9$ and $14 - 8$
   c) $18 - 5$ and $15 - 2$ **d)** $11 - 7$ and $12 - 6$

3. Find each missing number.
   a) $16 - \square = 7$ **b)** $17 = 25 - \square$ **c)** $9 = \square - 10$

4. Find the number that makes each statement an equation.
   a) $15 - 6 = 13 - \square$ **b)** $8 - 3 = \square - 5$
   c) $\square - 14 = 10 - 8$ **d)** $17 - \square = 14 - 7$

5. Write 3 different pairs of numbers that
   make each statement an equation.
   How did you find the numbers?
   Show your work.
   a) $18 - 6 = \square - \square$
   b) $20 - 3 = \square - \square$

Numbers Every Day

Calculator Skills

Press: $+$ 50 $=$
Press: 3 $=$
Continue to press $=$.

Write the first 5 numbers
in the pattern.
What is the pattern rule?

Reflect

What strategies can you use to find the
missing number in an equation?

Strategies Toolkit

Explore ····································

These equations have figures in place of numbers.
Each figure represents a different number.
All the triangles represent the same number.
All the squares represent the same number.
All the circles represent the same number.

Find the number that each figure represents.

$$\blacksquare + \blacktriangle + \blacktriangle + \bullet = 17$$
$$\blacksquare + \blacktriangle + \bullet = 11$$
$$\blacksquare + \blacksquare + \blacktriangle = 8$$

Show *and* Share

Share the strategy you used to solve the problem.

Connect ·······························

Each figure represents a number.

$$14 = \heartsuit + \heartsuit + \blacktriangle + \blacktriangle$$
$$12 = \heartsuit + \heartsuit + \blacktriangle$$
$$10 = \bullet + \heartsuit + \blacktriangle$$

Find the number that each figure represents.

What do you know?
- Each figure represents a number.
- All the hearts represent one number.
- All the triangles represent one number.
- The circle represents one number.

Think of a strategy to help you solve the problem.
- You can **guess and check**.
- Guess a number for each figure.
  Check that the numbers fit the equations.

Strategies

- **Make a table.**
- **Use a model.**
- **Draw a picture.**
- **Solve a simpler problem.**
- **Work backward.**
- **Guess and check.**
- **Make an organized list.**
- **Use a pattern.**

What are good guesses for ♥ and for ▲?
If the first two sums are not 14 and 12,
think about your next guesses.
Should each number be greater than or
less than your first guess?

Check your work.
Are the sums 14, 12, and 10?
How could you solve this problem another way?

Choose one of the

Strategies

1. Each figure represents a different number.
   Find the number that each figure represents.
   ■ + ■ + ● = 26
   ■ + ● + ● + ▲ = 24
   ■ + ● + ▲ = 18

2. Each letter represents a different number.
   Find the number that each letter represents.
   12 = A + B + C
   14 = A + A + B + B
   11 = A + B + B

3. Which object has the greatest mass?
   The least mass? Show your work.

Reflect

Choose one question in *Practice*. Use words, numbers,
or pictures to explain how you found the answer.

Number the Blocks

You will each need 4 of each of these Pattern Blocks.

6 points   4 points   4 points   3 points

Each block has the number of points shown.

➤ Place another yellow hexagon on the table.
➤ Take turns to place one of your blocks so it touches one side of the block on the table.

You can do this.   You *cannot* do this.

   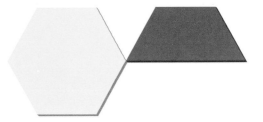

➤ Your score is the sum of the points for the block you placed and the block or blocks your block touches.

For example,
if you place the blue rhombus,
your score is $6 + 4 + 4 = 14$.

➤ Continue playing until both players have no blocks left.

➤ The winner is the player with the most points.

LESSON

1

1. Use a copy of a hundred chart and two different colours.
   Count on by 2s and by 5s on the same hundred chart.
   Colour the numbers as you count.
   Use the same start number each time.
   Write a pattern rule for the numbers that are shaded
   in both colours.

2

2. What is each pattern rule? Write the next three numbers.
   a) 2, 6, 10, 14, … **b)** 37, 34, 31, 28, … **c)** 18, 19, 20, 18, 19, 20, …

3. Janet used cubes to build a pyramid
   with 7 layers.
   The top 4 layers have these numbers
   of cubes: 1, 4, 9, 16.
   Record the pattern in a table.
   Suppose the pattern continues.
   How many cubes are in the 7th layer?
   How many cubes are in the pyramid?

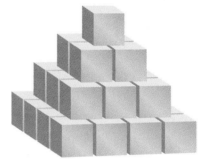

3

4. What is each pattern rule?
   Write the next three numbers.
   a) 5, 10, 20, 40, …
   b) 200, 188, 176, 164, 152, …

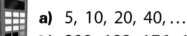

4

5. Find all the pairs of numbers that make
   each statement an equation.
   How do you know you have found
   all the pairs?
   a) $6 + 5 = \square + \square$ **b)** $\square + \square = 2 + 8$

5

6. Find the number that makes
   each statement an equation.
   a) $11 = 16 - \square$ **b)** $\square - 8 = 12$

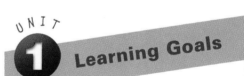

UNIT

1 Learning Goals

☑ use charts to display patterns
☑ identify the rule for a number pattern
☑ extend number patterns
☑ create number patterns
☑ use patterns to solve problems
☑ investigate equations

Calendar Patterns

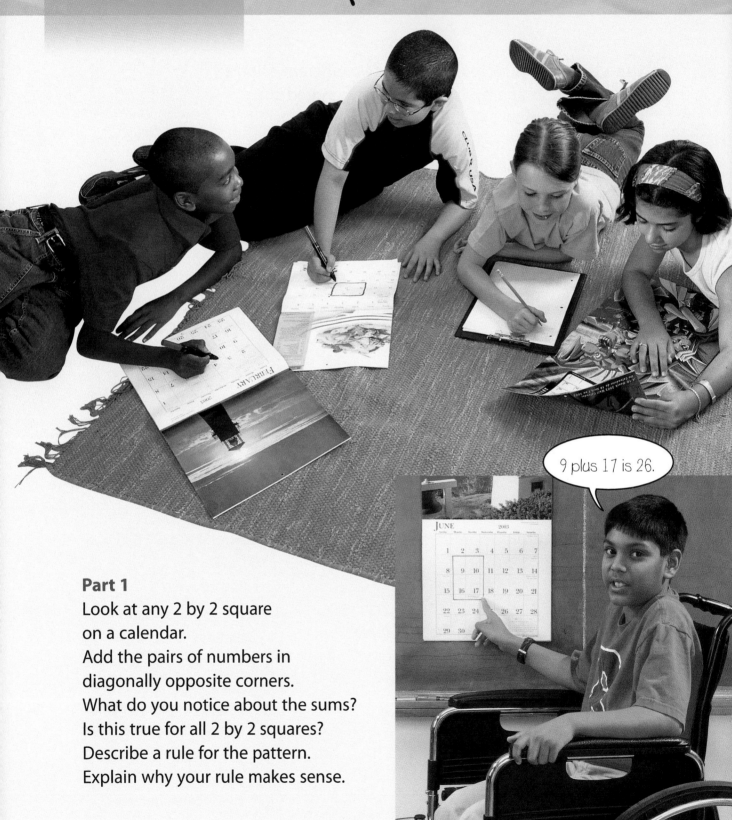

9 plus 17 is 26.

Part 1

Look at any 2 by 2 square
on a calendar.
Add the pairs of numbers in
diagonally opposite corners.
What do you notice about the sums?
Is this true for all 2 by 2 squares?
Describe a rule for the pattern.
Explain why your rule makes sense.

What patterns can you find in a 3 by 3 square?
A 4 by 4 square?

24 plus 12 is 36.

26 minus 10 is 16.

Part 2

Try subtracting instead of adding.
Use different sizes of squares.
Describe any patterns.

Part 3

Think of other ways to look for number patterns on a calendar.
Find as many different patterns as you can.
Use words and numbers to describe the patterns you found.

Reflect on the Unit

Describe one important idea you learned about number patterns.
How did you use this idea to solve problems?
Use words and numbers to explain.

2

Whole Numbers

Where Shall We Go?

Learning Goals

- recognize and read numbers from 1 to 10 000
- read and write numbers in standard form, expanded form, and written form
- use place value to represent numbers
- compare and order numbers
- estimate sums and differences
- add and subtract 3-digit numbers mentally
- add 4-digit numbers
- subtract a 3-digit number from a 4-digit number
- pose and solve problems

Angelie is a travel writer. She writes articles for newspapers and magazines. Angelie visits different places all over the world. Angelie plans a trip to Newfoundland.

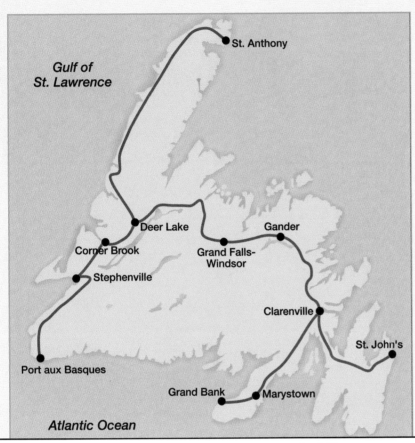

Distances in Kilometres					
	Corner Brook	Deer Lake	Gander	St. Anthony	St. John's
Corner Brook	—	55	355	444	652
Deer Lake	55	—	300	390	597
Gander	355	300	—	690	297
St. Anthony	444	390	690	—	987
St. John's	652	597	297	987	—

- Suppose Angelie travelled from St. John's to St. Anthony through Deer Lake.
  How could you find out how far she travelled?
- Suppose Angelie is in Gander.
  How could you find out if it's farther to St. John's or to Corner Brook?
- What else do you know from this map?

1

Whole Numbers to 10 000

The largest marching band
ever assembled had
4526 members.
There were students from
52 different school bands.

Explore

How many different ways can you show 4526?
Draw a picture to record each way you find.

Show and Share

Share your pictures with another pair
of students.
How do you know each picture shows 4526?

Connect

The largest marching band had 1342 majorettes, flag bearers,
and drill team members.
The rest of the band were musicians.
You can represent the number 1342 in different ways.

➤ Use Base Ten Blocks.
 To show the number 1342:

1 thousand   3 hundreds   4 tens   2 ones

LESSON FOCUS | Read and write whole numbers in standard, expanded, and word forms.

➤ Use a place-value chart.
To show the number 1342:

Thousands	Hundreds	Tens	Ones
1	3	4	2

1000	300	40	2

You can write the number 1342 as the sum of
the thousands, hundreds, tens, and ones.

$1342 = 1000 + 300 + 40 + 2$ ◀——— This is **expanded form**.

➤ Use words.

1342 is one thousand
three hundred forty-two.

The number 1342 is written in **standard form**.
Every digit has a place value, depending on its position.

Practice

1. The Canada – US border is about 8893 km long from west to east.
   Write this number in words.

2. The Mackenzie River is the longest
   river in Canada.
   It is about 4241 km long.
   Use Base Ten Blocks to show this number.
   Draw pictures of the blocks.

3. Mount Logan, Yukon, is the
   highest mountain in Canada.
   It is about 5959 m high.
   Use expanded form to show this number.

Numbers Every Day

Mental Math

Add.
Which strategies did you use?

$20 + 12$

$2 + 4 + 8 + 6$

$51 + 39$

$67 + 4$

4. Write each number in standard form.

a)

b)

5. Write each number in question 4 in words.

6. Write each number in standard form.
   a) 5000 + 600 + 40 + 3   **b)** 9000 + 700 + 80   **c)** 3000 + 200 + 9
   d) 8000 + 20   **e)** 7000 + 5   **f)** 4000 + 70 + 3

7. Write each number in standard form.
   a) one thousand seven hundred fifty-four
   b) nine thousand nine hundred ninety-nine
   c) four thousand seventy
   d) six thousand five hundred three

8. Write each number in expanded form.
   a) 5352   **b)** 7056   **c)** 8104   **d)** 4370

9. a) Press: 578. Make the screen show 508.
        How did you do it?
    b) Explain how to get each target number
        from each start number.

Start	394	156	4689
Target	94	106	4009

10. Tyler wrote 2005 in words as two hundred five.
       Explain Tyler's error.
       Show your work.

Reflect

Why is the order of the digits in a number important?
Use numbers, words, or pictures to explain.

2

Rounding Numbers

There are about 5000 people here today.

How did Athina estimate the number of people at the game?

Explore

You will need a copy of these number lines.

➤ Write the number that is halfway between the two given numbers.

➤ Use the number lines to answer each question.
  • Is 57 closer to 50 or 60?
  • Is 331 closer to 300 or 400?
  • Is 6500 closer to 6000 or 7000?
  Show your work.

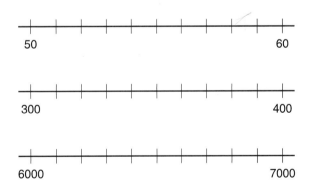

Show *and* Share

Share your answers with a classmate.
Talk about the strategies you used to find the closer number.

LESSON FOCUS | Round numbers to the nearest ten, hundred, and thousand.

33

There were 2371 people at a baseball game.
The number 2371 is exact because it is a count of the number of people.
To write an estimate for the number of people at the game,
you can **round**.

➤ Round 2371 to the nearest thousand.
Look at the thousands: 2 thousands
Look at 371. It is closer to 0 than to 1000.
So, 2371 rounds to 2 thousands, or 2000.

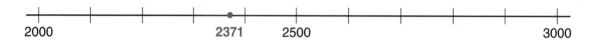

➤ Round 2371 to the nearest hundred.
Look at the hundreds: 23 hundreds
Look at 71. It is closer to 100 than to 0; so add 1 hundred.
So, 2371 rounds to 24 hundreds, or 2400.

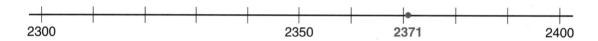

➤ Round 2371 to the nearest ten.
Look at the tens: 237 tens
Look at 1. It is closer to 0 than to 10.
So, 2371 rounds to 237 tens, or 2370.

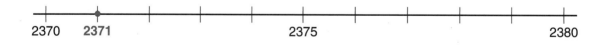

➤ Look at the number lines above.
To round the middle number on each number line, you round up.
To the nearest thousand, 2500 rounds to 3000.
To the nearest hundred, 2350 rounds to 2400.
To the nearest ten, 2375 rounds to 2380.

Use a number line when it helps.

1. The longest country line dance had 6275 people.
   Round this number to the nearest thousand.

2. The biggest game of Pass the Parcel had 3918 students.
   Round this number to the nearest hundred.

3. The biggest game of musical chairs
   began with 8238 students.
   Round this number to the nearest ten.

4. Round to the nearest thousand.
   How did you get each answer?
   a) 2376   b) 7891
   c) 6300   d) 4735
   e) 1999   f) 3087
   g) 5501   h) 9498

5. Round to the nearest hundred.
   a) 9876   b) 1509
   c) 3055   d) 1749
   e) 5465   f) 8230
   g) 4811   h) 1984

6. Round to the nearest ten.
   How did you get each answer?
   a) 2347   b) 6708
   c) 8973   d) 7597

7. Write three numbers that round to 600
   when rounded to the nearest hundred.

8. Write three numbers that round to 6000
   when rounded to the nearest thousand.

Numbers Every Day

Number Strategies
Order these numbers from
least to greatest.

• 73, 56, 41, 80
• 132, 231, 423, 312
• 501, 410, 609, 190

Use this table for questions 9 to 12.

Attendance at Silver Broom Tournament

Day	Number of People
Wednesday	4652
Thursday	5373
Friday	5546

9. Round each number to the nearest thousand.

10. Round each number to the nearest hundred.

11. Suppose a person wants to know about how many people attended each day. Would you give her the answer to question 9 or question 10? Explain.

12. The Saturday attendance was 5968.
    a) Round this number to the nearest thousand and nearest hundred.
       What do you notice?
    b) Write another number that rounds to the same number when rounded to the nearest hundred and nearest thousand.

 13. A number is rounded to the nearest ten, nearest hundred, and nearest thousand. All the rounded numbers are 5000. What was the number before it was rounded? How many possible numbers are there? Show your work.

At Home

Reflect

Is it possible that a 3-digit number rounds to 1000? Explain.

Look through newspapers and magazines.
Find examples of large numbers.
Write each number.
In which form is it written?
Is the number exact or rounded? Explain.

Comparing and Ordering Numbers

Use the digits 3, 5, 7, 8.
Write 3 different numbers using all these digits.
Order the numbers from greatest to least.
Show your work.

Show *and* Share

Share your numbers and ordering with another pair of students.
Take turns to describe the strategy you used for ordering.
What other strategies could you use to order the numbers?

Connect

To order the numbers 2143, 2413, and 1423 from least to greatest:

➤ Represent each number with Base Ten Blocks.

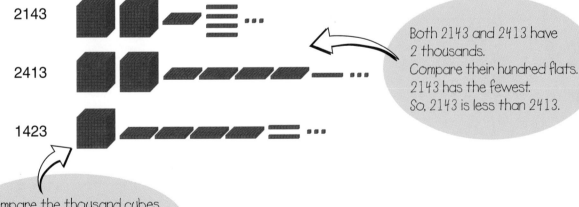

Both 2143 and 2413 have 2 thousands.
Compare their hundred flats. 2143 has the fewest.
So, 2143 is less than 2413.

Compare the thousand cubes. 1423 has the fewest.
So, 1423 is the least number.

From least to greatest: 1423, 2143, 2413

➤ Write each number in a place-value chart.

Thousands	Hundreds	Tens	Ones
2	1	4	3
2	4	1	3
1	4	2	3

1423 has the fewest thousands, so it is the least number.

Both 2143 and 2413 have 2 thousands. Compare their hundreds. 100 is less than 400. So, 2143 is less than 2413.

The arrow head points to the smaller number.

You can use < and > to show order.
1423 < 2143 means
1423 is less than 2143.

2413 > 2143 means
2413 is greater than 2143.

5 > 2

➤ Use a number line.
Mark a dot for each number on a number line.

1423   2143   2413

1000   1500   2000   2500   3000

Read the numbers from left to right.
From least to greatest: 1423, 2143, 2413

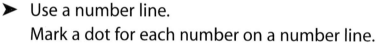

Practice

1. The Canadian Armed Forces have 80 F-18 Hornets. The US Navy has 200. Which has more F-18s? How do you know?

Numbers Every Day

Mental Math

What happens when you add 5 to a number with 5 in the ones place? Add.

35 + 5
65 + 5
85 + 5
25 + 5

2. Copy and complete. Write >, <, or =.
   How did you decide which symbol to use?
   a) 582 ☐ 589   b) 3576 ☐ 3476   c) 5754 ☐ 5745
   d) 792 ☐ 6082   e) 4110 ☐ 4101   f) 8192 ☐ 8291

3. Write the numbers in order from least to greatest.
   a) 862, 802, 869   b) 7656, 7665, 6756

4. Write the numbers in order from greatest to least.
   Explain how you did it.
   a) 9006, 9600, 9060   b) 5865, 895, 5685

5. Replace each ☐ with a digit so the statement is true.
   How many ways can you do this each time?
   a) 5762 < 5 ☐ 76   b) 7998 > ☐ 998   c) 6 ☐ 05 < 6604

6. Chantelle and Elena collect shells.
   Chantelle has 4325 shells. Elena has 4235.
   Who has more shells? How do you know?

7. Katie, Urvi, and Blake collect stamps.
   Katie has 2340 stamps; Urvi has 2304 stamps;
   and Blake has 2430 stamps.
   Who has the most stamps? The fewest stamps?
   How do you know?

8. Use the digits 3, 7, 8, 9.
   Write all the 4-digit numbers greater than 7000
   and less than 8000.
   Order the numbers from least to greatest.
   Show your work.

Reflect

Sue says that since 9 > 2, then 987 > 2134. Is she correct?
Use words, pictures, or numbers to explain.

Estimating Sums

Do you think doctors use an estimate when they prescribe medicine?

When you don't need an exact answer, you estimate. When would you use an estimate?

When you estimate a sum, you find a number that is close to the sum.

Explore

➤ About how much will it cost to buy a TV set and a DVD player?
➤ What could you buy if you had $700 to spend?

Estimate to find out. Record your answers.

ZAP electronics superstore

TV set	$589
DVD player	$204
VCR	$162
Computer	$998
Printer	$126
Keyboard	$119

SAVE $$$

Show and Share

Compare your answers with those of another pair of students.
Are your estimates higher or lower? Explain.
What strategies did you use to estimate?

Connect

An electronics store had 395 customers on Friday
and 452 customers on Saturday.
About how many customers did the store have for those 2 days?

When a question asks "about how many," you can estimate.
Estimate: $395 + 452$

When you estimate, you use numbers that are close but easier to work with.

➤ You could round each number to the nearest 100.
395 rounds to 400.
452 rounds to 500.

Add the rounded numbers: 400 + 500 = 900
Both numbers were rounded up; so this estimate is high.
The store had about 900 customers for the 2 days.

➤ You could cluster.
Both 395 and 452 are about 400.
So, 395 + 452 is about 400 + 400 = 800.
The store had about 800 customers for the 2 days.

➤ You could use front-end estimation.
Add the first digits of the numbers.
395 + **4**52 is about 300 + 400 = 700.

For a better estimate:
Think about 95 + 52.
This is about 100 + 50 = 150.
So, 395 + 452 is about 700 + 150 = 850.
The store had about 850 customers for the 2 days.

Practice

1. How many digits do you think each answer will have?
   Explain.
   a) 714 + 621   b) 375 + 496   c) 265 + 661

2. Raji estimated each sum.
   Is each estimate high or low?
   How do you know?
   a) 517 + 475 as 900   b) 316 + 442 as 800

3. Estimate each sum.
   How did you decide how to round each number?
   a) 71 + 847   b) 165 + 72   c) 192 + 192

4. Sam wants a lunch with less than 1000 calories. He has a hamburger with 445 calories, an apple pie with 405 calories, and ice cream with 270 calories.
   a) About how many calories are in the lunch?
   b) Did Sam make his goal? Explain.

5. Write a story problem where you would *not* use estimation to solve it.
   Explain why you would not estimate.

6. Look at these two addition questions:

   449 + 449   451 + 451

   a) Round to the nearest hundred to estimate each sum.
   b) Use a calculator.
      Are the two sums as different as the estimates make them seem? Explain.
   c) How might you get a better estimate for each sum?

7. When you estimate to add, how can you tell if the estimated sum is greater than or less than the exact sum?

8. The estimated sum of two numbers is 600.
   What might the numbers be?
   Show your work.

9. Suppose you want to know if you have enough money to buy 3 items. Would you estimate the price of each item by rounding up or rounding down? Explain.

Numbers Every Day

Reflect

When you estimate to add, how do you decide if you should round to the nearest ten or to the nearest hundred? Use words and numbers to explain.

Number Strategies

Replace □ with >, <, or =.

2 + 4 + 6 □ 3 + 5 + 7

6 + 6 + 6 □ 6 × 3

50 − 30 □ 50 − 20

Using Mental Math to Add

Explore

Students from two schools went on a field trip.
There were 227 students in one school,
and 134 students in the other school.
How many students went on the field trip?

Use mental math to find out.
Record your answer.

Show *and* Share

Share your strategies for adding with another pair of students.

Connect

➤ Use mental math to add: 137 + 298
   Use the strategy of make a "friendly" number.
   137 + 298
   298 is 300 − 2.
   Add 300, then take away 2.
   137 + 300 = 437
   437 − 2 = 435
   So, 137 + 298 = 435

> 300 is a friendly number because it is easy to add 300.

➤ Use mental math to add: 170 + 343
   Make a friendly number.
   170 + 30 = 200
   343 − 30 = 313
   So, 170 + 343 = 200 + 313 = 513

> I know
> 170 + 30 is 200, and
> 343 − 30 is 313.

➤ Use mental math to add: 264 + 323
Use the strategy of adding on.
Add on hundreds, add on tens, then add on ones.
Start with the greater number.
323 + 264

Think: 323 + 200 + 60 + 4

Count on by 100 two times: 323, 423, 523
Count on by 10 six times: 523, 533, 543, 553, 563, 573, 583
Then add 4: 583 + 4 = 587
So, 264 + 323 = 587

Practice

Use mental math.
1. Add. Try to use a different strategy each time.
   a) 179 + 234   b) 266 + 313   c) 348 + 434   d) 536 + 299

2. Add. For which questions would you "make a friendly number"?
   a) 263 + 328   b) 439 + 544   c) 691 + 180   d) 270 + 438

3. There were 168 children in the park on Friday morning.
   There were 273 children in the park on Friday afternoon.
   How many children were in the park on Friday?

4. Make up an addition problem you can solve
   using mental math. Tell which strategy
   you used to solve the problem, and why.

Numbers Every Day

Reflect

You know several strategies to add mentally.
Which is your favourite strategy?
Can you always use it?
Use words and numbers to explain.

Mental Math

Add.
What patterns do you see?

12 + 21
23 + 32
34 + 43
45 + 54

Adding 3-Digit Numbers

 **Explore**

Madhu uses the two sets of building blocks together.
How many pieces does she have?

Use Base Ten Blocks to find out.
Draw pictures to show your work.

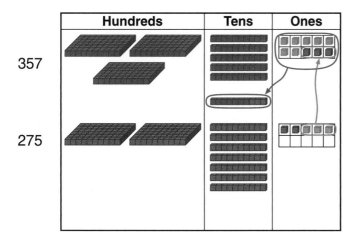

Show *and* Share

Share your results with another pair of students.
Did you get the same answer? Explain.
How could you solve the problem without using Base Ten Blocks?

Connect

One jigsaw puzzle has 357 pieces. Another puzzle has 275 pieces.
How many pieces are there altogether?

Add: 357 + 275

➤ Use Base Ten Blocks on a place-value mat to add.

	Hundreds	Tens	Ones
357			
275			

• Make 10.
• Trade 10 ones for 1 ten.

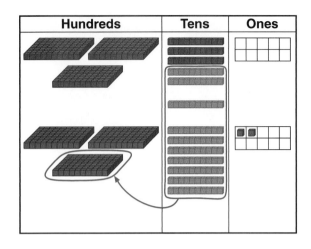

• Trade 10 tens for 1 hundred.

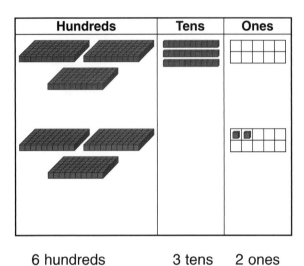

6 hundreds   3 tens   2 ones

$357 + 275 = 632$

➤ Use expanded form to add.

357 ————————→ 300 + 50 + 7
+ 275 ————————→ + 200 + 70 + 5
                500 + 120 + 12 = 620 + 12 = 632

➤ Use place value to add.

Add the ones: 12 ones Regroup 12 ones as 1 ten 2 ones.	Add the tens: 13 tens Regroup 13 tens as 1 hundred 3 tens.	Add the hundreds.
$\begin{array}{r} ^{1} \\ 357 \\ +\ 275 \\ \hline 2 \end{array}$	$\begin{array}{r} ^{1\ 1} \\ 357 \\ +\ 275 \\ \hline 32 \end{array}$	$\begin{array}{r} ^{1\ 1} \\ 357 \\ +\ 275 \\ \hline 632 \end{array}$

There are 632 jigsaw pieces altogether.

1. Estimate first.
   Then add the numbers for which the sum will be greater than 600.
   a) 503   b) 817   c) 199   d) 765
      + 365   + 179   + 52   + 384

2. Estimate first.
   Then add the numbers for which the sum will be less than 500.
   a) 384   b) 174   c) 305   d) 491
      + 765   + 89   + 168   + 256

3. A video store rented 165 more DVDs than video games.
   The store rented 258 video games.
   How many DVDs did the store rent?

4. The sum of two numbers is 756.
   What might the numbers be?
   How do you know?
   Can you find more than one pair of numbers?
   Explain.

5. Each letter in this sum represents
   a different digit.
   What is the value of each letter?
   How do you know?

   ```
     S E E
   + Y O U
   -------
   S O O N
   ```

6. What is the greatest number you can
   add to 365 *without* having to regroup
   in any place? Show your work.

Numbers Every Day

Number Strategies

Use the numbers in the box.

| 34 22 11 15 16 41 |

Find two numbers whose:
- sum is 63
- difference is 11
- sum ends in 0
- difference ends in 0

Reflect

You know 3 ways to add.
How are these ways the same? Different?
Use words and numbers to explain.

Adding 4-Digit Numbers

People set up dominoes in patterns.
So, when 1 domino topples, the rest topple.

Explore

There are 1275 dominoes in one set-up.
There are 2168 dominoes in another set-up.
How many dominoes are there altogether?

Use what you know about adding 3-digit numbers
to solve this problem. Show your work.

Show *and* Share

Share your solution with another pair of students.
How did you add without using Base Ten Blocks?

Connect

Scott Suko is a world famous "domino toppler."
On his Website, there are photos of his set-ups.
One of Scott's set-ups had 1976 dominoes.
Another set-up had 2868 dominoes.
How many dominoes were there altogether?

Add: 1976 + 2868

➤ Use expanded form to add.

$$1976 \longrightarrow 1000 + 900 + 70 + 6$$
$$+ 2868 \longrightarrow + 2000 + 800 + 60 + 8$$
$$3000 + 1700 + 130 + 14$$

$$4700 + 144 = 4844$$

➤ Use place value to add.

Step 1
Add the ones: 14 ones
Regroup 14 ones
as 1 ten 4 ones.

$$\begin{array}{r} {}^{1} \\ 197\mathbf{6} \\ + 286\mathbf{8} \\ \hline \mathbf{4} \end{array}$$

Step 2
Add the tens: 14 tens
Regroup 14 tens as
1 hundred 4 tens.

$$\begin{array}{r} {}^{1\,1} \\ 19\mathbf{7}6 \\ + 28\mathbf{6}8 \\ \hline \mathbf{4}4 \end{array}$$

Step 3
Add the hundreds: 18 hundreds
Regroup 18 hundreds as
1 thousand 8 hundreds.

$$\begin{array}{r} {}^{1\,1\,1} \\ 1\mathbf{9}76 \\ + 2\mathbf{8}68 \\ \hline \mathbf{8}44 \end{array}$$

Step 4
Add the thousands: 4 thousands

$$\begin{array}{r} {}^{1\,1\,1} \\ \mathbf{1}976 \\ + \mathbf{2}868 \\ \hline \mathbf{4}844 \end{array}$$

There are 4844 dominoes altogether.

You estimate to check that the sum
is reasonable.
1976 rounds to 2000.
2868 rounds to 3000.

$2000 + 3000 = 5000$
Since 4844 rounds to 5000, the sum is reasonable.

Numbers Every Day

Calculator Skills

Use the digits 2, 3, and 4.
Find the product closest
to 75.

$$\begin{array}{r} \square\,\square \\ \times \square \\ \hline \end{array}$$

49

1. Find each sum. Estimate to check.
   a) 4167   b) 3974   c) 5287
       + 2534   + 4382   + 3756

2. Add. How do you know each sum is reasonable?
   a) 7865   b) 3198   c) 9999
       + 1987   + 6751   + 324

3. Estimate each sum, then add.
   a) 2496   b) 1976   c) 1285
       3758   2627   352
       + 1832   3499   6007
                       + 1863   + 128

4. a) Write a story problem that could be solved by adding: 4267 + 1398
   b) Estimate the sum. How did you get your estimate?
   c) Is your estimate high or low? How do you know?
   d) Find the sum. What strategy did you use?
   e) How do you know your answer is reasonable?
   Show your work.

5. Three thousand six hundred forty-two people
   went to the Fall Fair on Friday.
   Four thousand seven hundred ninety-five people
   went on Saturday.
   How many people went to the Fall Fair on these 2 days?

6. The sum of two 4-digit numbers is 3456.
   What might the two numbers be? Explain.

Reflect

Think about the mental math strategies you know for adding
3-digit numbers. Which strategies could you use to add
4-digit numbers mentally? Use words and numbers to explain.

8 Estimating Differences

Explore ....

An arena has 594 seats.
Three hundred eight tickets have been sold for a concert.
About how many tickets are left?
Estimate to find out. Record your answer.

Show *and* Share

Compare your estimate with that of another pair of students.
Did the strategies you used affect your answers? Explain.

Connect ....

➤ Estimate: 612 − 387
Round each number to the nearest 100.
612 rounds to 600.
387 rounds to 400.
Subtract:
600 − 400 = 200
So, 612 − 387
is about 200.

Make friendly numbers before you subtract.

You get a better estimate if you round only one number.
Round 387 to 400.
612 − 400 = 212
So, 612 − 387 is about 212.

➤ Estimate: 387 − 49
One number has only 2 digits,
so round to the nearest ten.
387 rounds to 390.
49 rounds to 50.
Subtract: 390 − 50 = 340
So, 387 − 49 is about 340.

A better way to estimate is to round only the number you subtract.
387 − 50 = 337
So, 387 − 49 is about 337.

Practice

1. Use rounding to estimate each difference.
   a) 871 − 263   b) 610 − 429   c) 734 − 591   d) 990 − 625

2. Kyle estimated each difference. Is each estimate high or low?
   How do you know?
   a) 576 − 392 as 100   b) 911 − 188 as 800   c) 736 − 187 as 600

3. Estimate each difference by rounding.
   How did you decide how to round each number? Explain.
   a) 983 − 407   b) 772 − 695   c) 918 − 75   d) 447 − 293

4. Charlotte looks at this survey.
   She says, "About 300 more students
   chose biking over walking."
   a) How might Charlotte have estimated?
      Explain.
   b) Is the estimate high or low?
      Explain.

5. Write a subtraction problem that can be
   solved by estimating.
   Solve the problem.

6. The estimated difference of two numbers is 300.
   What might the numbers be?
   Explain how you found the numbers.

Reflect

When does rounding to the nearest
hundred not give a good estimate
when you subtract?
Use words and numbers to explain.

Numbers Every Day

Mental Math

Is each statement an equation?
How do you know?

5 + 7 = 1 + 2 + 9
20 − 3 = 19 − 2
20 − 2 = 19 − 3
4 + 3 + 2 = 3 + 3 + 3

LESSON

9

Using Mental Math to Subtract

Explore

Anita used 354 cards to make a house of cards.
Christopher used 198 to make his house.
How many more cards are in Anita's house
than Christopher's?
Use mental math to find out. Record your answer.

Show and Share

Share the strategy you used with another pair of students.

Connect

➤ Use mental math to subtract: 516 − 299
Use the strategy of "make a friendly number."
Add 1 to 299 to make 300.
Add 1 to 516 to make 517.
Write 516 − 299 as:
        517 − 300 = 217
So,   516 − 299 = 217

> I use this strategy when
> the number I take away is
> close to a friendly number.

➤ Use mental math to subtract: 347 − 205
Use a friendly number.
Subtract 200 instead of 205.

Think: 347 − 200 = 147

Then subtract 5.
147 − 5 = 142
So, 347 − 205 = 142

> I took away 200,
> then I took away 5.

➤ Use mental math to subtract: 432 – 220
Use the strategy of "counting on."
For 432 − 220, count on from 220.

Count: 220, 320, 420, 430, 432

+ 100 + 100 + 10 + 2   = 212

So, 432 − 220 = 212

I use this strategy when there are not too many steps to count on.

Practice

Use mental math.

1. Subtract. Which strategy did you use each time?
   a) 536 − 399 **b)** 635 − 188 **c)** 822 − 216 **d)** 423 − 298

2. Subtract 715 − 197 mentally as many different ways as you can.
   Which strategy was easiest? Explain.

3. How much change will you get from $100 when you
   buy something that costs $68? How do you know?

4. The answer to a subtraction problem is 127.
   Use mental math to find what the problem might be.
   How many different problems can you find?
   Show your work.

5. Write a subtraction problem you can solve
   using mental math. Solve the problem.

Reflect

Can you always use mental math to
subtract?
Use words and numbers to explain the
different strategies.

Numbers Every Day

Mental Math

Subtract.
What patterns do you see?

21 − 12
32 − 23
43 − 34
54 − 45

Subtracting 3-Digit Numbers

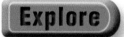 **Explore** ....

There are 430 students at Plymouth School.
Two hundred sixty-five students are boys.
How many are girls?

Use Base Ten Blocks to find out.
Draw pictures of the blocks to show your work.

Show *and* Share

Share your answer with another pair of students.
How could you have subtracted without using blocks?

Connect ....

Glendale School has 400 students.
Two hundred eighty-six students are girls.
How many are boys?

Subtract: 400 − 286

➤ Use Base Ten Blocks on a
   place-value mat to subtract.

You cannot take 6 ones
from 0 ones.
There are no tens to trade.
So, trade 1 hundred for 10 tens.

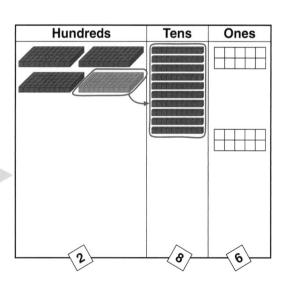

Hundreds	Tens	Ones

LESSON FOCUS | Use different strategies to subtract 3-digit numbers.

55

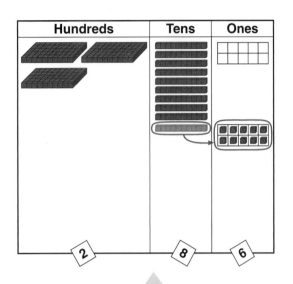

Hundreds	Tens	Ones
2	8	6

Trade 1 ten for 10 ones.

Numbers Every Day

Mental Math

Estimate each sum.
Which strategies did you use?

$73 + 22$

$155 + 156$

$307 + 199$

Hundreds	Tens	Ones
2	8	6

Take away 6 ones.
Take away 8 tens.
Take away 2 hundreds.

So, $400 - 286 = 114$

➤ Use place value to subtract.

You cannot take 6 ones from 0 ones.
There are no tens to regroup.
Regroup 1 hundred as 10 tens.
Regroup 1 ten as 10 ones.

$$\begin{array}{r} \overset{3}{\cancel{4}}\,\overset{9}{\cancel{0}}\,\overset{10}{\cancel{0}} \\ -\ 2\ 8\ 6 \\ \hline \end{array}$$

Subtract the ones.
Subtract the tens.
Subtract the hundreds.

$$\begin{array}{r} \overset{3}{\cancel{4}}\,\overset{9}{\cancel{0}}\,\overset{10}{\cancel{0}} \\ -\ 2\ 8\ 6 \\ \hline 1\ 1\ 4 \end{array}$$

➤ Use mental math to subtract.
Count on from 286 to 400.

Count: 286, 386, 396, 400

         + 100   + 10   + 4   = 114

So, 400 − 286 = 114

There are 114 boys.

You can check by adding.
The total number of boys and girls must equal
the number of students.

Add: 286 + 114
The sum should be 400.
Since 286 + 114 is 400, the answer is correct.

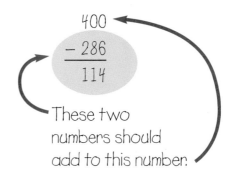

$$\begin{array}{r} 400 \\ -\ 286 \\ \hline 114 \end{array}$$

These two
numbers should
add to this number.

Practice

1. Subtract. What patterns do you see in the questions and answers?
    a) 857 − 100   **b)** 857 − 200   **c)** 857 − 300   **d)** 857 − 400

2. Estimate first. Then subtract the numbers for which the answer
will be less than 200.

    a) $\begin{array}{r} 255 \\ -\ 76 \\ \hline \end{array}$ **b)** $\begin{array}{r} 426 \\ -\ 158 \\ \hline \end{array}$ **c)** $\begin{array}{r} 678 \\ -\ 298 \\ \hline \end{array}$ **d)** $\begin{array}{r} 382 \\ -\ 192 \\ \hline \end{array}$

3. Subtract. How do you know each answer is reasonable?

    a) $\begin{array}{r} 565 \\ -\ 317 \\ \hline \end{array}$ **b)** $\begin{array}{r} 700 \\ -\ 189 \\ \hline \end{array}$ **c)** $\begin{array}{r} 101 \\ -\ 96 \\ \hline \end{array}$ **d)** $\begin{array}{r} 861 \\ -\ 178 \\ \hline \end{array}$

4. Sadiq read 315 pages.
Laura read 248 pages.
How many more pages does
Laura need to read to catch up
with Sadiq?

5. The largest gorilla has a mass of about 275 kg.
   The largest orangutan has a mass of about 90 kg.
   What is the difference in their masses?

6. The world records for barrel jumps
   are held by Canadians.
   The longest barrel jump by a woman is 670 cm.
   The longest barrel jump by a man is 882 cm.
   How much farther is the man's jump?
   How do you know your answer is reasonable?
   Show your work.

7. **a)** The answer to a subtraction problem is 375.
      What might the problem be?
      How many problems can you find?
   b) The answer to an addition problem is 375.
      What might the problem be?
      How many problems can you find?

Math Link

History

The abacus is used for counting.
You can add, subtract, multiply, and
divide with it.
The abacus was invented in China
over 800 years ago.
In North America, blind children are
taught to use the abacus.

Reflect

Tell why you can check a subtraction problem by adding.
Use words and numbers to explain.

Subtracting from a 4-Digit Number

Explore

Matthew's school created a Website.
One day, the site had 1531 visitors. The next day it had 867 visitors.
How many more people visited the site the first day?

Use what you know about subtracting
3-digit numbers to solve this problem.

Show *and* Share

Share your solution with another pair of students.
How did you subtract without using Base Ten Blocks?

Connect

How many more people visited the Website
on Friday than on Saturday?

Subtract: 2031 − 856

Day	Visitors to Website
Friday	2031
Saturday	856

Use place value to subtract.

You cannot take 6 ones from 1 one. Regroup 1 ten as 10 ones. Then, subtract the ones.	You cannot take 5 tens from 2 tens. There are no hundreds to regroup. So, regroup 1 thousand as 10 hundreds. Then, regroup 1 hundred as 10 tens.	Then, subtract the tens. Subtract the hundreds. Subtract the thousands.
$$\begin{array}{r} {\scriptstyle 2\ 11} \\ 203\overset{}{1} \\ -\ \ 856 \\ \hline 5 \end{array}$$	$$\begin{array}{r} {\scriptstyle 9\ 12} \\ {\scriptstyle 1\ 10\ 2\ 11} \\ 2031 \\ -\ \ 856 \\ \hline 5 \end{array}$$	$$\begin{array}{r} {\scriptstyle 9\ 12} \\ {\scriptstyle 1\ 10\ 2\ 11} \\ 2031 \\ -\ \ 856 \\ \hline 1175 \end{array}$$

There were 1175 more visitors on Friday than on Saturday.

Check.
➤ By adding
  Add the answer to the number you subtracted.

$$\begin{array}{r} 856 \\ + \ 1175 \\ \hline 2031 \end{array}$$ ← The sum is the number you started with. So, the answer is correct.

➤ By estimating
  2031 rounds to 2000.
  856 rounds to 900.
  $2000 - 900 = 1100$

1100 is close to 1175; so, the answer is reasonable.

Practice

1. Estimate, then subtract.
   Is each answer reasonable? Explain.
   a) $\begin{array}{r} 8274 \\ - \ \ \ 96 \\ \hline \end{array}$ b) $\begin{array}{r} 6328 \\ - \ \ 937 \\ \hline \end{array}$ c) $\begin{array}{r} 4028 \\ - \ \ 639 \\ \hline \end{array}$

2. Subtract. Check your answer.
   a) $\begin{array}{r} 3102 \\ - \ \ 428 \\ \hline \end{array}$ b) $\begin{array}{r} 5287 \\ - \ \ 931 \\ \hline \end{array}$ c) $\begin{array}{r} 7000 \\ - \ \ 476 \\ \hline \end{array}$

3. Subtract.
   a) $\begin{array}{r} 7130 \\ - \ 2864 \\ \hline \end{array}$ b) $\begin{array}{r} 9345 \\ - \ 6898 \\ \hline \end{array}$ c) $\begin{array}{r} 6005 \\ - \ 4816 \\ \hline \end{array}$

4. Subtract.
   a) Seven thousand one minus three hundred fifty-six
   b) Eight thousand twelve minus four hundred twenty-eight

5. It's 450 km from Fredericton to Halifax.
It's 4625 km from Fredericton to Edmonton.
How much closer is Fredericton to Halifax than to Edmonton?

6. Is it possible to subtract a 3-digit number from a
4-digit number and get a 4-digit number as the answer?
A 3-digit number as the answer?
A 2-digit number as the answer?
A 1-digit number as the answer?
Give an example for each possible answer.
Show your work.

7. In 1215, the Magna Carta was signed.
How many years ago is that?

8. Use eight different digits from 1 to 9.

□ □ □ □
− □ □ □ □
‾‾‾‾‾‾‾‾‾‾

a) What is the greatest difference you can make?
b) What is the least difference you can make?
c) How do you know the answer you found in
part a is the greatest? In part b is the least?

9. Each letter in this problem
represents a different digit
from 0 to 9.
What is the value of each letter?
How do you know?

S H H H
−   S
‾‾‾‾‾‾‾
Z Z Z

Reflect

What is the difference between checking
if your answer is reasonable and
checking if your answer is correct?
Use words and numbers to explain.

Strategies Toolkit

Explore

Fiona is 5 cm taller than Zac.
Together their heights total 299 cm.
How tall is Fiona? How tall is Zac?

Work together to solve this problem.
Use any materials you think will help.

Show and Share

Describe the strategy you used to
solve the problem.

Connect

Yael and Victor collect postcards.
Yael has 10 more postcards than Victor.
Together, they have 420 postcards.
How many postcards does each person have?

Understand

What do you know?
- There are 420 postcards in all.
- Yael has 10 more postcards
  than Victor.

Plan

Think of a strategy to help you
solve the problem.
- You can **make an organized list**.
- Find two numbers that add to 420.
  One number must be 10 more than
  the other.

Strategies

- **Make a table.**
- **Use a model.**
- **Draw a picture.**
- **Solve a simpler
  problem.**
- **Work backward.**
- **Guess and check.**
- **Make an organized
  list.**
- **Use a pattern.**

Make an organized list to show
the numbers.
Choose a number for Yael's postcards; such as 220.
Subtract 220 from the total:
420 − 220 is 200 postcards for Victor.
Subtract the numbers of postcards:
220 − 200 = 20 This is too high.

> Try 1 less for Yael
> and 1 more for
> Victor.

Yael's postcards	Victor's postcards	Difference
220	200	220 − 200 = 20 Too high
219	201	219 − 201 = 18 Too high

Continue this strategy until the difference is 10.

Could you have added and subtracted 2 or 3 instead?
Explain.

Practice

Choose one of the

Strategies

1. The Huda family drove 800 km in two days.
   They drove 20 km farther on the first day than on the
   second day. How far did the family drive each day?

2. Raphie has $1.75 in quarters and dimes.
   She has the same number of each coin.
   How many of each coin does Raphie have?

Reflect

What is the difference between "making a list" and
"making an organized list"?
Which is the better strategy for solving problems? Explain.

LESSON

1

1. The highest score in a Scrabble game is 1049.
   Write this number in words and in expanded form.

2. Write each number in standard form.
   a) eight thousand twenty-six   **b)** 6000 + 800 + 7

2

3. The deepest a submarine has gone
   is 6526 m below the surface of the ocean.
   Round this number:
   a) to the nearest thousand
   b) to the nearest hundred
   c) to the nearest ten

3

4. Write these numbers in order from least to greatest.
   5242, 5232, 5223

4
8

5. Estimate each sum or difference.
   a) 680 + 213   **b)** 276 − 178   **c)** 176 + 412
   d) 597 − 237   **e)** 276 + 566   **f)** 911 − 499

5
9

6. Use mental math to add or subtract.
   a) 256 + 172   **b)** 385 − 189   **c)** 247 + 338   **d)** 421 − 298

4

7. For a Read-A-Thon, Natalie read 786 pages.
   Kevin read 815 pages. Mario read 623 pages.
   Altogether, they read over 2000 pages.
   a) Is 2000 exact or an estimate? How do you know?
   b) About how many more pages did Kevin read than Mario?

6
7
11

8. Add or subtract. Check your answers.

   a)   2211   **b)**   452   **c)**   800   **d)**   4579
          − 878   + 348   − 298   + 3975

9. The tallest unicycle is 3053 cm high.
   The shortest unicycle is 20 cm high.
   How much taller is the tallest unicycle?

10. Canada was founded in 1867.
    Which birthday will Canada celebrate
    in 2006?
    How do you know?

Use the following information to answer
questions 11 to 13.
   Container A holds 2500 mL of water.
   Container B holds 1875 mL of water.

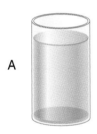 

A   B

11. How much do the two containers hold
    together?

12. Rhonda uses 725 mL from
    container A to make lemonade.
    Then Marilyn uses 925 mL
    to make juice, and Everett uses
    375 mL for his water bottle.
    How much is left in container A?

13. Is there enough room now in
    container A to pour in the water
    from container B? Explain.

UNIT
2 Learning Goals

- ✓ recognize and read numbers from 1 to 10 000
- ✓ read and write numbers in standard form, expanded form, and written form
- ✓ use place value to represent numbers
- ✓ compare and order numbers
- ✓ estimate sums and differences
- ✓ add and subtract 3-digit numbers mentally
- ✓ add 4-digit numbers
- ✓ subtract a 3-digit number from a 4-digit number
- ✓ pose and solve problems

Where Shall We Go?

You will need an atlas or a map of Canada,
or maps of the territories and provinces.

Plan a 7-day car trip anywhere in Canada.

Decide on the city where you will begin your trip.

You can travel up to 500 km per day.
Decide which cities you will stop at on each day of your trip.
(You do *not* have to plan your return trip.)

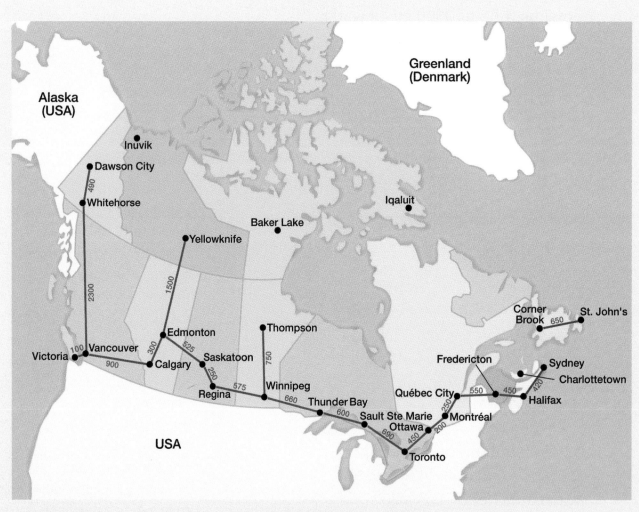

All distances are approximate and measured in kilometres.

➤ Plan your trip. Include:
- The cities you will travel to on each day of your trip
- The distance you will travel each day
- How much farther you will travel on one day than the next
- The total distance you will travel for the week

Show your work.

➤ Suppose you have $1000 for the trip. Do you think you will have any money left at the end of the trip? Explain.

Your work should show
- ☑ a plan of your trip and how you did what you were asked
- ☑ your thinking in words, numbers, or pictures
- ☑ how you added and subtracted correctly
- ☑ a clear record of your answers

Reflect on the Unit

Write about the different strategies you know for adding and subtracting.

Geometry

3

Under Construction

Learning Goals

- construct congruent figures
- measure angles
- sort and classify figures
- identify similar figures
- explore solids
- build skeletons

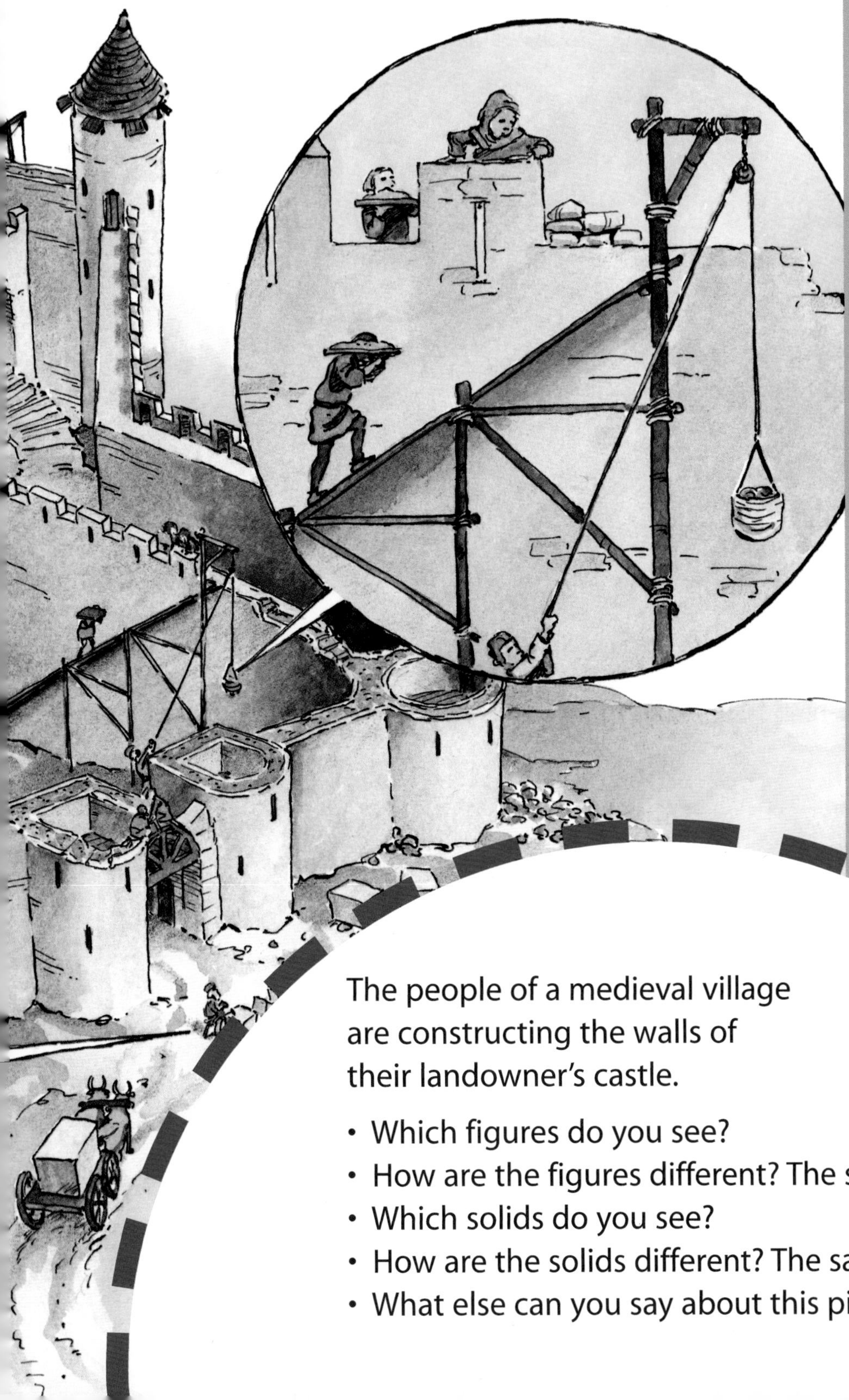

congruent figures

protractor

degree

quadrilateral

diagonal

kite

adjacent sides

parallel lines

similar figures

vertex, vertices

skeleton

volume

The people of a medieval village are constructing the walls of their landowner's castle.

- Which figures do you see?
- How are the figures different? The same?
- Which solids do you see?
- How are the solids different? The same?
- What else can you say about this picture?

Congruent Figures

What can you say about the figures in this picture?

Explore

You will need 2 geoboards, geobands, and dot paper.

➤ Take turns to make a figure on the geoboard, in secret. Then describe the figure to your partner.

➤ Your partner makes the same figure on her geoboard. When she has finished, look at the two figures. Are the figures congruent? How do you know?

➤ Draw the figures on dot paper.

Show and Share

Compare your figures with those of another pair of students.
Explain how you know if your classmates' figures are congruent.

Congruent figures have the same size and shape.

➤ The figures in each pair are congruent.

  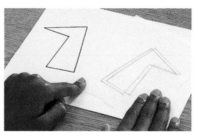

You may have to flip a figure, or turn a figure, to show it is congruent to another figure.

➤ You can use tracing paper to find out if two figures are congruent.

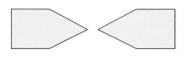

1. Use a copy of the figures below.
   Find pairs of congruent figures.
   Explain how you know the figures are
   congruent. Use tracing paper to check.

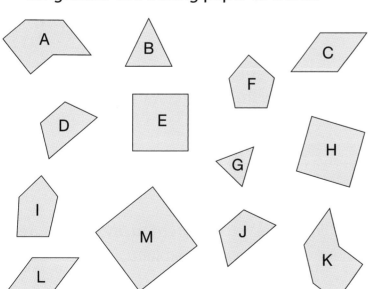

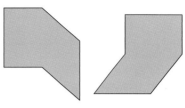 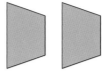

Numbers Every Day

Number Strategies

In the number 1234, which digit is in:

- the tens place?
- the hundreds place?
- the thousands place?
- the ones place?

Your World

A decorator uses a stencil to make a border with congruent figures. The decorator makes a repeating pattern with the figures.

2. Are the figures in each pair congruent? Explain how you know.

   a) 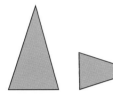   **b)** 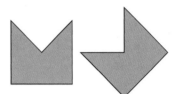   **c)**

3. Draw a figure.
   Use tracing paper to make a figure congruent to the figure you drew.

4. Use a geoboard or dot paper.
   Make each figure. Join the dots to divide each figure:
   a) into 3 congruent triangles
   b) into 3 congruent rectangles
   c) into 4 congruent figures

   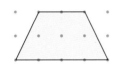   

   Which figure can you divide in different ways?
   Why can you not divide the other figures in different ways?
   Show your work.

Reflect

Suppose you want to create a figure that is congruent to another figure. How would you do it? Use pictures and words to explain.

Exploring Angles

An angle is formed when 2 lines cross.

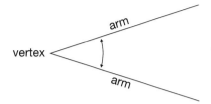

vertex

arm

arm

Explore

You will need Pattern Blocks.

➤ Look at each block.
Which blocks have a right angle?
Which blocks have an angle greater than a right angle?
Which blocks have an angle less than a right angle?
Record your work.

➤ Use the smaller angle in the tan block
as a unit of angle measure.
Measure each angle in each Pattern Block
in terms of the tan block angle.
Record your work in a table.

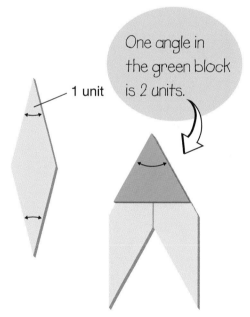

1 unit

One angle in
the green block
is 2 units.

Pattern Block	Angle Measure
	2 units

Show and Share

Share your angle measures with another pair of students.
What is the measure of each angle in the orange square?
The yellow hexagon? How do you know?

It is easier to measure an angle when the units are not separate pieces.

➤ We can put 6 tan blocks together to make an angle measurer.

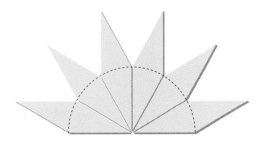

The angle measurer is called a **protractor**.
We can draw the protractor on tracing paper.

Number the units from 0 to 6 clockwise
and counterclockwise.

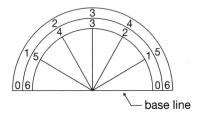

base line

➤ To measure this angle, count how many units
fit the angle:
  • Place the protractor on the angle.
  • Line up one arm of the angle with the
    base line of the protractor.
    The vertex of the angle is at the centre
    of the base line.
  • Use the scale, starting at 0, to count the units
    that fit between the arms.

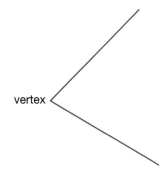

vertex

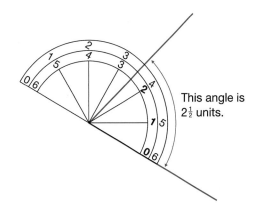

This angle is
$2\frac{1}{2}$ units.

The angle is between 2 units and 3 units.
The angle is about $2\frac{1}{2}$ units.

Use Pattern Blocks for questions 1 to 3.

1. Use one angle in the green triangle as a unit of angle measure.
   Measure the angles in:
   a) the yellow hexagon
   b) the blue rhombus
   c) the red trapezoid
   Record your measures.

2. You can measure the angles of some
   Pattern Blocks by combining other blocks.

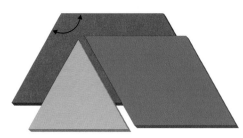

   Pattern Block Fact:
   The large angle of the red
   trapezoid is equal to one angle of
   the green triangle and one smaller
   angle of the blue rhombus.

   List three more angle facts about Pattern Blocks.

3. How is the orange square different from
   the other blocks?
   Write two facts about the angles of the
   orange square.

Math Link

Your World

A land surveyor
measures and maps
land. She uses a
distance meter to
measure distances
and a theodolite to
measure angles.

Numbers Every Day

Number Strategies

Use 1, 3, 5, and 7 to make:
- the smallest sum possible
- the largest sum possible

$$\begin{array}{c} \square\,\square \\ +\,\square\,\square \end{array}$$

4. Say if each angle is a right angle, less than a right angle, or greater than a right angle.

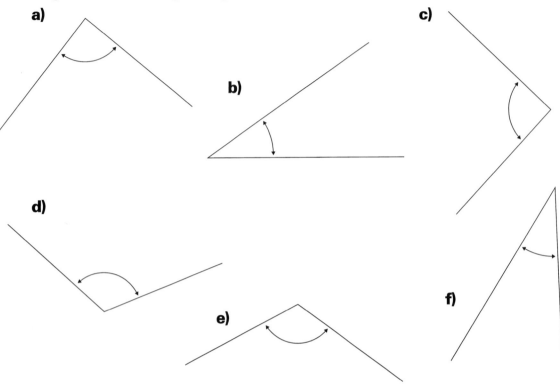

a)

b)

c)

d)

e)

f)

For questions 5 and 6, use the protractor your teacher gives you.

5. Measure each angle in question 4.

6. Use a ruler.
Draw an angle.
Use the protractor to measure the angle.
Explain how you did it.
Show your work.

Reflect

How can you tell if an angle is greater than or less than a right angle?
How many ways can you find out?
Use words and pictures to explain.

Measuring Angles

Each of you will need a piece of tracing paper or wax paper
measuring about 12 cm by 24 cm.
You will fold the paper to make a protractor.
You will then use the protractor to measure angles.

➤ Fold the paper in half and make a crease along the fold.

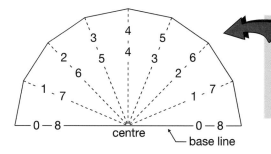

Fold the paper in half again and make a crease.
Fold the paper in half once more and make a crease.
Cut as shown. Then open out the paper.
It should look like this:

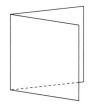

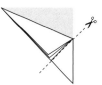

The protractor is divided into 8 equal slices.
The unit of angle measure is 1 slice.
Label the slices from 0 to 8 clockwise and
counterclockwise.

How is this protractor like the protractor you used in Lesson 2?
How is it different?

➤ Use your protractor to measure each angle.

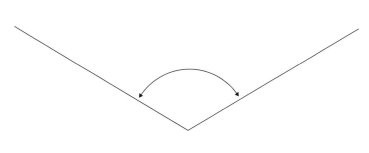
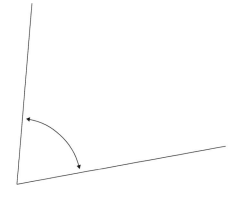

Show *and* Share

Compare your protractor with that of your partner.
Did you measure the angles the same way? Explain.
Did you get the same measures? Explain.

Connect

➤ The protractor you made has 8 congruent slices.
The protractor in Lesson 2 had 6 congruent slices.
You use a **standard protractor** to measure an angle more accurately.

The standard protractor has 180 congruent slices.
Each slice is 1 **degree**. You write: 1°

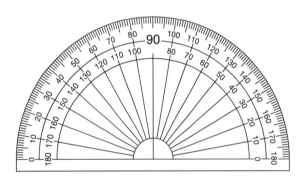

On the standard protractor, the measures go from 0° to 180° clockwise and counterclockwise.

The standard protractor shows angle
measures from 0° to 180°.
From now on, you will use a
standard protractor;
and we drop the name "standard."

➤ This angle is a right angle.
To measure this angle using a protractor:

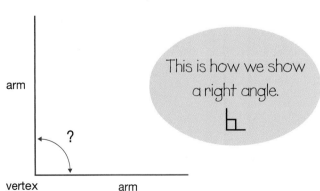

arm

?

vertex   arm

This is how we show
a right angle.

Step 1.

Place the protractor on top of the angle.

The vertex of the angle is at the centre of the protractor.

One arm of the angle lines up with the base line of the protractor.

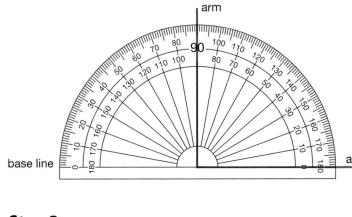

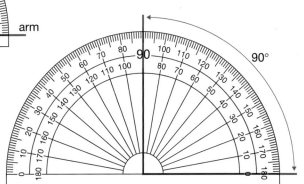

90°

Step 2.

Find where the other arm of the angle meets the protractor.

Start at 0° on the arm along the base line.

Read the measure.

The angle measures 90°.

A right angle measures 90°.

Practice

1. **a)** Which angle is greater than 90°? Less than 90°? Equal to 90°?

A

B

C

b) Use a protractor to measure the angles.
   Record the measurements.

c) Order the angles from largest to smallest.

2. Use capital letters.
Print your first and last names.
Look at the letters that have no curved parts.
   a) Which letters have all angles of 90°?
   b) Which letters have some angles that are greater than 90°?
   Less than 90°?
   c) Write a word with letters that have all angles of 90°.
   d) Write a word with letters that have no angles of 90°.

3. The hands of a clock make an angle at the centre of the clock.
Measure each angle.

a) **b)** **c)**

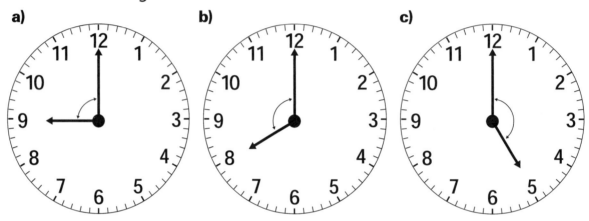

4. Use a ruler.
   a) Draw an angle you think is less than 90°.
   b) Draw an angle you think measures 90°.
   c) Draw an angle you think is greater than 90°.
   How can you check to see if you are correct?
   Show your work.

At Home

Reflect

Use a ruler. Draw an angle.
Explain how to measure the angle
using a protractor.

Look at different street signs.
Draw pictures of signs that have
angles less than 90°.

Exploring Sides in Quadrilaterals

A **quadrilateral** is a figure with 4 sides.

Explore ....

You will need a ruler and a copy of the quadrilaterals below.
Share the work.

➤ How are the quadrilaterals alike? How are they different?
   Identify each quadrilateral.
➤ Measure the lengths of the sides of each quadrilateral.
   What do you notice?
➤ A **diagonal** joins two opposite vertices.
   Draw the diagonals in each quadrilateral. What do you notice?
Record your results.

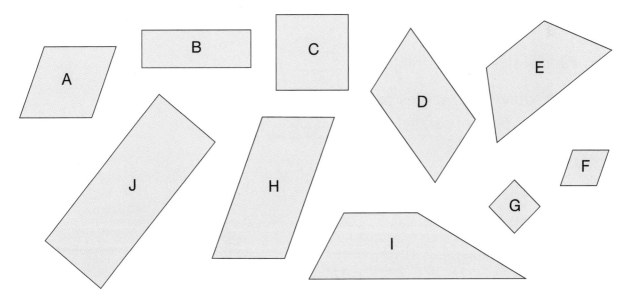

Show *and* Share

Make a class list of the attributes of each quadrilateral.

LESSON FOCUS | Discover attributes of quadrilaterals related to side lengths.

81

➤ Equal sides in quadrilaterals

- All squares have 4 sides equal.

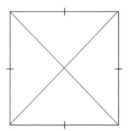

  The diagonals of a square are equal.

- All rectangles have 2 pairs of opposite sides equal.

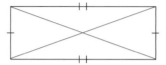

  The diagonals of a rectangle are equal.

- All rhombuses have 4 sides equal.

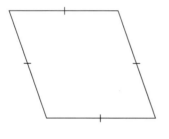

- All parallelograms have 2 pairs of opposite sides equal.

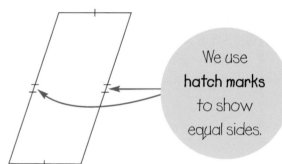

  We use **hatch marks** to show equal sides.

➤ Parallel sides in quadrilaterals

- All squares, rectangles, parallelograms, and rhombuses have 2 pairs of parallel sides.

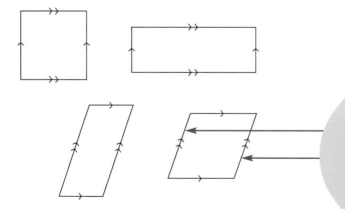

  Parallel lines are always the same distance apart and never meet. You draw arrows on lines to show they are parallel.

• All trapezoids have 1 pair of parallel sides.

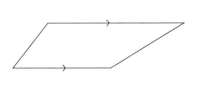

Practice •

1. Use a geoboard.
   Make 5 different rectangles.
   Draw the rectangles on dot paper.
   Write how each rectangle is different.

2. Use a geoboard.
   How many different quadrilaterals
   can you make:
   a) with 4 equal sides?
   b) with 2 pairs of parallel sides?
   c) with no equal sides and 2 parallel sides?
   Draw each quadrilateral on dot paper.

3. Here are two **kites**.
   Measure the sides of each kite.
   What attributes can you see?

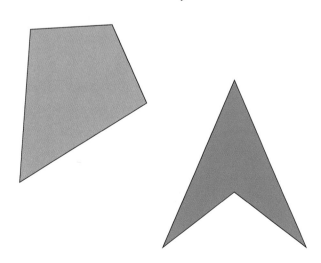

Numbers Every Day

Number Strategies

What patterns do you see?
Find each sum.

66 + 55

77 + 88

33 + 99

Is there a pattern in
the answers?
Explain.

4. Sort the quadrilaterals below.
 a) Use the attributes: "Has diagonals of different lengths"
 and "Has 2 pairs of equal sides."

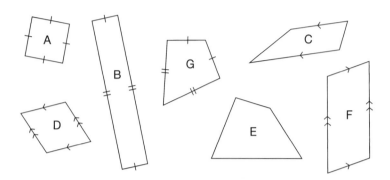

 b) Choose two different attributes.
 Sort the quadrilaterals a different way.

5. Copy this figure on dot paper.
 a) Join the dots to divide the figure into
 5 congruent rectangles.
 b) Can you join the dots to make
 4 congruent rectangles?
 How do you know?

6. Use dot paper. Draw a parallelogram.
 Write something about a parallelogram that is:
 a) Never true   **b)** Sometimes true   **c)** Always true
 Explain your work.

7. Use the words "all," "some," or "no."
 Complete each sentence to make it true.
 a) ☐ rhombuses are parallelograms.
 b) ☐ squares are rhombuses.
 c) ☐ rhombuses are squares.
 d) ☐ parallelograms have diagonals of equal length.

Reflect

How can you use the lengths of the sides of a quadrilateral
to identify it? Use words and pictures to explain.

Exploring Angles in Quadrilaterals

Explore

You will need a protractor and a copy of the quadrilaterals below.

Share the work.

➤ How are the angles in the quadrilaterals the same?
  How are they different?
  Identify each quadrilateral.

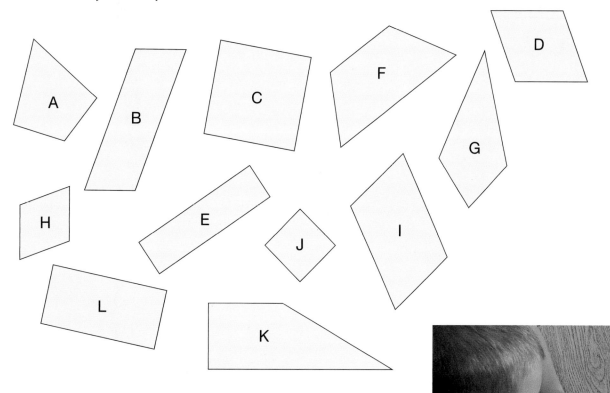

➤ Measure the angles in each quadrilateral.
  What do you notice?
Record your results.

Show *and* Share

Continue your class list of the attributes of each quadrilateral.

➤ All squares and rectangles have 4 equal angles.
Each angle is 90°.

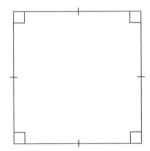

➤ All parallelograms and rhombuses have opposite angles equal.

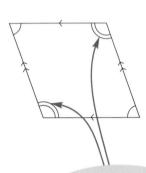

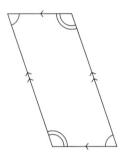

We use matching arcs to show equal angles in a figure.

➤ All kites have 2 equal angles.

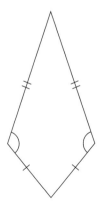

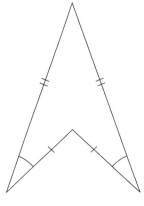

Numbers Every Day

Number Strategies

Order these numbers from least to greatest.

- 683, 694, 670, 609

- 3256, 2536, 6253, 2635

1. You will need a geoboard and dot paper.
Try to make a quadrilateral with each attribute.
   a) Only 1 right angle
   b) Only 2 right angles
   c) Only 3 right angles
Record each figure on dot paper.
Which figure could you not make? Explain.

2. How many different ways can you name each quadrilateral?

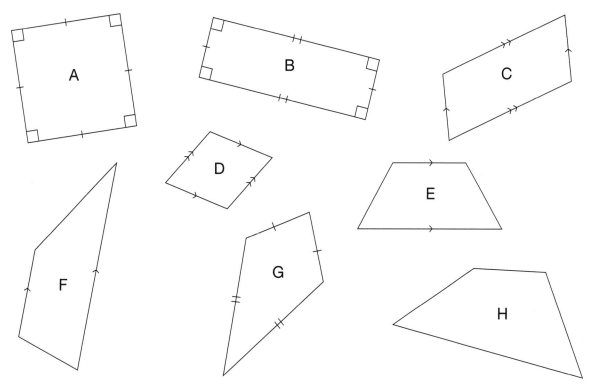

3. Use the quadrilaterals in question 2.
   a) Sort the quadrilaterals.
      Use the attributes: "Has all sides equal" and
      "Has an angle greater than a right angle."
      Record your sorting.
   b) Choose 2 different attributes.
      Sort the quadrilaterals again.
      Record your sorting.

Your World

You see parallel lines in rail road tracks, rails on a fence, and double yellow lines on a road.

4. a) Why is this quadrilateral not a square?

b) Why is this quadrilateral not a rectangle?

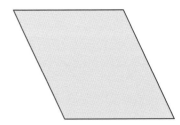

c) Why is this quadrilateral not a rhombus?

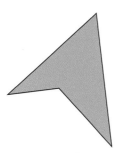

d) Why is this quadrilateral not a kite?

Show your work.

Reflect

What did you know about quadrilaterals before this lesson? Write 3 new things you learned about quadrilaterals.

Attributes of Quadrilaterals

Explore ••

➤ Draw a large copy of this diagram.

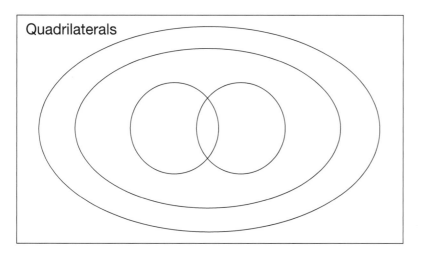

Quadrilaterals

Think about the attributes of each of these quadrilaterals.

square	parallelogram	rhombus	rectangle	trapezoid

➤ Write the name of each quadrilateral in the diagram so it is true for all quadrilaterals enclosed by that loop. In each loop, sketch a quadrilateral that belongs there.

Why does kite not fit in a loop?

Show and Share

Share your results with the class.
Explain why each name is in the correct loop.

Name	Attributes	Examples
Trapezoid	1 pair of parallel sides	
Parallelogram	2 pairs of parallel sides opposite sides equal opposite angles equal	
Rectangle	2 pairs of parallel sides opposite sides equal all right angles	
Square	2 pairs of parallel sides all sides equal all right angles	
Rhombus	all sides equal opposite angles equal 2 pairs of parallel sides	
Kite	2 pairs of equal adjacent sides 1 pair of equal angles	These sides are *adjacent*.

1. How are these figures the same? How are they different?

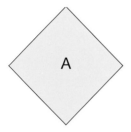
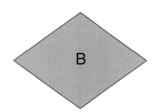

2. **a)** Why is a parallelogram a trapezoid?
   b) Why is a trapezoid not a parallelogram?
   c) Why is a rectangle a trapezoid?
   d) Why is a trapezoid not a rectangle?

3. Use a geoboard.
   Make a trapezoid with only 1 pair of parallel sides.
   How can you change the trapezoid to a square in the
   fewest moves?
   Draw the trapezoid and the results of each move on dot paper.

4. Solve each riddle.
   All figures are quadrilaterals.
   How many different figures
   can you find each time?
   a) I do not have any right angles.
       All my sides are the same length.
       What am I?
   b) All 4 of my angles are right angles.
       I have 2 pairs of equal sides.
       What am I?
   c) I have 2 parallel sides.
       I have 2 right angles.
       What am I?
   d) Make up your own riddle.
       Trade riddles with a classmate.
       Solve your classmate's riddle.
   Show your work.

Numbers Every Day

Calculator Skills

Enter the number 3. Enter ⊞
20 ⊟ ⊟ ⊟ ⊟ to
make an addition pattern.

Predict the next four terms
in the pattern. Check your
prediction.

5. Use a geoboard. Show how you can divide:
   a) a rectangle to make 3 smaller rectangles
   b) a parallelogram to make 3 smaller parallelograms
   Record your work on dot paper.
   Could you divide a square and rhombus in a similar way? Explain.

6. Use a tangram.
   a) Identify and name the tangram pieces that are quadrilaterals.
   b) Combine 2 tangram pieces to make a quadrilateral. Try to do this as many different ways as you can.
   Trace, then name each new figure you made.

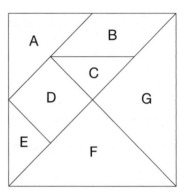

7. Use the clues to help you find the mystery attribute.
   • All these quadrilaterals have the attribute.

   • None of these quadrilaterals has the attribute.

   • Which of these figures have the attribute?

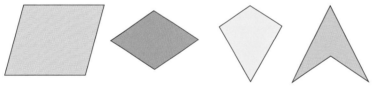

What is the attribute?

Reflect

Choose 2 quadrilaterals. Draw each one on dot paper.
Write all you know about it.

Similar Figures

Lisa had 2 sizes of photographs for her school pictures.

These photos have the same shape but different sizes.
Figures that have the same shape are **similar**.

Explore

➤ Which figures on these grids are similar? How do you know?

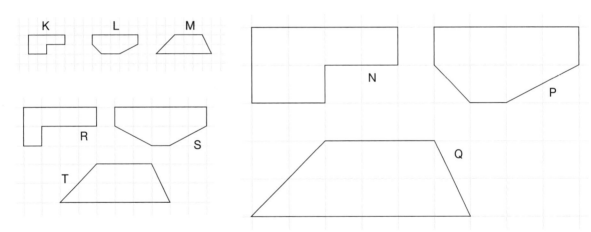

➤ Which figures on this grid are similar? How do you know?

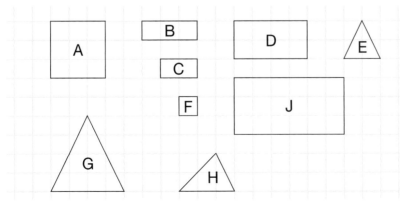

Show *and* Share

Compare your answers with those of
another pair of students.
How did you decide if 2 figures
were similar?

Connect

These figures are similar.
They have the same shape.

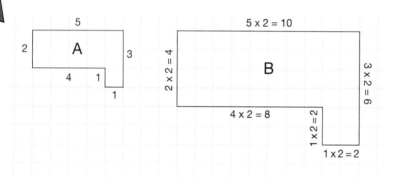

Each side of Figure B is 2 times the length of a corresponding side
of Figure A.
Each angle in Figure B is equal to a corresponding angle in Figure A.

These figures are *not* similar.
They do *not* have the same shape.

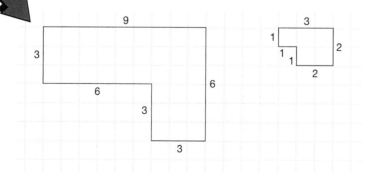

Math Link

Literacy

In language arts, two things
are similar if they are alike in
some way.
In math, the word "similar"
has a special meaning:
two figures are similar if they
have the same shape.

94

1. Which figures are similar? How do you know?

   a)

   b)

   c)

   d)

2. Which of these rectangles are similar? How do you know?

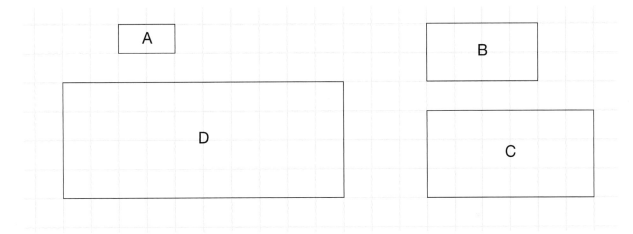

3. **a)** Are all squares similar?

   b) Are all rectangles similar?

   c) Are all triangles similar?

   Use words and pictures to show your answer to each question.

4. **a)** Do two rectangles always have the same shape? Explain.

   b) Are two rectangles always similar? Explain.

Reflect

How can you tell if 2 figures are similar?
Use words, numbers, or pictures to explain.

Using a Computer to Explore Pentominoes

Here are three pentominoes.

A pentomino is a figure made by joining 5 congruent squares.
There are twelve different pentominoes.
Use AppleWorks. Work with a partner.

Follow these steps to create pentominoes on a computer.

1. Open a new document in AppleWorks. Click:
   Drawing

2. If a grid appears on the screen, go to Step 3.
   If not, click: Options

   Click: Show Graphics Grid

3. Check that Autogrid is on.
   Click: Options

   If **Turn Autogrid Off** appears in the menu, Autogrid is on.
   If not, click: Turn Autogrid On   Ctrl+Y

4. Check the ruler units are centimetres.
   Click: Format

   Click: Rulers   ▶

   Click: Ruler Settings...

   Choose these settings:

   Click **OK**.

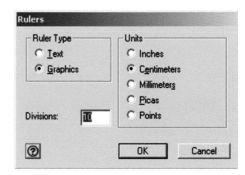

5. To **draw a square**, click the Rectangle Tool: ☐ .
   The cursor will look like this: **+**

   Hold down the Shift key while you click
   and hold down the mouse button.
   Drag the cursor. Release the mouse button.

6. To **change the size** of the square, click the square to select it.

   Click: | Options |

   Then click: ▐ Object Size... ▐

   Enter 2 cm for the width and 2 cm for the height.

   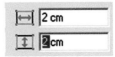

   Click: ☒ . This closes the Object Size box.

7. To **colour a square**, click the square.

   Click the Fill formatting button: ☐

   Click the Color palette button: ▦
   Select a colour.

8. To **copy a square**, click the square.

   Click: | Edit | Click: ▐ Copy   Ctrl+C ▐

   Click: | Edit | Click: ▐ Paste   Ctrl+V ▐

   The copy shows on top of the square.
   Click and drag the copy to where you want it.

9. To **move a square**, put the cursor inside the square.
   Click and hold down the mouse button.
   Drag the square to where you want it.
   Release the mouse button.

10. Use Steps 5 to 9 to create 12 different pentominoes.

11. Save your pentominoes.

Click: | File |

Click: Save As...   Shft+Ctrl+S

Name your file. Then click **Save**.

12. Print your pentominoes.

Click: | File |

Click: Print...   Ctrl+P

Click **OK**.

13. Use your pentominoes to make a puzzle.
Trade puzzles with a classmate.
Solve your classmate's puzzle.

14. Use your pentominoes to make a pattern.
Print your pattern.
Describe your pattern.

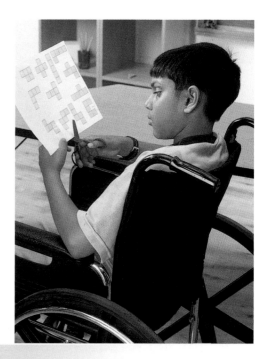

Reflect

How did you find 12 different pentominoes?
Write about how you know they are different.

Faces of Solids

A pyramid and a prism are named for their bases.
The bases are shaded in the pictures below.

- A pyramid has 1 base.

Square pyramid

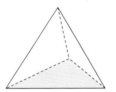

Triangular pyramid

- A prism has 2 bases.

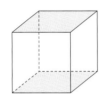

Square prism or cube

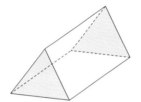

Triangular prism

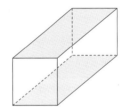

Rectangular prism

Explore

 Game

The Face-Off Game!

The goal of this game is to show
all the faces of each solid above.

Game Rules
You need 3 players and 36 cards.
Each card shows the face of one of the solids.

1. The dealer deals 3 cards to each player.
   The deck of remaining cards is placed
   face down.

LESSON FOCUS | Identify and sketch the faces of solids.

2. The dealer places one of her cards face up.
This is one face of one of the solids shown on page 99.

3. Each time a player places a card face up,
the player takes a new card from the deck.

4. The second player selects a card from his hand
that shows another face of the solid started by the dealer.
(If a player does not have a card that can be used,
he takes a new card from the deck. The player loses his turn.)

5. The third player selects a card from her hand
that is another face of the solid.

6. Play continues until all faces of the solid are shown.

7. The player who places the last card to complete all faces
of the solid, names the solid, and gets a point.

8. All the cards are shuffled and a new round begins.

9. Play continues for 4 more rounds.
The player with the most points wins.

In each round, players must build a new solid with their face cards.

Show *and* Share

Show how you matched the faces to each solid.
Talk about the faces for each solid.
Which faces are congruent? How do the faces fit together?

Here are some solids and their faces.

Solid	Faces in Pictures	Faces in Words
Rectangular prism		3 pairs of congruent rectangles
Rectangular pyramid		1 rectangle 2 pairs of congruent triangles
Cube		6 congruent squares
Triangular pyramid		4 congruent triangles
Triangular prism		2 congruent triangles 3 congruent rectangles

Use models of solids when you can.

1. Name each solid. Identify the shape of the face that is shaded blue.

    a)

    b)

    c)

    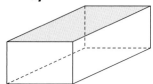 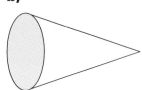 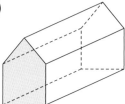

2. Sketch and name the different faces of each solid in question 1.

3. Name three solids that have at least one rectangular face.
    Sketch all the different faces of each solid you name.

4. Identify the solid that has each set of faces.
    Explain how you know. Show your work.

    a)

    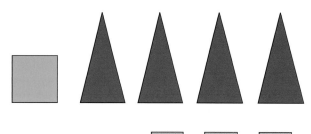

    b)

Reflect

Compare a prism and a pyramid.
How are they the same? Different?
Use words and sketches of faces to explain.

Numbers Every Day

Number Strategies

39 is ...

☐ ones

☐ tens and ☐ ones

4 groups of 10 minus ☐

1 ten and ☐ ones

 9 Solids in Our World

Think about some of the objects you see around you.

What makes one object different from another?

Explore

➤ Go on a scavenger hunt.
Find as many classroom items as you can that match each solid below. Explain why each item matches a solid.

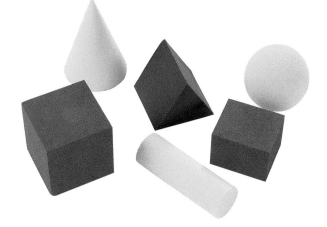

➤ Sort the items and solids. Record your sorting.

Show **and** Share

Show another pair of students your sorting.
Talk about the attributes you used to sort.
Find other ways to sort.

Here are some ways to sort solids.

➤ You can sort by the numbers of faces, edges, and vertices.

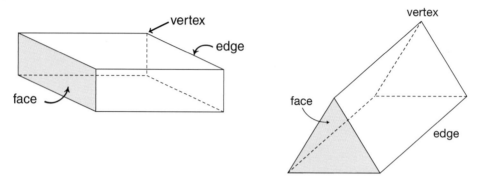

The solids below have been sorted by the numbers of faces.

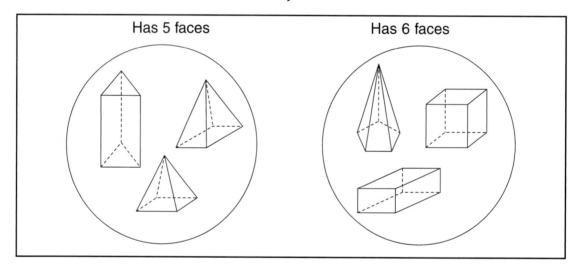

➤ You can sort by the shapes of the faces.

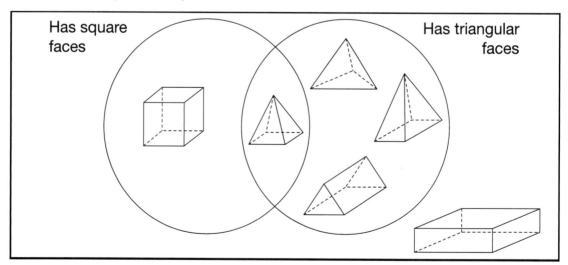

1. Match each solid on the left to an item on the right.

For each pair, name the solid.
How are the solid and the item alike? Different?

2. Name the solid that best represents each item.

a)

b)

c)

Numbers Every Day

Mental Math

Subtract.

456 − 322
329 − 150
601 − 349

Which strategies did
you use?

3. a) Sort the solids below.
Use the attributes: "Has circular faces" and "Has more than 6 faces."

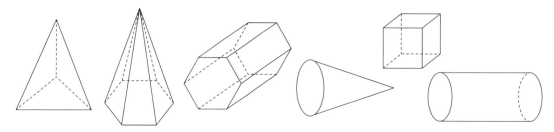

b) Sort the solids above.
Choose 2 attributes different from those in part a.
Record your sorting.

4. Use the words "all," "some," or "no" in place of ☐.
Copy and complete each sentence.
How do you know each sentence is true?
  a) ☐ rectangular prisms have 6 vertices.
  b) ☐ cubes are rectangular prisms.
  c) ☐ rectangular prisms are cubes.
  d) ☐ triangular prisms have 5 congruent faces.
Show your work.

5. Look at a sharpened pencil.
Which two solids best represent it?
Sketch a picture.

Reflect

When you look at an object,
how can you tell which solid or
solids best represent it?
Use words and pictures to explain.

At Home

Find an object that represents
each solid you know.
List the solids and the
matching objects.

Designing Skeletons

When a building is constructed, the first step is to build a frame or **skeleton** of the building.

Which figures can you see in this skeleton?

Explore

You will need scissors, straws, and Plasticine.

➤ Take turns to choose one of these solids.

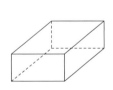 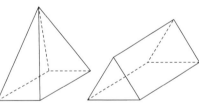 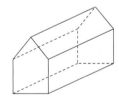

➤ Without your partner seeing, make a skeleton of the solid.
Take turns to describe your skeleton to your partner.
Your partner makes the skeleton, then tells what the solid is.

➤ Choose a different solid.
Make a skeleton of it.
Write how you made your skeleton.
Trade notes with your partner.
Use your partner's notes to make a skeleton of his solid.

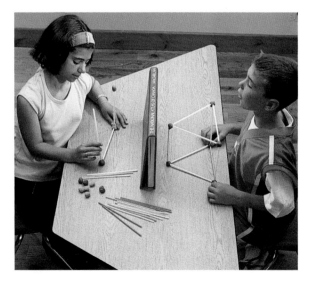

Show *and* Share

Talk with your partner about how you described each skeleton.
How was your partner able to identify it?

A skeleton can be described by how many vertices it has,
and its equal edges.

Skeleton	Number of Vertices	Types of Edges
Rectangular prism	8	4 equal lengths 4 equal heights 4 equal widths
Rectangular pyramid	5	The base has 2 pairs of equal edges. There are 4 equal edges from the base.

We use hatch marks to show equal edges.

Practice

1. Jo made skeletons using toothpicks and marshmallows.
   She counted edges and vertices.
   This table shows some of Jo's results. Copy and complete this table.
   What do the toothpicks represent?
   What do the marshmallows represent?

Number of Toothpicks	Number of Marshmallows	Skeleton
6		triangular pyramid
8	5	
9	6	
	8	rectangular prism
12		cube

2. **a)** Suppose you build a cube using marshmallows and toothpicks.
How many marshmallows would you need?
Draw a picture to show your thinking.

   b) Suppose you made a skeleton of 3 connected cubes.
How many marshmallows and toothpicks would you need?
Sketch the skeleton.

   c) Look at the skeleton in part b.
Join 3 cubes in a way that uses a different number
of marshmallows.
Sketch the new skeleton.
Explain how it is different from the skeleton in part b.

3. Suppose you have 20 toothpicks and 6 marshmallows.
You can use some or all of these materials.
Which solids could you make skeletons of?
Sketch all possible skeletons.
Show your work.

4. Why can you not make a skeleton for a cone, a cylinder,
or a sphere? Explain.

Numbers Every Day

Number Strategies

Write four different number
patterns that begin
with 1, 2, ...

Write each pattern rule.

Reflect

Which attributes of prisms and
pyramids make it easy to create
skeletons? Use words, pictures, or
numbers to explain.

Strategies Toolkit

Explore

Liam and Sophie have 36 Snap Cubes. They use all the cubes to build a rectangular prism.
The **volume** of the prism is 36 cubes. How many different rectangular prisms can they build?

Show *and* Share

Explain how you solved this problem.

Connect

Here is a similar problem.
How many different rectangular prisms can you build with a volume of 24 Snap Cubes?

Understand

What do you know?
- There are 24 cubes.
- The cubes are used to build a rectangular prism.

Think of a strategy to help you solve the problem.
- You can **use a model**.
- Use the cubes to make different rectangular prisms.

Plan

Strategies

- **Make a table.**
- **Use a model.**
- **Draw a picture.**
- **Solve a simpler problem.**
- **Work backward.**
- **Guess and check.**
- **Make an organized list.**
- **Use a pattern.**

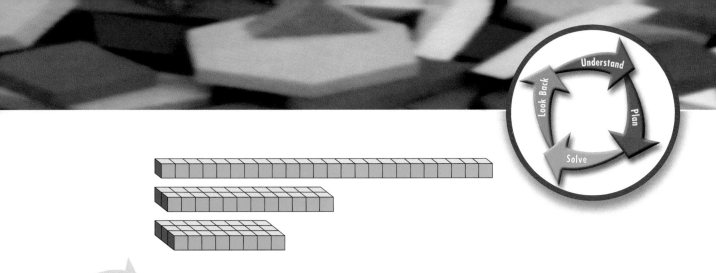

Start with a prism that is 1 cube high.
How many different prisms can you build?
Then try to build different prisms that are 2 cubes high,
3 cubes high, and so on.
How many different rectangular prisms did you make?
Record each prism that you made.

How do you know you have found all possible
rectangular prisms?
Think of another way you could have solved this problem.

Practice

Choose one of the

Strategies

1. You have 100 Snap Cubes. How many larger cubes
   can you make using any number of the small cubes?
   Record your work. What patterns do you see?

2. A rectangular prism has a volume of 9 Snap Cubes.
   How many different prisms can be made with these cubes?
   Suppose the number of cubes were doubled.
   How many different prisms can be made now?

Reflect

How can building a model help you solve a problem?
Use examples to explain.

LESSON

2
3

1. Measure each angle.

a)   b)   c)

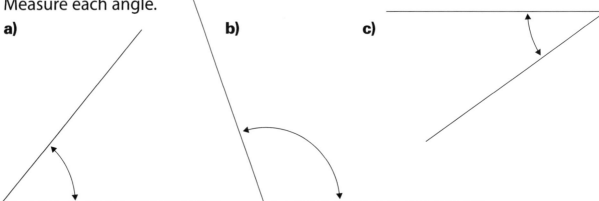

4
5
6

2. Choose 2 attributes. Sort these figures.

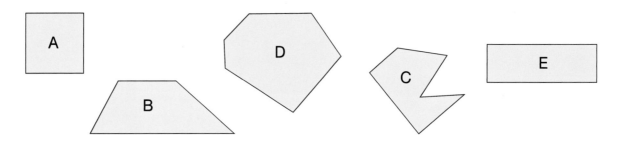

3. Identify each quadrilateral in question 2.
List the attributes of each quadrilateral.

4. Answer each question. Explain how you know.
   a) Is a rectangle a square?   **b)** Is a square a rectangle?
   c) Is a rhombus a square?   **d)** Is a rhombus a parallelogram?

7

5. Are these figures similar? Explain how you know.

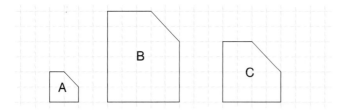

6. Name each solid. Sketch the faces of each solid.
Name the faces. Say if any faces are congruent.

a)

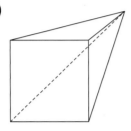

b)

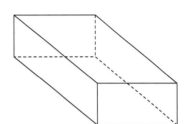

7. Name the solid that best represents each item.
Sketch the different faces of each solid you name.

a)

b)

c)

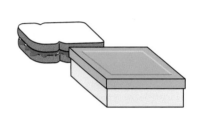

8. Suppose you have 10 toothpicks and 6 marshmallows.
Design a skeleton that uses some or all of these materials.
Use Plasticine and straws to make the skeleton.
Sketch the skeleton.

9. Use 20 Snap Cubes.

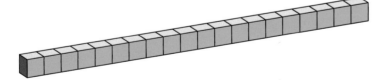

How many different rectangular prisms
can you make with a volume of
20 Snap Cubes?
Record your work.

UNIT

3 Learning Goals

☑ construct congruent figures
☑ measure angles
☑ sort and classify figures
☑ identify similar figures
☑ explore solids
☑ build skeletons

Unit Problem

Under Construction

Part 1

- Design a medieval castle.
- Use Plasticine and straws to make a skeleton of your castle.
- Sketch the skeleton; then write about it.

Part 2

- Design one wall of your castle.
- Use grid paper to sketch windows with different shapes and sizes.
- Try to include all the figures you have learned about in this unit.
- Include congruent figures in your design.
- Measure the angles of the figures in your design.
- Write about your wall.

Reflect on the Unit

Sketch the different figures you have worked with.
Write about each figure and how you can identify it.

The Icing on the Cake

You will need Snap Cubes and a calculator.

My piece has icing on three faces.

My piece has icing on one face.

My piece has icing on two faces.

Part 1

➤ Use Snap Cubes to model different-sized, square, one-layer "cakes."
  Start with a 2 by 2 square.
  Make larger and larger squares.
➤ Imagine that the top and sides are covered in icing.
  Each Snap Cube represents one piece of cake.
➤ For each cake, how many pieces have icing on one face?
  How many pieces have icing on two faces? Three faces?
Record your work in a table.

Size of Cake	Number of Pieces	Number of Faces with Icing		
		3 Faces	2 Faces	1 Face
2 by 2	4			

Part 2

➤ What patterns can you find in the table?

➤ What do you notice about the numbers of pieces that have icing on three faces?

➤ One cake has 16 pieces with icing on two faces. How many pieces are there in the whole cake?

➤ Suppose you made a 10 by 10 cake. How many of each kind of piece would there be?

Display Your Work

Make a poster display to show all the patterns you found.

Take It Further

Model rectangular cakes with 24 Snap Cubes.

➤ How many different cakes can you model using all 24 cubes?

➤ How many cakes have pieces with icing on four faces?

➤ Which cake has the greatest number of pieces with icing on one face? Two faces? Three faces?

➤ Write about what you found out.

117

At the
Garden Centre

Learning Goals

- skip count
- recall basic multiplication and division facts
- use different strategies to multiply and divide
- relate multiplication and division
- identify patterns in multiplication and division
- multiply by 10, 100, and 1000
- multiply and divide a 2-digit number by a 1-digit number
- pose and solve problems using multiplication and division

and Division

May-Lin works in a garden centre. She has planted seeds that grow into seedlings.

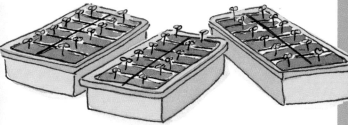

- How many seedlings are there?
- How did you find out?
- How many different ways can you find the answer?

May-Lin will replant the seedlings into other boxes like this:

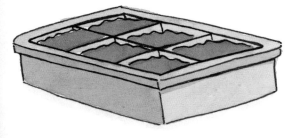

- How many smaller boxes does May-Lin need for all the seedlings?
- How do you know?

Key Words
· · · · · · · · · · · · · · · ·

multiples

multiplication fact

factor

product

array

multiplication sentence

related facts

remainder

division sentence

short division

Skip Counting

You will need copies of these charts.

Hundred Chart

1	2	3	4	5	6	7	8	9	10
11	12	13	14	15	16	17	18	19	20
21	22	23	24	25	26	27	28	29	30
31	32	33	34	35	36	37	38	39	40
41	42	43	44	45	46	47	48	49	50
51	52	53	54	55	56	57	58	59	60
61	62	63	64	65	66	67	68	69	70
71	72	73	74	75	76	77	78	79	80
81	82	83	84	85	86	87	88	89	90
91	92	93	94	95	96	97	98	99	100

Multiplication Chart

x	1	2	3	4	5	6	7	8	9	10
1	1	2	3	4	5	6	7	8	9	10
2	2	4	6	8	10	12	14	16	18	20
3	3	6								
4	4	8								
5	5	10								
6	6	12								
7	7	14								
8	8	16								
9	9	18								
10	10	20								

➤ Use the hundred chart.
   Start at 3 and count on by 3s.
   Use the numbers you count to fill in the next row
   and column in the multiplication chart.

➤ Repeat the activity.
   Start at 4 and count on by 4s.
   Start at 5 and count on by 5s.
   Count on by other numbers until you have filled in the chart.

Which patterns do you see in the multiplication chart?

Show and Share

Share the patterns you found with another pair of students.
Which patterns did you find in the ones digits? The tens digits?

Look at the row for 6 in the multiplication chart.

6	6	12	18	24	30	36	42	48	54	60

You say these numbers when you start at 6 and count on by 6s.
These numbers are **multiples** of 6.

Practice
· ·

1. Use a hundred chart.
   a) Start with 3.
      Colour all the numbers you say
      when you count on by 3s.
   b) Use a different colour.
      Colour all the multiples of 6.
      What patterns do you see?
   c) Use a different colour.
      Colour all the multiples of 9.
      What patterns do you see?

Use a multiplication chart for questions 2 and 3.

2. a) Start at 4.
      List multiples of 4.
   b) Start at 8.
      List multiples of 8.
   c) Compare the numbers in both lists.
      What patterns do you see?

3. a) List the multiples of 10.
   b) List the multiples of 5.
   c) Compare the numbers in both lists.
      What patterns do you see?

Numbers Every Day

Number Strategies

Skip count to find the missing numbers.

3, 6, 9, □, □, □
10, 20, 30, 40, □, □, □
7, 14, 21, 28, □, □, □
12, 17, 22, 27, □, □, □

4. Play this game with a partner.
   You will need a number cube labelled 4, 5, 6, 7, 8, 9;
   a counter; and a hundred chart.
   Choose a target number between 50 and 100.
   Put the counter on that number.
   Roll the number cube to find the start number.
   Use the same number to count on.
   Have your partner say if you will "hit" the target
   when you count on.
   Count on to check. Or, explain how you know.
   Trade roles. Take turns to roll and check.

5. Is each statement true or false?
   Give an example to support each answer.
   a) A multiple of 4 is also a multiple of 2.
   b) A multiple of 2 is also a multiple of 4.
   c) When a number is even, all its multiples are even.
   d) When a number is odd, all its multiples are odd.
   Show your work.

6. List all the multiples of 2 to 50.
   List all the multiples of 3 to 50.
   What numbers are in both lists?
   How would you describe these numbers?

7. a) Use a copy of a hundred chart.
      Colour all the numbers in which the ones digit
      and the tens digit are the same.
   b) What multiples have you coloured? Explain.

8. A student says that 36 is a multiple of 3.
   How can you check if she is correct?

Reflect

How can you find multiples?
Use words and numbers to explain.

Multiplying by Numbers to 9

You can use a multiplication chart to write multiplication facts.
For example,

$$6 \times 7 = 42$$

↑

This is a **multiplication fact**.

x	1	2	3	4	5	6	7
1	1	2	3	4	5	6	7
2	2	4	6	8	10	12	14
3	3	6	9	12	15	18	21
4	4	8	12	16	20	24	28
5	5	10	15	20	25	30	35
6	6	12	18	24	30	36	42
7	7	14	21	28	35	42	49

Explore

Look at this multiplication chart.
How is it the same as the chart above?
How is it different?
Use the chart to write ten multiplication facts.

x	0	1	2	3	4	5	6	7	8	9
0	0	0	0	0	0	0	0	0	0	0
1	0	1	2	3	4	5	6	7	8	9
2	0	2	4	6	8	10	12	14	16	18
3	0	3	6	9	12	15	18	21	24	27
4	0	4	8	12	16	20	24	28	32	36
5	0	5	10	15	20	25	30	35	40	45
6	0	6	12	18	24	30	36	42	48	54
7	0	7	14	21	28	35	42	49	56	63
8	0	8	16	24	32	40	48	56	64	72
9	0	9	18	27	36	45	54	63	72	81

Show and Share

Share your facts with another pair of students.
What is a quick way to multiply by 0? By 1?

➤ In a multiplication fact, you multiply **factors** to get a **product**.

5 × 4 = 20

factor ↑   factor ↑   product ↑

➤ You can use symmetry to help you remember multiplication facts.

The multiplication chart has a line of symmetry along the diagonal from 0 to 81.

x	0	1	2	3	4	5	6	7	8	9
0	0	0	0	0	0	0	0	0	0	0
1	0	1	2	3	4	5	6	7	8	9
2	0	2	4	6	8	10	12	14	16	18
3	0	3	6	9	12	15	18	21	24	27
4	0	4	8	12	16	20	24	28	32	36
5	0	5	10	15	20	25	30	35	40	45
6	0	6	12	18	24	30	36	42	48	54
7	0	7	14	21	28	35	42	49	56	63
8	0	8	16	24	32	40	48	56	64	72
9	0	9	18	27	36	45	54	63	72	81

If you know:	then you know:
7 × 6 = 42	6 × 7 = 42
8 × 5 = 40	5 × 8 = 40
9 × 4 = 36	4 × 9 = 36

➤ When you multiply by 1, the product is the other factor.

3 × 1 = **3**   1 × **5** = **5**

➤ When you multiply by 0, the product is 0.

7 × **0** = **0**   **0** × 6 = **0**

➤ You can use patterns to remember multiplication facts with 9.

The number multiplied by 9 is always 1 more than the tens digit in the product; for example:

6 is 1 more than 5. ⟶ **6 × 9 = 54**
7 is 1 more than 6. ⟶ **7 × 9 = 63**

$1 \times 9 = 9$
$2 \times 9 = 18$
$3 \times 9 = 27$
$4 \times 9 = \textbf{36}$ ⟶ $3 + 6 = 9$
$5 \times 9 = \textbf{45}$ ⟶ $4 + 5 = 9$
$6 \times 9 = \textbf{54}$
$7 \times 9 = \textbf{63}$
$8 \times 9 = 72$
$9 \times 9 = 81$

The digits in the product always add to 9; for example:

Practice

1. Multiply.
   a) 7×1
   b) 0×3
   c) 1×2
   d) 1×0

2. Multiply.
   a) 1×2
   b) 2×2
   c) 2×3
   d) 2×4
   e) 5×2
   f) 2×6
   g) 7×2
   h) 2×8

   Which strategies did you use to multiply by 2?

3. Multiply.
   a) 1×5
   b) 5×2
   c) 3×5
   d) 5×4
   e) 5×5
   f) 6×5
   g) 7×5
   h) 5×8

   Which strategies did you use to multiply by 5?

4. How can you use patterns to find each product?
   a) 7×9
   b) 8×9
   c) 9×9
   d) 9×6
   e) 8×2

5. If you know 8×3, what else do you know?

6. Show how you find each product.
   a) 8×5
   b) 8×6
   c) 6×9
   d) 7×8
   e) 6×3

7. Multiply.
   a) 4×8
   b) 5×9
   c) 8×7
   d) 2×9
   e) 1×8

Try to remember as many facts as you can.

8. How many days are in 8 weeks? 9 weeks?

9. Write a multiplication fact for each product.
How many different facts can you find?
   a) 12   **b)** 16   **c)** 18   **d)** 24   **e)** 36

10. Emi walks her dog every day for 2 hours.
How many hours does Emi walk in 5 weeks?
Show your work.

11. Find each product.
What patterns do you see in the products?
   a) $12 \times 9 = \square$ **b)** $13 \times 9 = \square$
   c) $14 \times 9 = \square$ **d)** $15 \times 9 = \square$
   e) $16 \times 9 = \square$ **f)** $17 \times 9 = \square$
   g) $18 \times 9 = \square$ **h)** $19 \times 9 = \square$
   i) $20 \times 9 = \square$

Reflect

A student cannot remember that
$7 \times 6 = 42$.
How do *you* remember this
multiplication fact?
Use words, pictures, or numbers to explain.

Numbers Every Day

Mental Math

Find each sum. What strategy
did you use?

19 + 2

24 + 3

33 + 2

48 + 3

3 Other Strategies for Multiplying

Explore · 👫 Game

Play this game with a partner.

Cross-Out Product

You will need a number cube labelled 4, 5, 6, 7, 8, 9; and 2 copies of this game board.

4	6	9	12	14
18	20	24	27	32
35	40	42	45	49
56	63	64	72	81

➤ One person rolls the number cube to get a factor.
   Each person thinks of a multiplication fact
   that uses that factor.
   Record the fact you use.
   Cross out the product on your game board.

➤ Take turns to roll the number cube.
➤ The first person to cross out all the products is the winner.

Show *and* Share

Talk with your partner about the strategies you used to multiply.
Did you use a multiplication chart?
Did you use mental math?

Here are some strategies to multiply.

➤ Use doubling to multiply by 4.
First multiply by 2, then double.

To find 4×9:

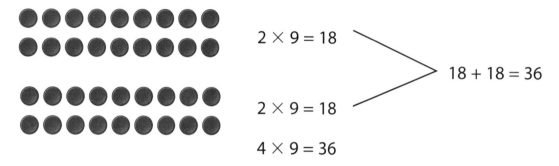

$2 \times 9 = 18$

$2 \times 9 = 18$

$18 + 18 = 36$

$4 \times 9 = 36$

This is an **array**.

➤ Use known facts to multiply by 6.
Use what you know about multiplying by 5 to multiply by 6.

To find 6×7:

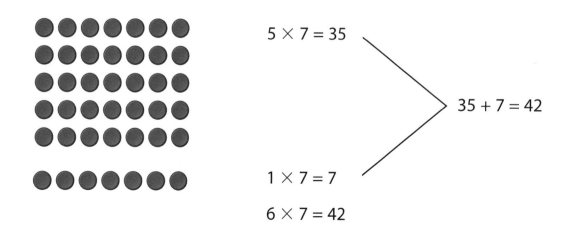

$5 \times 7 = 35$

$1 \times 7 = 7$

$35 + 7 = 42$

$6 \times 7 = 42$

➤ Use facts with 5 and 2 to multiply by 7.

To find 7 × 8:

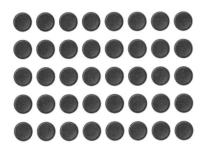

$5 \times 8 = 40$

$40 + 16 = 56$

$2 \times 8 = 16$

$7 \times 8 = 56$

Practice

Use counters when they help.

1. Make an array to find each product.
   a) 3×7 b) 7×3
   c) 6×4 d) 4×6

2. Multiply. What strategies did you use?
   a) 9×8 b) 7×5
   c) 8×4 d) 4×9

3. Children are jumping rope at recess.
   Three children share each rope.
   There are 9 jump ropes.
   How many children can jump rope?
   Show your work.

4. Name two facts that help you find the product of 8×6.

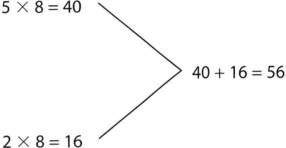

Numbers Every Day

Mental Math

Find each difference.
What strategy did you use?

$24 - 22$

$32 - 28$

$60 - 57$

$83 - 79$

Measurement

To find the area of a rectangle, count the squares.
6 rows of 3 squares = 18 squares

To find the product of 6×3, draw an array on a grid,
then count the squares.
$6 \times 3 = 18$

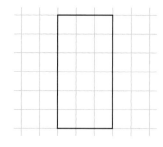

5. You have 6 nickels and 4 dimes.
How many cents do you have?
Draw a picture to help you.

6. How could you find the product of 9×7
if you know the product of 9×5?
Show your work.

7. There are stools and chairs in the classroom.
A stool has 3 legs.
A chair has 4 legs.
Liam counts 31 legs.
How many stools and chairs might there be?
How many different ways can you find the answer?

8. Write a story problem you can solve by multiplying.
Solve your problem. Show your work.

Reflect

How do you know that the product of 6×5 is less
than the product of 7×6 without multiplying?
Use words and pictures to explain.

Exploring Multiplication Patterns

Explore

You will need a calculator.

➤ Use a calculator to find each product.

4 × 1	9 × 1	5 × 5	2 × 3
4 × 10	9 × 10	5 × 50	2 × 30
4 × 100	9 × 100	5 × 500	2 × 300
4 × 1000	9 × 1000	5 × 5000	2 × 3000

What patterns do you see?

➤ Use patterns to find each product.
Check with a calculator.

7 × 1	8 × 1	4 × 2	2 × 9
7 × 10	8 × 10	4 × 20	2 × 90
7 × 100	8 × 100	4 × 200	2 × 900
7 × 1000	8 × 1000	4 × 2000	2 × 9000

30 is a multiple of 10.
300 is a multiple of 100.
3000 is a multiple of 1000.

Show *and* Share

Share the products and patterns
you found with a classmate.
How can you multiply by 10, by 100,
and by 1000 without using a calculator?
How can you multiply by multiples of 10,
of 100, and of 1000 without using a calculator?

Connect ....

➤ You can use place value to multiply by 10, by 100, and by 1000.
You know 3 × 1 = 3.
Use mental math to find 3 × 10, 3 × 100, and 3 × 1000.

3 × 1 ten = 3 tens
   3 × 10 = 30

3 × 1 hundred = 3 hundreds
3 × 100 = 300

3 × 1 thousand = 3 thousands
3 × 1000 = 3000

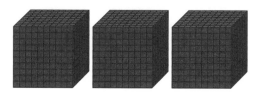

➤ You can use basic multiplication facts and place value
to multiply by multiples of 10, of 100, and of 1000.

You know 2 × 4 = 8.
Use mental math to find 2 × 40, 2 × 400, and 2 × 4000.

2 × 4 ones = 8 ones
    2 × 4 = 8

2 × 4 tens = 8 tens
    2 × 40 = 80

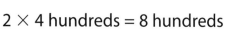
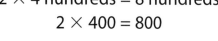

2 × 4 hundreds = 8 hundreds
    2 × 400 = 800

2 × 4 thousands = 8 thousands
    2 × 4000 = 8000

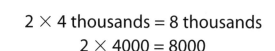

 **Practice**

Use Base Ten Blocks when they help.

1. Multiply.
   a) 3×10 **b)** 5×10
   c) 7×10 **d)** 9×10
   e) 10×4 **f)** 10×1
   g) 10×8 **h)** 10×0

2. Use a basic fact and patterns to find each product.
   a) $6 \times 1 = \square$
      $6 \times 10 = \square$
      $6 \times 100 = \square$
   b) $7 \times 3 = \square$
      $7 \times 30 = \square$
      $7 \times 300 = \square$
   c) $4 \times 6 = \square$
      $4 \times 60 = \square$
      $4 \times 600 = \square$

3. Multiply.
   a) 4×100 **b)** 100×6 **c)** 9×100
   d) 100×1 **e)** 7×100 **f)** 100×0

4. There are 60 cards in one box.
   Caitlin bought 8 boxes.
   How many cards did Caitlin buy?

5. Multiply.
   a) 3×50 **b)** 4×70 **c)** 9×30
   d) 90×8 **e)** 20×6 **f)** 80×3

6. There are 200 cents in 1 toonie.
   Clay has 6 toonies.
   How many cents does Clay have?

Numbers Every Day

Number Strategies

Write each number in expanded form.

384

987

6793

8384

7. Multiply.
　a) 2 × 300　　　**b)** 7 × 600　　　**c)** 5 × 200
　d) 1000 × 6　　 **e)** 2000 × 3　　 **f)** 4 × 1000

8. There are 1000 mL in 1 L.
　Jan has 6 L of juice.
　How many millilitres is that?

9. Make up some examples to show
　how you can multiply by:
　a) multiples of 10
　b) multiples of 100
　c) multiples of 1000
　Explain how you know your strategies work.

10. There are 50¢ in 1 roll of pennies.
　How many cents are in 9 rolls of pennies?

11. One tower is made with 100 red blocks,
　200 yellow blocks, and 200 white blocks.
　a) How many blocks of each colour
　　would you need to make 4 towers?
　b) How many blocks would you need altogether?

Reflect

Which patterns do you use when you multiply by 10,
by 100, or by 1000?
Use words, pictures, or numbers to explain.

5 Estimating Products

Explore

A Bombardier Challenger airplane holds 22 passengers.
About how many passengers will 8 of these planes hold?
Estimate to solve this problem.
Record your answer.

Show and Share

Share your strategies for estimating with
another pair of students. Did you get the same answer? Explain.

Connect

➤ A school bus holds 64 students.
About how many students can travel
on 7 school buses?

> 64 is close to 60.
> I round down to 60.

To estimate 7 × 64
↓
Think: 7 × 60 = 420

About 420 students can travel on
7 school buses.

➤ There are 87 pages in a book.
About how many pages are there in
5 of these books?

> 87 is close to 90.
> I round up to 90.

To estimate 5 × 87
↓
Think: 5 × 90 = 450

There are about 450 pages in 5 books.

1. Estimate each product.
   a) 3×21 b) 4×28 c) 5×35 d) 7×74

2. A can of soup costs 69¢.
   About how much will 7 cans cost?

3. Estimate each product.
   a) 62×4 b) 57×8 c) 28×2 d) 43×9

4. A belt is 77 cm long.
   About how long are 5 of these belts?
   How do you know?

5. Estimate to find out which is greater:
   6×72 or 7×66

6. Kyle's mother drives 47 km to work every day.
   About how far does she drive in 2 weeks?
   Show your work.

7. The estimated answer to a multiplication question is 360.
   What might the question be?
   How do you know?

Reflect

When you round to estimate,
how do you know when to round up
and when to round down?
Use words and numbers to explain.

Numbers Every Day

Number Strategies

Round each number to the nearest 10.

- 75
- 82
- 96
- 57

6 Strategies for Multiplication

Explore ....

There are 12 eggs in a carton.
How many eggs are there in 6 cartons?

Solve this problem.
Show your work.

Show *and* Share

Share your strategy with another pair of students.
How do you know you have the correct answer?

Connect ....

There are 36 envelopes in a package. You buy 4 packages.
How many envelopes do you have?

4 packages of 36 envelopes = 4 × 36
Here are three ways to multiply.

➤ Use Base Ten Blocks.
   Arrange 4 groups of 36.

Multiply the tens. ⟶ 4 × 30   4 × 6 ⟵ Multiply the ones.
Add.   120   +   24   = 144

4 × 36 = 144 ⟵ This **multiplication sentence** is an equation.

➤ Use grid paper to show an array.

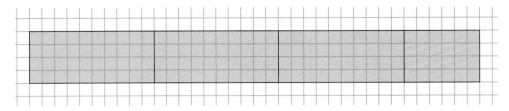

4 rows of 30   4 rows of 6
4 × 30 = 120   4 × 6 = 24

120 + 24 = 144

➤ Break a number apart to multiply.

$$
\begin{array}{r}
36 \\
\times\ 4 \\
\end{array}
$$

Multiply the ones: 4 × 6 ⟶ 24
Multiply the tens: 4 × 30 ⟶ + 120
Add.   144

You have 144 envelopes.

Practice

Numbers Every Day

Number Strategies

Make the greatest difference using the digits 4, 6, 7, and 9. Use each digit only once.

☐ ☐ ☐
−   ☐

Use Base Ten Blocks when they help.

1. Write a multiplication sentence for each array.

a)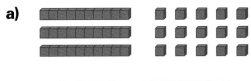

b)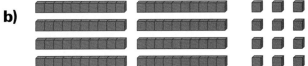

2. Multiply.

a)   23   b)   36   c)   62   d)   72   e)   47
   × 3   × 2   × 4   × 6   × 3

3. Multiply.

a) 5 × 61   b) 2 × 93   c) 45 × 4   d) 6 × 25   e) 18 × 4

4. Gita works at a garden centre.
She plants 15 seedlings in each row.
Gita plants 7 rows.
How many seedlings does Gita plant?

5. How much greater is 7×23 than 6×23? Explain.

6. Eva says to find 3×29, she would use mental math
to find 3×30, then subtract 3.
Is Eva correct? Explain.

7. Tom is buying candles for his
great grandmother's 90th birthday.
There are 24 candles in a box.
Tom buys 4 boxes of candles.
a) Will he have enough candles? Explain.
b) Will Tom have any candles left over? Explain.
Show your work.

8. Write a story problem that can be solved by multiplying.
Solve your problem. Show your work.

9. Chris wrote this product to find 62×6:

$$\begin{array}{r} 62 \\ \times\ 6 \\ \hline 12 \\ 360 \\ \hline 372 \end{array}$$

Explain each step of Chris' work.

At Home

Reflect

How can you use addition
to help you multiply?
Use words, numbers,
or pictures to explain.

Ask relatives and friends what
strategies they use to multiply
two numbers such as 74×5.
Write about their strategies.

Strategies Toolkit

Explore

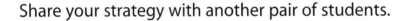

Marcus makes a "penny triangle."
He puts 1 penny in the 1st row, 2 pennies in the
2nd row, 3 pennies in the 3rd row, and so on.
How many pennies does Marcus need to make
a triangle with 8 rows?

Show *and* Share

Share your strategy with another pair of students.

Connect

There are 7 students in an inter-school math
competition. When they meet, each student shakes
hands with every other student.
How many handshakes will there be?

Understand

What do you know?
• There are 7 students.
• When student A shakes hands with
  student B, that's *one* handshake.
• You have to find how many
  handshakes there will be in all.

Strategies

• **Make a table.**
• **Use a model.**
• **Draw a picture.**
• **Solve a simpler problem.**
• **Work backward.**
• **Guess and check.**
• **Make an organized list.**
• **Use a pattern.**

Plan

Think of a strategy to help you solve the problem.
• You could **solve a simpler problem**.
• Count how many handshakes for 2 people, then for
  3 people, and so on. Look for a pattern in the answers.

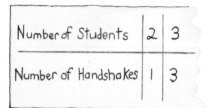

For 2 students, there is 1 handshake.
For 3 students, there are 3 handshakes.

Copy and continue this table.
How many handshakes are there
for 7 students?

Number of Students	2	3
Number of Handshakes	1	3

How could you solve this problem another way?
Each student shakes hands with 6 other students.
Why is the total number of handshakes not 7×6?

Practice

Choose one of the

Strategies

1. Here is a pattern with Colour Tiles.
   Suppose the pattern continues.

How many tiles would be in the 7th figure?
How many tiles are there in the first 7 figures?

2. How many squares can you see in this picture?
   Remember to count big squares as well as small squares.

Reflect

Explain how you used the strategy of solve a simpler problem
to solve one of the problems in this lesson.

141

LESSON

Dividing by Numbers from 1 to 7

Explore ··· 👥

There are 56 students who want to play basketball.
There are 7 players on a school team.
How many teams can be made?
Solve this problem.
Use any materials you need.
Record your work.

Show *and* Share

Share your answer with another pair of students.
What strategy did you use to solve the problem?

Connect ···

Thirty students want to play volleyball.
There are 6 players on a team.
How many teams can there be?

To find how many teams, divide: 30 ÷ 6

➤ Make an array of 30 counters with 6 counters in each row.
There are 5 rows.

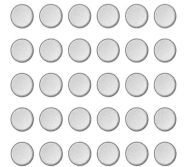

So, 30 ÷ 6 = 5
There can be 5 teams.

➤ To find 30 ÷ 6

To divide, you can think about multiplication.

Think: 6 times which number is 30?

You know 6 × 5 = 30

So, 30 ÷ 6 = 5

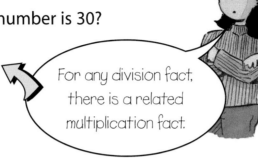

For any division fact, there is a related multiplication fact.

Practice

Use counters when they help.

1. Write a multiplication fact and a division fact for each array.

   a)

   b)

   c)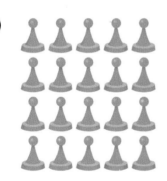

   d)

2. a) Draw an array to show 5 ÷ 1.
   b) Draw an array to show 5 ÷ 5.

3. Use related multiplication facts to help you divide.

   a) 6 × 4 = 24   b) 5 × 7 = 35   c) 4 × 2 = 8
      24 ÷ 4 = ☐   35 ÷ 7 = ☐   8 ÷ 2 = ☐

4. Divide. Draw a picture to show your work.

   a) 7 ÷ 1   b) 14 ÷ 2   c) 20 ÷ 4   d) 42 ÷ 7
   e) 25 ÷ 5   f) 24 ÷ 6   g) 21 ÷ 3   h) 6 ÷ 6

5. Dimitra works in a hardware store.
   She makes packages of washers.
   Dimitra puts 6 washers in each package.
   She has 36 washers.
   How many packages can Dimitra make?

6. Use a related multiplication fact to divide.
   a) 15 ÷ 3   b) 30 ÷ 5   c) 49 ÷ 7   d) 12 ÷ 2
   e) 28 ÷ 4   f) 42 ÷ 6   g) 6 ÷ 1   h) 16 ÷ 4

7. Write a story problem you can solve using division.
   Trade problems with a classmate.
   Solve your classmate's problem.

8. A class made equal teams of 5 for basketball,
   and equal teams of 6 for volleyball.
   Each student in the class was on a team.
   How many students might be in the class?

9. Joe has 35 cubes.
   He shares the cubes equally among 7 students.
   Each student needs 6 cubes.
   Does Joe have enough cubes? Explain.
   Show your work.

Reflect

How can you use multiplication to divide?
Use words, numbers, or pictures to explain.

Dividing by Numbers from 1 to 9

Explore ....

Use the multiplication chart.

➤ Write the multiplication facts that have 8 as a factor.
Use these facts to write all the division facts where you divide by 8.
Draw arrays to show some of these facts.

➤ Repeat the activity for multiplication facts that have 9 as a factor.

x	1	2	3	4	5	6	7	8	9
1	1	2	3	4	5	6	7	8	9
2	2	4	6	8	10	12	14	16	18
3	3	6	9	12	15	18	21	24	27
4	4	8	12	16	20	24	28	32	36
5	5	10	15	20	25	30	35	40	45
6	6	12	18	24	30	36	42	48	54
7	7	14	21	28	35	42	49	56	63
8	8	16	24	32	40	48	56	64	72
9	9	18	27	36	45	54	63	72	81

Show *and* Share

Share your facts and arrays with another pair of students.
How do you know if you found all the facts?

Connect ....

➤ To find $72 \div 9$

Think multiplication: $\qquad 9 \times \square = 72$

You know: $\qquad 9 \times 8 = 72$
So, $\qquad\qquad 72 \div 9 = 8$
Also, $\qquad\quad 72 \div 8 = 9$

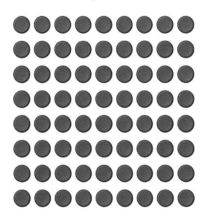

➤ To find 64 ÷ 8

Think
multiplication: $8 \times \square = 64$

You know: $8 \times 8 = 64$
So, $64 \div 8 = 8$

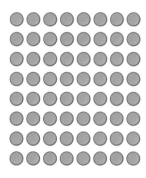

For most multiplication facts,
you know two division facts.

For some multiplication facts,
you know one division fact.

$7 \times 8 = 56$
$8 \times 7 = 56$ These are **related facts**.
$56 \div 8 = 7$
$56 \div 7 = 8$

$7 \times 7 = 49$
$49 \div 7 = 7$

 Practice

Use counters or grid paper when they help.
1. Write two multiplication facts and two division facts for each array.

   a)

   b)

2. Find each product.
   Then write a related multiplication fact and two division facts.
   a) $7 \times 3 = \square$ b) $8 \times 6 = \square$ c) $5 \times 9 = \square$ d) $9 \times 7 = \square$

3. Write four related facts for each set of numbers.
   a) 9, 6, 54   b) 5, 8, 40   c) 4, 7, 28   d) 1, 7, 7

4. a) One number in a set of related facts is 63. What could the set of facts be?
   b) One number in a set of related facts is 8. What could the set of facts be?

5. Divide.
    a) 24 ÷ 8   **b)** 36 ÷ 9   **c)** 56 ÷ 8   **d)** 9 ÷ 1   **e)** 16 ÷ 8
    f) 72 ÷ 8   **g)** 63 ÷ 9   **h)** 27 ÷ 3   **i)** 8 ÷ 8   **j)** 64 ÷ 8

6. Write all the multiplication facts for which there is
only one division fact.
Where are these products on the multiplication chart?
Write each related division fact.

7. Divide.
    a) 40 ÷ 5   **b)** 45 ÷ 9   **c)** 81 ÷ 9   **d)** 18 ÷ 6
    e) 20 ÷ 4   **f)** 36 ÷ 9   **g)** 54 ÷ 9   **h)** 63 ÷ 9

8. If you know that 63 ÷ 9 = 7, what else do you know?

9. Grade 4 students are going on an activities day.
There are 32 students in the class.
Eight students can go in each canoe.
How many canoes will be needed?

10. There are 9 marbles in each bag.
Heidi wants to buy 54 marbles.
How many bags does Heidi need to buy?

11. Write a story problem that you can solve by dividing.
Trade problems with a classmate. Solve your classmate's problem.

12. a) How do you know that 48 ÷ 8 is more than 40 ÷ 8?
    b) How do you know that 72 ÷ 8 is more than 72 ÷ 9?
    Show your work.

Reflect

How can you use an array to show how
multiplication and division are related?

Numbers Every Day

Calculator Skills

Find the product closest
to 100 using the digits 2,
4, and 6.

LESSON

10

Division with Remainders

Explore

· ·

Monica works in a market.
She arranges fruit baskets.
Monica has 41 oranges.
She puts 6 oranges in each basket.
How many baskets can Monica make up?
Use any materials that help. Show your work.

Show *and* Share

Share your answer with another pair of students.
How is this problem different from the problems in Lesson 9?

Connect

· ·

➤ Monica has 25 apples.
   She puts the same number of apples in each of 4 baskets.
   How many apples are there in each basket?

   Share 25 apples equally among 4 baskets.
   Divide: 25 ÷ 4

Monica puts 6 apples in each basket.
There is 1 apple left over.

You write: 25 ÷ 4 = 6 R1 ⟵ This is a **division sentence.**
You say: 25 divided by 4 is 6 remainder 1.

R stands for remainder.

148   **LESSON FOCUS** | Use counters to divide with remainders.

➤ Twenty-five students go on a field trip.
Six students can fit in each van.
How many vans are needed?

Divide: $25 \div 6$

Think about the division fact
that is closest to $25 \div 6$.
You know that $24 \div 6 = 4$.
So, $25 \div 6 = 4\,R1$

The nearest multiple
of 6 to 25 is 24.
I know $24 \div 6 = 4$.

But, if 4 vans are used, then 1 student cannot go.
So, 5 vans are needed.

Practice

Use counters when they help.

1. Write a division sentence for each picture.
   a)

   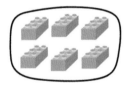

   b)

2. Divide. Draw a picture to show how you got each answer.
   a) $17 \div 2$ b) $28 \div 5$ c) $21 \div 3$ d) $20 \div 6$

3. Caleb is putting his markers into packages.
   He has 43 markers.
   Each package holds 8 markers.
   a) How many packages will Caleb fill?
   b) How many markers will he have left over?

4. Which division statements have an answer greater than 6?

a) 50 ÷ 8   **b)** 45 ÷ 7   **c)** 76 ÷ 9   **d)** 13 ÷ 2

e) 20 ÷ 4   **f)** 50 ÷ 6   **g)** 61 ÷ 8   **h)** 36 ÷ 5

5. Elizabeth takes 2 apples to school each day for her snack.
She has 15 apples.
How many days can Elizabeth take her snack to school?
Show your work.

6. Divide.

a) 14 ÷ 7   **b)** 15 ÷ 7   **c)** 16 ÷ 7   **d)** 17 ÷ 7

e) 18 ÷ 7   **f)** 19 ÷ 7   **g)** 20 ÷ 7   **h)** 21 ÷ 7

What is the greatest remainder when you divide by 7? Explain.

7. Write a story problem that has a remainder when you divide
to solve the problem. Solve the problem.
How did you deal with the remainder?

8. Amina solves a division problem this way: 21 ÷ 4 = 5 R1
Tyler solves the problem this way: 21 ÷ 4 = 4 R5
Who is correct? How do you know?
Show your work.

9. Bottles are packaged 6 to a carton. Every bottle must be in a carton.
There are 32 bottles to be packaged.
a) How many cartons are needed?
b) Does the number of cartons change
if there are 35 bottles instead of 32?
Explain.

Reflect

When you solve a division problem,
what might you do when there is a
remainder? Use examples to show
your ideas.

Numbers Every Day

Mental Math

Copy and complete.

$99 is about ☐ $10 bills.

$99 is ☐ quarters.

99 days is about ☐ weeks.

99 weeks is about
☐ months.

Using Base Ten Blocks to Divide

Explore

Felipe has 76 books.
He divides them equally among 4 boxes.
How many books are in each box?
Show your work.

Suppose Felipe had 78 books.
Could he divide them equally among 4 boxes?
How do you know?

Show and Share

Share your answers with those of another
pair of students.
What strategies did you use to solve the problem?

Connect

➤ Divide: 36 ÷ 3
Use Base Ten Blocks to show 36.

Divide the blocks into 3 equal groups.

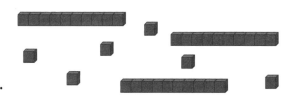

In each group, there is 1 ten rod and 2 unit cubes.
So, there are 12 in each group.

$36 \div 3 = 12$

➤ Divide: 57 ÷ 4

Use Base Ten Blocks to show 57.

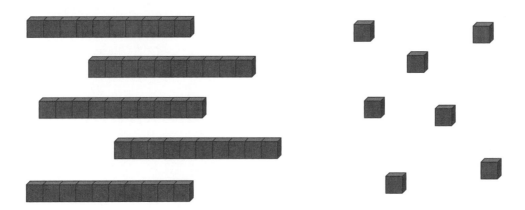

Divide the blocks into 4 equal groups.

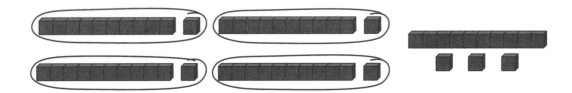

There is 1 ten rod and 1 unit cube in each group.
There is 1 ten rod and 3 unit cubes left over.
Trade the ten rod for 10 unit cubes.

There are 13 unit cubes.
Divide these cubes among the 4 equal groups.

There is 1 ten rod and 4 unit cubes in each group.
There is 1 unit cube left over.

So, 57 ÷ 4 = 14 R1

Use Base Ten Blocks when they help.

1. Divide.
    a) 69 ÷ 3   b) 68 ÷ 4   c) 87 ÷ 2   d) 64 ÷ 4   e) 75 ÷ 6

2. Aidan is collecting eggs at a farm. He puts the eggs in cartons.
   Each carton holds 6 eggs. Aidan collects 34 eggs.
   How many cartons does he need?

3. Divide. Draw a picture to show how you got each answer.
    a) 93 ÷ 3   b) 49 ÷ 4   c) 96 ÷ 8   d) 56 ÷ 5   e) 91 ÷ 7

4. Write a story problem that can be solved using 78 ÷ 6.
   Solve the problem. Show your work.

5. Divide.
    a) 40 ÷ 2   b) 41 ÷ 2   c) 42 ÷ 2   d) 43 ÷ 2
    e) 44 ÷ 2   f) 45 ÷ 2   g) 46 ÷ 2   h) 47 ÷ 2
   How can you tell *before* you divide by 2 if there will be a remainder?

6. Divide.
    a) 40 ÷ 5   b) 42 ÷ 5   c) 45 ÷ 5   d) 46 ÷ 5
    e) 50 ÷ 5   f) 54 ÷ 5   g) 55 ÷ 5   h) 57 ÷ 5
   How can you tell *before* you divide by 5 if there will be a remainder?

7. Chin-Tan found 52 action figures for his yard sale.
   He wants to put them in more than 1 box,
   but fewer than 5 boxes. Each box will have
   the same number of figures.
   How many boxes can Chin-Tan use? Explain.

Numbers Every Day

Number Strategies

Order each set of numbers
from greatest to least.

- 357, 573, 735, 753
- 456, 564, 654, 546
- 7352, 7532, 5723, 5732
- 2801, 1802, 8021, 8012

Reflect

Which numbers have no remainder when
they are divided by 2? By 5?
Use words, numbers, or pictures to explain.

Another Strategy for Division

Explore

There are 63 trees.
They are to be planted in 4 equal rows.
How many trees will there be in each row?
Do you think there will be any trees left over?
Explain. Show your work.

Show *and* Share

Talk with another pair of students about
the strategy you used to solve this problem.
How did you deal with any leftover trees?

Connect

There are 76 plants.
They are to be planted in 3 gardens.
Each garden will have the same number of plants.
How many plants will there be in each garden?

Divide: $76 \div 3$
Use 7 ten rods and 6 unit cubes.

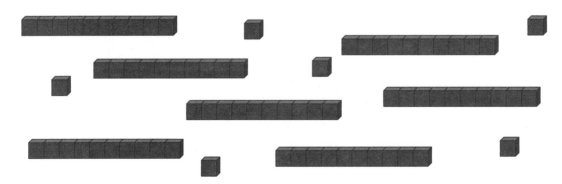

Arrange the 7 rods in 3 equal rows.

You see:

You think:

7 rods ÷ 3
is 2 rods each
with 1 left over.

You write:

3⌐7¹6
2

Trade 1 ten rod for 10 ones.

You have 16 unit cubes.

Share these 16 cubes equally among the 3 rows.

You see:

You think:

16 ÷ 3 is 5 cubes
each with 1 left
over.

You write:

3⌐7¹6
2 5 R1

So, 76 ÷ 3 = 25 R1

There will be 25 plants in each garden.
There will be 1 plant left over.

When you show division
like this, it is called
short division.

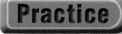 **Practice**

Use Base Ten Blocks when they help.

1. Find 3 division statements that have an answer greater than 11.
   a) 27 ÷ 2   b) 47 ÷ 4   c) 61 ÷ 6   d) 84 ÷ 8
   e) 52 ÷ 5   f) 36 ÷ 3   g) 99 ÷ 9   h) 73 ÷ 7

2. Victoria shares 49 crayons equally among 8 students.
How many crayons does each student get?

3. Divide.
   a) 56 ÷ 6   **b)** 29 ÷ 9   **c)** 47 ÷ 7   **d)** 74 ÷ 4
   e) 92 ÷ 2   **f)** 83 ÷ 3   **g)** 38 ÷ 8   **h)** 65 ÷ 5

4. Emma is collecting a series of books.
Each book costs $6.
How many books can Emma buy with $53?

5. Trenton has to feed 8 cats.
Each large can of cat food feeds 2 cats per day.
Trenton has 45 large cans of cat food.
How many days of cat food does Trenton have?
Show your work.

6. Divide.
   a) 36 ÷ 3   **b)** 38 ÷ 3   **c)** 39 ÷ 3   **d)** 40 ÷ 3
   e) 42 ÷ 3   **f)** 43 ÷ 3   **g)** 45 ÷ 3   **h)** 46 ÷ 3
   How can you tell *before* you divide by 3 if there will be a remainder?

7. Suppose you have 60 straws.
How many of each figure could you make?
   a) triangles
   b) squares
   c) pentagons
   d) hexagons

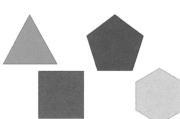

Reflect

You have used Base Ten Blocks and short
division to divide.
Which method do you prefer?
Use words, numbers, or pictures to explain.

Numbers Every Day

Number Strategies

Which questions have the
answer 42?
How do you know?

  • 4 + 2
  • 88 ÷ 2
  • 6 × 7
  • 21 × 2

Array, Array!

You will need scissors and several sheets of 1-cm grid paper.
Cut out an array for each multiplication fact from 2 × 2 to 9 × 9.
You should have 36 arrays.

For each array:
- Write the products of factors on one side.

		8 × 2		
		2 × 8		

- Write the product on the other side.

16

Game 1 Matching Arrays

➤ Spread out the arrays.
  18 cards should have grid side up.
  18 cards should have grid side down.
➤ Take turns to choose an array and say
  what is on its other side.
  If you are correct, you keep the array.
  If you are incorrect, put the array back
  on the table.
➤ The winner is the student with the
  most arrays at the end of the game.

Game 2 Who Has the Greater Product?

➤ Deal the cards, grid side up.
➤ Each student places one card on the table.
  The student with the greater product takes both cards.
➤ Subtract the products.
  The answer is the number of points the student gets.
  Use a tally chart to keep score.
➤ The winner is the student with the most points at the
  end of the game.

157

Show What You Know

LESSON

Use any materials when they help.

4, 8, 12...   3, 6, 9,...

1 1. **a)** List all the numbers you say when you start at 4 and count on by 4s to 50.
   b) List all the numbers you say when you start at 3 and count on by 3s to 50.
   c) What numbers are in both lists? What is special about these numbers?

2 3 4 2. Multiply. What strategies did you use?
   a) 5×8 **b)** 1×8 **c)** 9×0 **d)** 7×6
   e) 9×9 **f)** 8×10 **g)** 8×9 **h)** 7×8

4 3. Find each product.
   a) 6×700 **b)** 900×8 **c)** 5×60 **d)** 1000×4
   e) 200×5 **f)** 2×4000 **g)** 7×400 **h)** 90×2

4. The answer to a multiplication question is 4500. What might the question be?

5 5. Estimate each product.
   a) 5×31 **b)** 7×63 **c)** 8×56 **d)** 4×69

4 6. A radio station gives away a $300 prize every day for a week.
   How much will the station have given away at the end of the week?
   Show your work.

WE'VE GOT ANOTHER WINNER!

6 7. Multiply.
   a)   29
          $\times\,2$

   b) 73
          $\times\,3$

   c) 34
          $\times\,6$

   d) 95
          $\times\,4$

8. Divide.
   a) $45 \div 9$ b) $32 \div 8$ c) $56 \div 7$ d) $27 \div 3$ e) $9 \div 9$

9. Find each product.
   Then write a related multiplication fact and two division facts.
   a) $6 \times 7 = \square$ b) $8 \times 1 = \square$ c) $5 \times 9 = \square$

10. Write four related facts for each set of numbers.
    a) 5, 6, 30   b) 9, 7, 63   c) 8, 6, 48   d) 7, 8, 56

11. There are 72 Grade 4 students.
    The students are divided into 8 equal groups to work on a project.
    How many students will be in each group? How do you know?

12. Divide.
    a) $42 \div 3$ b) $52 \div 4$ c) $65 \div 5$ d) $78 \div 6$
    e) $91 \div 7$ f) $88 \div 8$ g) $99 \div 9$ h) $34 \div 2$

13. A TV series runs for 25 hours.
    One videotape can record 4 hours.
    How many tapes are needed
    to record the series?
    How do you know?

UNIT
4 Learning Goals

✓ skip count
✓ recall basic multiplication and division facts
✓ use different strategies to multiply and divide
✓ relate multiplication and division
✓ identify patterns in multiplication and division
✓ multiply by 10, 100, and 1000
✓ multiply and divide a 2-digit number by a 1-digit number
✓ pose and solve problems using multiplication and division

14. Divide.
    a) $76 \div 5$ b) $65 \div 3$
    c) $21 \div 2$ d) $32 \div 6$
    e) $98 \div 7$ f) $54 \div 8$
    g) $87 \div 9$ h) $43 \div 4$

15. Grade 4 students go on a wagon ride
    at a farm. Nine children can go on
    the wagon at one time.
    There are 97 students.
    How many wagon rides will there be?

At the Garden Centre

1. Jean works at a garden centre.
   He has an order for 72 petunias.
   The petunias are grown in boxes of 4 or 9.
   How many boxes of each size does Jean need?
   Can he deliver the order in more than one way?
   Explain.

2. The boxes of petunias fit on trays.
   One tray holds 6 boxes of 4 petunias or 3 boxes of 9 petunias.
   How many trays are needed for an order of 75 petunias?

Check List

Your work should show
- ✔ the strategies you used to solve each problem
- ✔ a clear explanation of each answer
- ✔ how you multiplied and divided accurately

3. The garden centre sells small plastic pots to grow seedlings.
The pots are sold in packages of 30 or 100.
One package of 30 pots costs $10.00.
One package of 100 pots costs $27.00.
One customer wants 180 pots.
What is the cheapest way she can buy the pots?

4. May-Lin is replanting trees.
She has 80 trees.
May-Lin will plant them in equal rows.
How many different ways can she do this?
Show each way as a multiplication fact, then a division fact.

Reflect on the Unit

How are multiplication and division related?
Use words, numbers, or pictures to explain.

Cumulative Review

UNIT

1

1. Describe each pattern. What is the pattern rule?
Write the next three terms for each pattern.
  a) 3, 5, 7, 9, 11, 13, …
  b) 3, 5, 7, 3, 5, 7, …
  c) 99, 94, 89, 84, 79, …

2. Which pattern in question 1 has a core? Write the core.

3. Find the number that makes each statement an equation.
  a) $6 + 9 = \square + 4$ **b)** $20 - \square = 9 - 5$
  c) $\square - 8 = 12 - 9$ **d)** $31 - 5 = 40 - \square$

2

4. Choose a 4-digit number.
Write it in:
  a) standard form   **b)** expanded form   **c)** words

5. Use the digits 3, 4, 5, 6.
Write all the 4-digit numbers greater than 4000
and less than 6000.
Order the numbers from greatest to least.

6. Estimate first.
Then add or subtract the numbers for which the answer
is greater than 500.
  a)   219   **b)**   627   **c)**   87   **d)**   786
       $-$ 195 $+$ 186 $+$ 256 $-$ 195

3

7. Use dot paper and a ruler.
Draw 2 congruent squares.

8. Use a protractor.
Measure each angle.

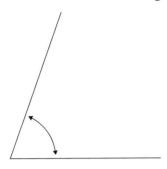

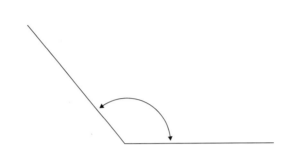

Use the figures below in questions 9 and 10.

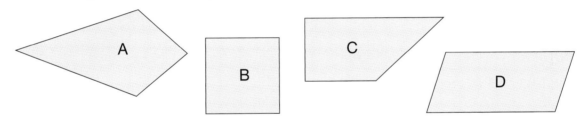

9. Identify each quadrilateral above.
List the attributes of each quadrilateral.

10. Use a Venn diagram.
Sort the quadrilaterals above.
Use the attributes: "Has opposite sides equal"
and "Has some angles equal"

11. Use a basic fact to find each product.

a) 6×7	**b)** 8×3	**c)** 5×9	**d)** 4×5
6×70	8×30	5×90	4×50
6×700	8×300	5×900	4×500

12. Find 2 division statements that have an answer greater than 9.

a) $37 \div 3$ **b)** $46 \div 9$ **c)** $58 \div 5$ **d)** $63 \div 8$

Data Management

At the Vet

Learning Goals

- read and interpret data in tables, pictographs, bar graphs, and circle graphs
- draw pictographs and bar graphs by hand and with a computer
- predict the results of a survey
- conduct a survey

Dr. Fernandez is a veterinarian.
She records data about pets in her care.

This tally chart shows the types of animals
she has cared for in the last month.

Key Words

pictograph

bar graph

title

labels

axis

key

scale

range

circle graph

trial

survey

- Which type of animal did Dr. Fernandez
  see most often? Least often?

- What other information do you know
  from looking at the tally chart?

- How else could you display these data?

- What other data might you record
  about a pet?

LESSON

1 Reading Data in Tables

 Explore

Harry Potter books were very popular in 2002.
Look at the table.

10 Best Selling Books for Children Ages 9 to 12, 2002

Rank	Title	Author	Jacket Type	Publisher	Publication Date
1	*Harry Potter and the Goblet of Fire*	J.K. Rowling	Paperback	Raincoast	July 2002
2	*The Thief Lord*	Cornelia Funke	Hardcover	Scholastic	August 2002
3	*The All New Captain Underpants Extra Crunchy Book O'Fun*	Dav Pilkey	Paperback	Zagat	August 2002
4	*Stage Fright on a Summer Night*	Mary Pope Osborne	Paperback	Random House	March 2002
5	*Holes*	Louis Sachar	Paperback	Seal	May 2000
6	*Harry Potter and the Prisoner of Azkaban*	J.K Rowling	Paperback	Raincoast	September 2001
7	*Artemis Fowl*	Eoin Colfer	Paperback	Disney	May 2002
8	*Harry Potter and the Chamber of Secrets*	J.K. Rowling	Paperback	Raincoast	August 2000
9	*The Giver*	Lois Lowry	Paperback	Bantam	July 1994
10	*The Magical Worlds of Harry Potter: A Treasury of Myths, Legends, and Fascinating Facts*	David Colbert	Paperback	Berkley	June 2002

Which book was published first? How do you know?
Which publisher appears most often in the table?

With your partner, write 3 questions you can answer using
the data in the table.

166 **LESSON FOCUS** | Read and interpret data in tables.

Show *and* Share

Exchange questions with another pair of classmates.
Answer your classmates' questions.
Discuss why a table is useful to show data.

Connect

This table shows the number of sign-outs and renewals of some
library books in Enzo's school in one year.

Title	Author	Number of Sign-Outs	Number of Renewals
Flat Stanley	Jeff Brown	32	4
The Giving Tree	Shel Silverstein	28	0
Harriet the Spy	Louise Fitzhugh	18	9
The Secret World of Og	Patsy and Pierre Berton	14	3
Top-Secret Personal Beeswax: A Journal By Junie B. (and Me!)	Barbara Park	24	2

From the table:
The book signed out most often was *Flat Stanley*.
The book signed out least often was *The Secret World of Og*.

Harriet the Spy was renewed most often.
The Giving Tree was never renewed.

Half of the people who signed out
Harriet the Spy renewed the book.
$\frac{1}{2}$ of 18 is 9.

Numbers Every Day

Mental Math

Find each product.
Describe the pattern.

2 × 10	64 × 10
2 × 100	64 × 100
2 × 1000	64 × 1000

Practice

1. Look at this table.

Top 10 Books for Children Ages 2 to12, 2002

Rank	Title	Author	Price
1	*If You Take a Mouse to School*	Laura Numeroff	$23.99
2	*Harry Potter and the Goblet of Fire*	J.K. Rowling	$18.95
3	*Back to School for Franklin: A Sticker Activity Book*	Scholastic	$7.00
4	*Harry Potter Paperback Boxed Set*	J.K. Rowling	$51.80
5	*The World Almanac for Kids 2003*	World Almanac	$17.95
6	*Coraline*	Neil Gaiman	$23.99
7	*Good Morning, Gorillas*	Mary Pope Osborne	$5.99
8	*Writing Smarts: A Girl's Guide to Journaling, Poetry, Storytelling, and School Papers*	Pleasant Company	$13.95
9	*The New Captain Underpants Collection*	Dav Pilkey	$29.95
10	*Walter, the Farting Dog*	William Kotzwinkle	$27.95

a) Which is the most expensive book?
Why do you think it's the most expensive?

b) Which is the least expensive book?

c) Which books cost less than $10 each?

d) Write a question about the data in the table.
Answer your question.

2. The Richter scale is used to describe the magnitude, or strength, of an earthquake.
This table shows how often earthquakes have occurred since 1900.

a) How do the numbers change in the third column? Why do you think this happens?

b) What other information does the table show?

c) Why do you think the number of minor earthquakes is estimated?

Type	Magnitude on Richter Scale	Typical Number Each Year
Great	8 and higher	1
Major	7 – 8	18
Strong	6 – 7	120
Moderate	5 – 6	800
Light	4 – 5	6 000 (estimated)
Minor	3 – 4	49 000 (estimated)

168

Math Link

Your World

In the last 100 years Canada has had only 1 great earthquake, but several major earthquakes. This table shows the top 6 Canadian earthquakes in that time.

Year	Location
1949	Offshore Queen Charlotte Islands, B.C.
1970	South of Queen Charlotte Islands, B.C.
1933	Baffin Bay, Nunavut
1946	Vancouver Island, B.C.
1929	Atlantic Ocean, south of Newfoundland
1979	Southern Yukon-Alaskan border

3. Here are the highest daily temperatures for October, 2002, in Fergus, Ontario.

October	1	2	3	4	5	6	7	8	9	10	11	12	13	14	15	16
Temperature°C	27	22	16	25	16	17	16	11	17	19	14	14	14	10	14	10

October	17	18	19	20	21	22	23	24	25	26	27	28	29	30	31	
Temperature°C	6	8	9	7	8	4	5	4	5	7	7	5	2	4	3	

a) Which day was the warmest? Coolest?

b) Why is the beginning of the month warmer than the end of the month?

c) Is the beginning of a month always warmer than the end of a month? Explain.

d) Look at the way the temperature changed. Predict the temperature on November 2.

Show your work.

Reflect

From a newspaper or magazine, cut out a table. Write two things you know from reading the table. Why do you think the data in the table were collected?

LESSON 2 Reading Pictographs and Bar Graphs

Explore ··

This **pictograph** and **bar graph** show data from March 2003.

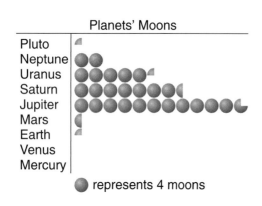

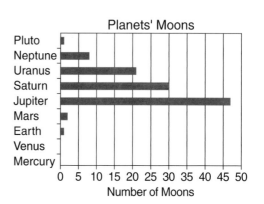

Which planet has the most moons? How do you know?
Write 5 other things you know from looking at the graphs.
How are the graphs the same? How are they different?

Show and Share

Write a question that could be answered using the graphs.
Exchange questions with another pair of classmates.
Answer your classmates' question.

Connect ··

The **title** of a graph tells you what the graph shows.
The **labels** on the **axes** tell you what data are displayed.

In a pictograph, symbols are used to show data.
In the pictograph above, the **key** is "⬤ represents 4 moons".
The key shows what each symbol represents.

170 LESSON FOCUS | Read and interpret pictographs and bar graphs.

In a bar graph, bars are used to show data.
The numbers on the axis show the **scale**.

➤ Use the pictograph to find how many moons Jupiter has.
1 circle represents 4 moons.
There are $11\frac{3}{4}$ circles for Jupiter on the graph.

Jupiter

Count by 4s eleven times: 4, 8, 12, 16, 20, 24, 28, 32, 36, 40, 44;
or multiply: $11 \times 4 = 44$
The $\frac{3}{4}$ circle represents 3 moons.
So, Jupiter has 44 + 3, or 47 moons.

➤ Use the bar graph to find how many moons Mars has.
The bar for Mars ends just less than halfway between 0 and 5.
So, Mars has 2 moons.

The **range** is the difference between the greatest value and the least value.
It tells how spread out the data are.

The greatest value is 47. The least value is 0.
$47 - 0 = 47$
So, the range is 47.

Practice

1. This graph shows the types of
gym shoes Grade 4 students wear
at Zeina's school.
   a) What is the most common type
   of gym shoe?
   b) How many students wear
   basketball shoes?
   c) Which 2 types of shoes are worn
   by the same number of students?
   How do you know?
   d) What is the range?

Types of Gym Shoes

Basketball	👟 👟 👟
Trail/Hiking	👟
Cross Trainers	👟 👟 👟 👟
Court	👟 👟 👟
Running	👟 👟 👟 👟 👟

👟 represents 3 students

2. This graph shows the number of goals scored by 10 NHL players in the 2001/2002 season.

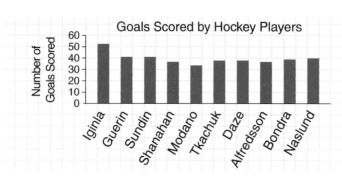

a) Who scored the most goals?

b) Who scored the fewest goals?

c) What is the range?

d) Which players had the same number of goals? How do you know?

e) Which player had 12 goals more than Naslund?

f) Which player had 6 goals fewer than Naslund?

3. This graph shows the typical number of sunny days each year for 6 cities.

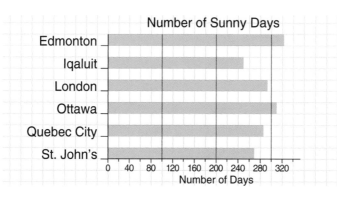

a) Which cities have more than 300 sunny days?

b) Which cities have between 200 and 300 sunny days?

c) Which city has the most sunny days?

d) Suppose the numbers on the axis were not given. Could you still answer part c? Explain.

e) How many sunny days does Quebec City have? Is your answer exact or approximate? Explain.

Show your work.

4. This graph shows how much animal actors get paid for one day of work.

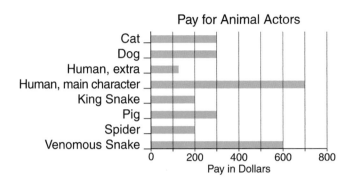

Pay for Animal Actors

Cat
Dog
Human, extra
Human, main character
King Snake
Pig
Spider
Venomous Snake

0   200   400   600   800
Pay in Dollars

a) Which animal actors receive the same rate of pay?

b) Which actors' pay is one-half that of a venomous snake's?

c) Why do humans appear twice in the graph? What is the difference in their pay?

d) Why do some animal actors get paid more than others?

5. Look at this pictograph.

a) Find two birds whose combined life spans are less than that of a cockatoo.

b) A canary's life span is 25 years. How would you show 25 years on this graph?

c) Suppose the key was ❤ represents 20 years. Would there be more hearts or fewer hearts in the pictograph? How do you know?

Life Spans of Birds in Captivity	
Cockatoo	❤ ❤ ❤ ❤ ❤ ❤ ❤ ❤
Rhea	❤ ❤ ❤ ❤
Vulture	❤ ❤ ❤
Ostrich	❤ ❤ ❤ ❤
Swan	❤ ❤ ❤ ❤ ❤
Bald Eagle	❤ ❤ ❤ ❤ ❤

❤ represents 10 years

Reflect

How are bar graphs and pictographs alike?
How are they different?
Use words, pictures, or numbers to explain.

Reading Circle Graphs

Explore ·

Look at the graphs below.
Which graph do you think represents the data better?
Explain your thinking.

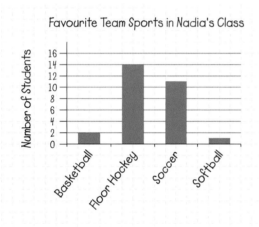

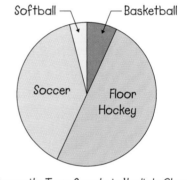

Favourite Team Sports in Nadia's Class

Show *and* Share

Write 3 questions about each graph.
Exchange questions with a classmate.
Answer your classmate's questions.

Connect ·

This **circle graph** shows the activity each
student in Al's class chose for winter fun day.

A circle graph shows parts of a whole.
In the graph, the circle represents
Al's whole class.

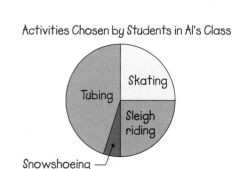

To find which activity most students chose, find the largest sector of the circle graph.

Since the purple sector is the largest, most students chose tubing.

Snowshoeing was the activity chosen by the fewest students.

Since the yellow and orange sectors are the same size, equal numbers of students chose skating and sleigh riding.

The yellow sector represents about $\frac{1}{4}$ of the circle.
The orange sector represents about $\frac{1}{4}$ of the circle.
So, about $\frac{1}{4}$ of the class chose skating,
and about $\frac{1}{4}$ chose sleigh riding.

Practice

1. This graph shows where Grades 4 to 7 students, from Alice's school, go after school.

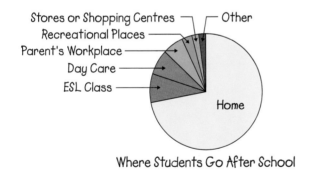

Stores or Shopping Centres
Recreational Places
Parent's Workplace
Day Care
ESL Class
Other
Home

Where Students Go After School

a) Where do most students go after school?
b) Is your answer to part a more or less than one-half of the students? How do you know?
c) What are some possible places that come under "Other"?

Numbers Every Day

Number Strategies

How many different two-digit numbers can you write using the digits 1 to 9?

2. These circle graphs show the mass of the fruits and nuts in two types of snack mix.

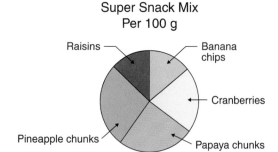

Morning Snack Mix
Per 100 g

Super Snack Mix
Per 100 g

a) Order the foods in Morning Snack Mix from least mass to greatest mass.

b) About what fraction of Morning Snack Mix are almonds?

c) Which snack mix has more raisins? How do you know?

3. This circle graph shows what students in Lee's class did on Sunday night.

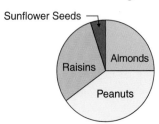

Sunday Night Activities

a) Which activity did the fewest students do?

b) Estimate the fraction of students who read a book.

c) Did one-half of the students watch TV? Explain.

d) Which two activities were done by about the same numbers of students?

e) Write a question about this graph. Answer your question.

Show your work.

Reflect

What is one advantage of circle graphs?
What is one disadvantage?
Record your ideas.

At Home

Look through newspapers and magazines. Find a circle graph. What does the whole circle represent?

4 Drawing Pictographs

Explore

You will need a bag of 20 two-colour counters.

➤ Empty the counters onto a desk.
➤ Choose one colour.
   Record the number of counters showing this colour.
   This is your first **trial**.
➤ Return the counters to the bag. Do 4 more trials.
   Count the same colour each time.
   Record the results of each trial.
➤ Graph your findings in a pictograph. Use a key.
➤ What do you know from looking at the pictograph?

Show and Share

Did you have fractions of symbols
in your pictograph? Explain.
Could you have chosen a key
so there would be no fractions? Explain.

Numbers Every Day

Number Strategies

Show two ways to find
14 × 5.

Aliyah asked Grades 4 and 5 students in her school
how they travel to school each day.
Here are her results:

Type of transportation to School	Walk	Bus	Bike	Car
Number of Students	30	45	5	25

Aliyah chose 🕴 for the symbol because she collected data
on the number of students.

To make sure her graph was not too large,

Aliyah chose 🕴 to represent 10 students.

Then, 𝒇 represents 5 students.

To show 30 students, Aliyah needed 3 symbols: 🕴🕴🕴

To show 45 students, Aliyah needed $4\frac{1}{2}$ symbols: 🕴🕴🕴🕴𝒇

To show 5 students, Aliyah needed $\frac{1}{2}$ a symbol: 𝒇

To show 25 students, Aliyah needed $2\frac{1}{2}$ symbols: 🕴🕴𝒇

To draw the pictograph, Aliyah wrote each type of transportation
on the vertical axis.
Then, she drew the correct number of symbols beside
each type of transportation.

Aliyah completed the pictograph with a key, a label on the axis, and a title.

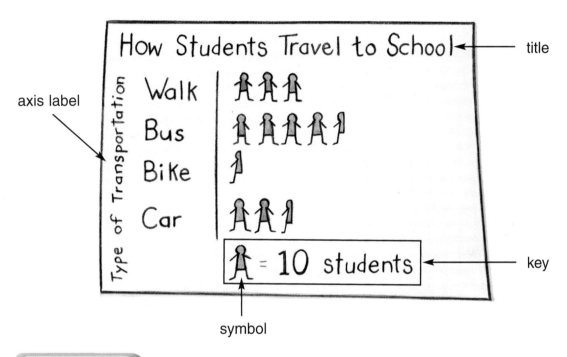

axis label

title

key

symbol

Practice

1. Each table has data for a pictograph.
   Suppose you drew each pictograph. What key would you use? Why?

a)

Favourite Type of Movie	Number of Students
Action	6
Comedy	12
Drama	8
Horror	2
Mystery	4

b)

Favourite Colour	Number of People
Red	15
Yellow	25
Blue	10
Green	25
Orange	40

c)

Activity	Number of Students
High Jump	60
200-m Dash	50
Long Jump	80
Ball Throw	70
100-m Dash	100

2. **a)** Draw a pictograph to display these data.

Students in the Band

Grade	4	5	6	7	8
Number of Students	9	5	6	11	13

b) How did you choose your key?
c) Write what you know about the band.

3. **a)** Draw a pictograph to display these data.

Time That People Take the Bus in the Morning

Time of Day	6:00	7:00	8:00	9:00	10:00	11:00	12:00
Number of People	4	8	14	2	5	8	10

b) What is the range of the data?
c) Write two questions using the data from the graph.
Exchange questions with a classmate.
Answer your classmate's questions.

4. This table shows the typical number of eggs some animals lay.
   a) Draw a pictograph.
   How did you choose your key?
   b) A seahorse lays about 200 eggs.
   How would you include this data
   on your pictograph?
   Would you need to change anything?
   Explain.
   Show your work.

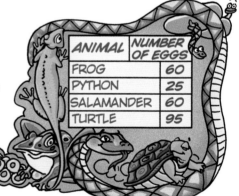

ANIMAL	NUMBER OF EGGS
FROG	60
PYTHON	25
SALAMANDER	60
TURTLE	95

Reflect

How is a pictograph useful to show data?
Use words, pictures, or numbers to explain.

Making Pictographs Using *Graphers*

Nat's soccer club wants to design team T-shirts.
The students voted to choose
the colour of the T-shirts.

Use *Graphers*. Work with a partner.

Follow these steps to create a pictograph
on a computer.

Colour	Number of Students
Red	4
Blue	10
Yellow	1
Green	8
Purple	7

1. Open Graphers. Click:

2. To enter the data:

Click: , then click:

Click: , then click:

Click: , then click:

Click: , then click:

Click:

Look at the data table above.
Click each colour button once for each
student who chose that colour.
For example, click the red symbol 4 times.
Repeat this for each colour.

Click: **Done**

3. To draw a pictograph:

Click: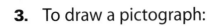

Click:  , then click: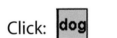

4. To change the axis label, click on the text box, Color .

Type: Colour, then click: OK

To change the title, click on the text box, Colors .

Type: T-shirt Votes, then click: OK

5. To add the colour names, click: Tools

Click: dog

This converts the colour symbols on the axis to text.

To convert text to symbols, click: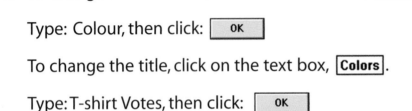

6. To display the data table on the same screen, click: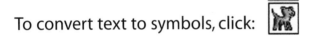

Click: 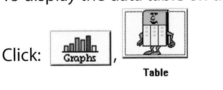 ,

then click: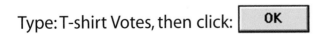

7. To change the title of the table, click on the text box, Colors .

Type: T-shirt Votes, then click: OK

182

8. To add your name, click:

Type your name and click:

9. To print the pictograph, click:

Click: , then click: **Put In**

Click: , then click: **Put In**

Click: , then click: **Put In**

Click: **Done**

Select the normal print size:

Print Size

⊙ **Normal (8.5 x 11 sheet)**

Click: **OK**

10. Look at the graph and table.
Complete each exercise in your notebook.
a) Which T-shirt colour was the most popular?
b) How many students were surveyed?
Is this shown on the graph?
c) What colour was twice as popular as red?
d) Suppose the T-shirts could be 2 colours.
What colours should they be? Explain your choice.

Reflect

Which is easier: graphing by hand or by computer?
Explain your choice.

Drawing Bar Graphs

 **Explore**

This table shows the typical
life spans of some animals.

Use grid paper. Draw a bar graph.
Choose a suitable scale.

Animal	Typical Life Span
Asian elephant	40 years
Black rhinoceros	15 years
Killer whale	65 years
Polar bear	20 years

Show and Share

Share your graph with another
pair of students.
How are your graphs the same? Different?

The typical life span of a Galapagos tortoise is 100 years.
Suppose you wanted to add the life span of this tortoise to your graph.
Discuss how you might have to change your graph.

Connect

Bar graphs may be drawn vertically or horizontally.
You can graph the data below on grid paper.
Draw 2 axes. Label the axes "Animal" and "Typical Life Span in Years."

Animal	Typical Life Span
Bottle-nosed dolphin	40 years
Brown bear	22 years
Fin whale	85 years
Potbelly seahorse	8 years

There are 20 squares along one side of the 1-cm grid paper.

If we count by 1s, the scale will go only to 20. The highest number in the table is 85.

If we count by 2s, the scale will go only to 40.

➤ Count by 5s for the scale. The scale is 1 square represents 5 years.

➤ Draw a vertical bar for each animal in the table. Estimate the lengths of the bars for 22 years and 8 years. The bar for 22 years ends less than halfway between 20 and 25. The bar for 8 years ends slightly more than halfway between 5 and 10.

➤ Write a title for the graph.

Life Spans of Some Animals

Typical Life Span in Years

Animal

Practice

1. The number of wins in 2002 is shown for 4 Major League Baseball teams.
   a) Draw a bar graph to show the number of wins. For the scale, count by 5s.
   b) Write two things you know from looking at your graph.

Teams	Number of Wins
Blue Jays	78
Expos	83
Tigers	55
Yankees	103

2. This table shows the heights of some players from the 2002 Canadian women's hockey team.
  a) Draw a bar graph to display these data.
  b) Explain why each of these parts of your graph is important: title, bars, labels, scale

Name	Height
Antal	170 cm
Botterill	175 cm
Brisson	170 cm
Heaney	173 cm
Ouellette	180 cm
St. Pierre	173 cm
Wickenheiser	175 cm

3. a) Draw a bar graph to display these data.
  b) Which city had the fewest wet days?
  c) Why do you think Victoria had more wet days than Edmonton?
  d) Write a question you can answer using the table or the graph. Answer the question.
  Show your work.

City	Typical Number of Wet Days Each Year (1961–1990)
Charlottetown	177
Edmonton	123
Fredericton	156
Montreal	162
Ottawa	159
Victoria	153

Math Link

Your World

The driest town in Canada is Osoyoos, B.C. It typically receives less than 20 cm of rainfall each year.

In the Inkaneep native dialect, the name Osoyoos means "where the water narrows."

Reflect

Jacob missed class today.
Write clear instructions for him on how to draw a bar graph.

Making Bar Graphs Using *Graphers*

TECHNOLOGY

This table shows the movies that Paula's classmates rented in one week.

Use *Graphers*.
Work with a partner.

Follow these steps to create a bar graph on a computer.

Day	Number of students who rented movies
Monday	1
Tuesday	1
Wednesday	2
Thursday	4
Friday	9
Saturday	8
Sunday	3

1. Open Graphers. Click:

2. To enter the data:

   Click: **Work Out** , then click:

   Click: **Create New Data** , then click:

   Click: **Time Data** , then click:

   Click: **Days**  , , then click:

   Click: **Data Maker**

   Look at the data table above.
   On the **Data Maker** window, click each day of the week once for each student who rents a movie on that day.
   For example, click on Sunday 3 times.
   Repeat this for each day of the week. Click: **Done**
   Ignore the days followed by a number, like Thu2.

3. To draw a bar graph:

Click:

Click: , then click:

4. To change the title, click on the text box, Days .

Type: Most Popular Day to Rent Movies,

then click: OK

5. To change the scale, click: Axis

Change Step to 2, then click: OK
How did the graph change?

6. Click: Axis

Change Max. to 20.

How did the graph change?

7. Click: Axis

Set Max. to 10, Step to 1, and Min. to 0.

8. To display the data table on the same screen, click:

Click:  , ,
Table

then click: Go

9. To change the title of the table, click on the text box, Days .

Type: Most Popular Day to Rent Movies, then click: OK

10. To add your name, click: Notebook

Type your name and click: ✕|

11. To print the bar graph, click: Print

Click: Graph , then click: Put In

Click: Graph , then click: Put In

Click: abc NB , then click: Put In

Click: Done

Select the normal print size: **Print Size**
⊙ **Normal (8.5 × 11 sheet)**

Click: OK

12. Look at the graph and table.
   a) What day was the most popular to rent a movie. Why?
   b) On which day do students rent two times as many movies as on Thursday?

Reflect

Which makes a better bar graph: graphing by hand or by computer?
Explain your choice.

Conducting a Survey

A **survey** is conducted to collect and record data on some topic.

How well do you know your classmates?
Can you predict which TV show is most popular in your class?
Can you predict the number of pets each classmate has?

As a class, discuss what you would like to find out about one another.
Choose one topic.

Explore

You will conduct a survey to collect data on your topic.
Plan how you will conduct the survey.
What question will you ask?
Predict the results.

Show *and* Share

As a class, conduct the survey.
Record the data on a tally chart.
Graph the data. Look at the graph.
How accurate were your predictions?

Connect

Nadia wanted to know how many hours
her classmates spent watching TV
on Wednesday nights.
Nadia wrote a survey question to ask
her classmates: "How many hours of TV
do you watch on Wednesday nights?"
Then, Nadia made a tally chart to record the data.

Numbers Every Day

Number Strategies

Use the digits from 1 to 7.
Make the difference
as close to 0 as possible.

☐☐☐☐
−　☐☐☐

In the first column, Nadia listed her classmates' possible answers. As each classmate answered the question, Nadia made a tally mark in the second column.

From the tally chart, Nadia knows that 1 hour of TV is watched by most children on Wednesday nights.

Number of hours	Number of students
0	₩₩₩₩ I
½	III
1	₩₩₩₩ ₩₩₩₩ I
1½	I
2	II
2½	I
3	I
3½	II
4	I

Practice

1. Write 4 possible answers for each survey question.
   a) What is your shoe size?   b) What is your favourite fruit?

2. Write a survey question for each topic.
   Give 4 possible answers for each question.
   a) Favourite ice cream flavour   b) Number of sisters

3. Work in groups of four.
   a) Conduct a class survey.
      Use a topic from question 1 or 2.
   b) Display the results in a tally chart.
      Draw a graph.
   c) Describe the results of the survey.
   d) How might the results change if you conducted the survey in a different class? A different school?
   Show your work.

At Home

Reflect

Write the steps on how to conduct a survey.

Look through newspapers and magazines. Find a bar graph. What is the scale of the bar graph?

Strategies Toolkit

Explore

The Grade 4 music class has 26 students.
Each student plays the clarinet, recorder, or trumpet.
There are 12 boys in the class.
Of the 8 students who play the recorder, 5 are girls.
Three boys play the trumpet.
Eight students play the clarinet.
How many girls and boys play each instrument?

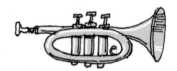

Show *and* Share

Describe the strategy you used to solve the problem.

Connect

At a track and field meet, 42 students won medals.
• 18 medals were won in field events.
• 9 gold medals were won in field events.
• 15 silver medals were won in track events.
• 10 bronze medals and 14 gold medals were won.
How many gold, silver, and bronze medals were won
in track events? In field events?

Strategies

• **Make a table.**
• **Use a model.**
• **Draw a picture.**
• **Solve a simpler problem.**
• **Work backward.**
• **Guess and check.**
• **Make an organized list.**
• **Use a pattern.**

Understand

What do you know?
• Some of the data are given above.
• Use those data to find the unknown data.

Plan

Think of a strategy to help you solve the problem.
• You can **make a table**.
• Fill in what you know. Use addition and subtraction to
find the missing numbers in the table.

Copy and complete the table.

Medals	Gold	Silver	Bronze`	Total
Track		15		
Field	9			18
Total	14		10	42

How many of each type of medal was won?

How do you know your answers are correct?
How could you have solved this problem another way?

Practice

Choose one of the

Strategies

1. There are rainy days, sunny days, and cloudy days.
   - September and October had the same number of rainy days.
   - There were 6 cloudy days in September.
   - There were 10 rainy days in total for both months.
   - There were 3 more cloudy days in October than in September.

   How many sunny days were there in September? In October?

2. Mr. Chu's class counted animals on its field trip.
   How many of each type of animal were seen in the woods?
   In the stream?
   - 30 animals were counted. There were 16 animals in the woods.
   - 2 omnivores were in the stream, and 4 omnivores were seen in total.
   - There were 3 times as many herbivores as omnivores in the stream.
   - There were half as many carnivores in the stream as in the woods.

Reflect

How can a table help you solve a problem?
Use words and numbers to explain.

LESSON

1

1. This table shows the leading hitters for Major League Baseball, 2002.

Player	Team	Position	Number of Hits
Soriano	New York Yankees	Second Base	209
Suzuki	Seattle Mariners	Outfield	208
Guerrero	Montreal Expos	Outfield	206
Tejada	Oakland Athletics	Short Stop	204
Williams	New York Yankees	Outfield	204

a) Which position do most of the leading hitters play?

b) Which team has the most leading hitters?

c) Both Tejada and Williams had 204 hits.
   Why is Tejada listed before Williams in the table?

2

2. This graph shows the eye colours of students in Sara's class.

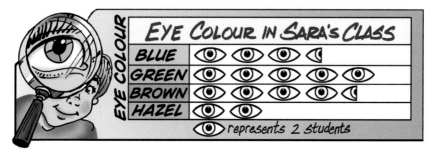

a) How many students are in Sara's class?

b) What is the range of the data?

c) How many more students have green eyes than hazel eyes?

3

3. a) What does this circle graph show?

   b) What might the survey question have been?

   c) How many books were read by most students?

   d) What else do you know from the graph?

4. For a physical education project, Jenny had to find
the most popular sport during the school year.
She conducted a survey and recorded the results in a table.

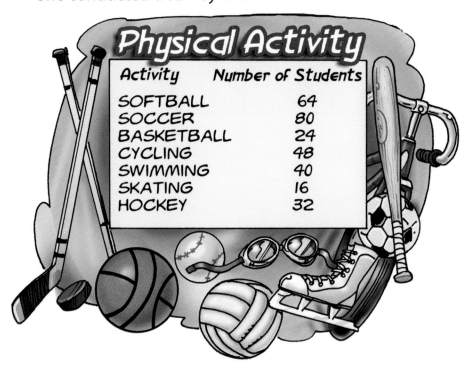

Activity	Number of Students
SOFTBALL	64
SOCCER	80
BASKETBALL	24
CYCLING	48
SWIMMING	40
SKATING	16
HOCKEY	32

a) Graph the data.

b) What are the results of the survey?

c) What else do you know from the graph?

d) How might the results change
if Jenny conducted the survey in a
different school?

5. Conduct a class survey.

a) The survey question is:
"What is your favourite school subject?"
Predict the results of surveying
your classmates.

b) Conduct the survey.

c) Display the results.

d) Write what you found out.

UNIT

5 Learning Goals

☑ read and interpret data in
tables, pictographs, bar
graphs, and circle graphs

☑ draw pictographs and bar
graphs by hand and with a
computer

☑ predict the results of a
survey

☑ conduct a survey

Unit Problem

At the Vet

Veterinarians record data about pets.
You will conduct a survey to collect data about pets.

Part 1

Work in groups of four.
Choose a survey topic on pets.
Predict the results of your survey.

Part 2

Conduct a class survey.
Remember to:
- write a survey question
- make a tally chart
- use a computer or grid paper
  to draw a graph
- label and title your graph
- write the results of the survey

Part 3

Present your results to the class.
Write how someone might use the results
of your survey.
Write about how you think the results
might change if you conducted the survey:
- in a different class
- in a different school
- in a different province or territory

Reflect on the Unit

Why do you draw graphs to display data?
Explain your thinking.

The Cooking Show

Learning Goals

- relate units of time
- estimate and measure time intervals
- tell time to the nearest minute
- estimate and count money
- make purchases and make change
- estimate and measure capacity
- estimate and measure mass
- compare and order objects by mass

You and a friend have been invited to be guest chefs on the "Kids Can Cook" TV show! You will appear on the show on Wednesday, April 8th from 7:30 p.m. to 8:15 p.m.

You plan to make your favourite dish, Polka-Dotted Macaroni and Cheese.

You will buy the ingredients. You must not spend more than $20.

Here are the ingredients you need to buy:

decade

century

millennium

elapsed time

capacity

litre

millilitre

mass

gram

kilogram

- Suppose you do the shopping 3 days before the show. What day and date will that be?
- Is $20 enough to buy all the ingredients? How could you find out?
- Which ingredients are sold by mass? Which by capacity?
- How long will you be on camera?

Exploring Units of Time

King Tutankhamen ruled Egypt over 3000 years ago.
That's 30 **centuries** or 3 **millenniums** ago.
He was only 9 years old when he became king.
Archaeologists discovered "King Tut's" tomb in 1922.
That's over 80 years, or 8 **decades**, ago.
The tomb was filled with many priceless treasures!

Millenniums, centuries, and decades are long units of time.
- What other units of time do you know?
- How are they related?

Explore

➤ Choose one of these units of time:

days	minutes	months	weeks	hours

years	millenniums	decades	centuries

➤ Write a sentence using the unit of time.
   Here are some ideas:
   - how long ago an event happened
     (or when it will happen)
   - someone's age
   - how long it takes to do an activity
➤ Leave a blank in your sentence for
   the unit of time.
➤ Repeat with other units of time.

Show and Share

Show your sentences to a classmate.
Have your classmate fill in the blanks.
Share how you chose the units to fill in the blanks.
Were there any blanks that could have been filled
with different units of time? How do you know?

Numbers Every Day

Mental Math

Find each product.
Describe any patterns.

1×5	1×10
2×5	2×10
3×5	3×10
4×5	4×10

Connect

Time is measured in different units.

A decade is 10 years.
A century is 100 years.
A millennium is 1000 years.

Here are some units of time from shortest to longest:

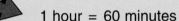

minute	hour	day	week	month	year	decade	century	millennium

This is how some units of time are related:

1 hour = 60 minutes	1 year = 12 months or 52 weeks or 365 days
1 day = 24 hours	1 decade = 10 years
1 week = 7 days	1 century = 10 decades or 100 years
1 month = about 4 weeks	1 millennium = 10 centuries or 1000 years

When you measure time, choose a reasonable unit.

It's more reasonable to say:

It's more reasonable to say:

I slept for 10 hours. **than** I slept for 600 minutes.

Sandy is 9 years old. **than** Sandy is 3287 days old.

1. Which unit would you use to measure each period of time?
   a) how long it takes to get to school
   b) how long ago mammoths lived
   c) how long the sun shines on a clear day
   d) the age of a baby when she can first sit up on her own
   e) how long it takes a tree to grow five metres

2. Which is longer? How do you know?
   a) 1 hour or 35 minutes   b) 46 weeks or 1 year
   c) 309 years or 3 centuries   d) 5 decades or 1 century

3. Copy and complete. Use >, <, or =.
   a) 485 days ☐ 1 year   b) 13 years ☐ 1 decade
   c) 24 months ☐ 2 years   d) 20 days ☐ 3 weeks
   e) 40 years ☐ 4 decades   f) 1 millennium ☐ 6000 years

4. Rewrite each sentence.
   Write the time in a different way.
   a) This house was built 6 decades ago.
   b) Daphne spent 49 days in Switzerland last summer.
   c) Ito's great uncle is 80 years old.
   d) It took Ron 24 months to make this quilt.
   e) I am 9 years old.
   Show your work.

5. Canada celebrated its centennial in 1967.
   What do you think centennial means?

Social Studies

The Magna Carta was signed on June 15, 1215. That's about 800 years or 8 centuries ago.

Reflect

The third millennium started on January 1, 2001.
Do you think you'll celebrate the fourth millennium?
Explain.

Telling Time

Maria can do 25 push-ups in 1 minute.
What can you do in 1 minute?

Explore · **Game**

Make a set of 6 clock cards.
The minute hand on each clock should be between the 5-minute marks.

6:12

9:43

Now make a set of 6 time cards to match the times on the clock cards.

Play the Matching Time Game.
➤ Mix up the 12 cards.
   Place the cards face down
   in 3 rows of 4.
➤ Take turns turning over 2 cards.
➤ If the cards match, keep them.
➤ If the cards do not match,
   put them back, face down.
➤ Keep playing until all the cards
   have gone.

Show *and* Share

Talk about the strategies you used
to find matching pairs of cards.

It takes 1 minute for the minute hand to move from one mark on the clock to the next mark.

20 minutes after
7 o'clock

7:20

21 minutes after
7 o'clock

7:21

You can read times after the half-hour in two ways.

You say:
54 minutes after
11 o'clock

or 11:54

You say:
6 minutes before
12 o'clock

or 6 minutes to 12

We use a.m. for times from midnight to just before noon.
We use p.m. for times from noon to just before midnight.

Practice

1. Write the time shown on each clock.

a)

b)

c)

d)

Numbers Every Day

Mental Math

Multiply each number by 10, 100, and 1000.

- 7
- 10
- 30

2. Write each time two ways. Write a.m. or p.m.

a) school ends

b) dinner time

c) wake up

d) bed time

e) play baseball

f) lunchtime

3. Draw an analog clock to show each time.
How can you use fractions to help you?

a) quarter past three   b) quarter to two   c) half past seven

4. Draw a digital clock to show each time.

a) 14 minutes after 3   b) 8 minutes before 7
c) 36 minutes after 5   d) 7 minutes before 1
e) 25 minutes before 8   f) 10 minutes to 9

5. Sophie and Carmella agreed to meet at the music store.
Sophie arrived at 4:47 p.m.
Carmella arrived at quarter to 5.
Who arrived first?
How many minutes earlier was she than the other girl?
Show your work.

At Home

Reflect

Are 3:48 and 12 minutes to 4
the same time?
Use words and pictures to explain.

How is your sense of time?
Guess what time you think it
is right now.
Now go and check a clock.
How close was your guess?

LESSON

3

Estimating Time

z...y...x...w...v...u...t...s...

Arnold estimates that he can say
the alphabet backward in 2 minutes.

How long do you think
it would take you?

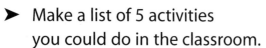

Explore

➤ Make a list of 5 activities
you could do in the classroom.
➤ Estimate how long it will take
to do each activity.
Record your estimates.
➤ Take turns doing each activity
while your partner times you.
Record each time to the
nearest minute.

I think it will
take me 3 minutes to
draw 100 stars.

I think it will take me
5 minutes to put a
tangram together.

Show *and* Share

One way to record your
work is to make a table.

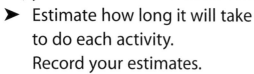

Activity	Estimated Time	Actual Time
Draw 100 stars.	3 minutes	4 minutes
Put a tangram together.	5 minutes	
Do 50 sit-ups.		

Share the strategies you used to estimate the times.
Were your actual times exact? Explain.

206　**LESSON FOCUS** | *Estimate and measure time intervals.*

The minute is a small unit of time.
Here are some benchmarks to help you estimate time in minutes.

It takes about 1 minute to brush your teeth.

It takes about 5 minutes to fill a bathtub.

It takes about 15 minutes to eat lunch.

Practice ●

1. Choose the better estimate for how long each activity would take.
   a) Drink a glass of milk.
      5 minutes or 40 minutes
   b) Do your homework.
      30 minutes or 5 hours
   c) Count to 100.
      2 minutes or 50 minutes
   d) Play a game of Monopoly.
      15 minutes or 50 minutes
   e) Wash the dishes.
      15 minutes or 2 hours
   f) Make your bed.
      2 minutes or 45 minutes

Numbers Every Day

Mental Math

When you add 999 to a number, add 1000 then subtract 1.
Try these:

- 999 + 80
- 999 + 75
- 687 + 999
- 22 + 999

2. Find how long it takes the minute hand to move:

a) from  to

b) from  to

3. Suppose you do not have a watch and the classroom clock is broken. How would you be able to tell when approximately 5 minutes had passed?

4. Jayne started skipping at 9:15 a.m. She stopped at 9:23 a.m. About how long did Jayne skip?

5. We finished dinner at 6:29 p.m. It took us about 20 minutes to eat. About what time did we start dinner?

6. Miguel left for his walk at 5:11 p.m. He returned 27 minutes later. About what time did Miguel return?

7. Dan estimated it would take 15 minutes to walk to the store. He left home at 10:14 a.m. and arrived at the store at 10:31 a.m. Was Dan's estimate reasonable? Explain.

Reflect

How could you explain to a 5-year-old how long 10 minutes is?
What are some benchmarks you could use?

LESSON 4

Exploring Elapsed Time

Explore ••

Plan a day at Funland Park.

➤ Choose 4 or 5 activities.

➤ Make a schedule of your day.

Estimate how long you'll spend at each activity.

Show the start and end times for each activity.

Allow 10 minutes between activities to get from one to the next.

Remember to schedule time for meals!

LESSON FOCUS | Use elapsed time to create a schedule.

209

Show *and* Share

Here is one way to record your schedule.

Activity	How Long	Start Time	End Time	Travel Time
Rock Climbing	1 hour and 15 minutes	9:30 a.m.	10:45 a.m.	10 minutes
Arts and Crafts	1 hour	10:55 a.m.		

Show your schedule to a classmate.
Explain how you found the start and end times for each activity.
What was the longest period of time you scheduled for an activity?
What was the shortest?

Connect

Darryl plans to go to the Water Park at 3:05 p.m.
He wants to spend 2 hours and 15 minutes there.
Here's how he found out what time to leave the Water Park.

He started at 3:05 and added 2 hours.	Then he added 15 minutes.

3:05 → 5:05

5:05 → 5:20

Darryl will leave the Water Park at 5:20 p.m.
The time between 3:05 p.m. and 5:20 p.m.
is the **elapsed time**.

210

Practice

1. Use copies of blank clock faces.
   Show the time on each clock after
   1 hour and 10 minutes. Write each new time.

a)

b)

c)

d)

e)

f)

Numbers Every Day

Calculator Skills

Make the largest product you
can using only 4, 6, 7, 9.

☐ ☐ ☐
×   ☐
‾‾‾‾‾‾‾‾

2. Copy and complete the table.

	Length of Activity	Start Time	End Time
a)	3 hours	11:25 a.m.	
b)	4 hours and 10 minutes	4:16 p.m.	
c)		7:20 a.m.	11:30 a.m.
d)		3:45 p.m.	5:50 p.m.
e)	1 hour and 30 minutes		10:00 a.m.

3. Dad cooked a turkey for 4 hours and 20 minutes.
   He put the turkey in the oven at 1:15.
   What time did Dad take it out?

4. Eva left Cambridge at 6:32 a.m.
   She arrived in Mississauga at 7:39 a.m.
   How long did it take Eva to travel from
   Cambridge to Mississauga?

211

5. Antonio and his sisters started a game of Monopoly
at 4:25 p.m. The game ended at 7:50 p.m.
How long did they play?

6. Petra took her dog for a walk.
She left home at 11:43 a.m. and returned at 12:30 p.m.
How long did Petra walk?

7. *The Flying Dog* is 2 hours and 5 minutes long.

The Flying Dog
starring Emily Curr - Michael Canine
Show times
1:45, 4:20, 6:45, 9:35

a) What time does each show end?
b) How much time is there between the end
of each show and the start of the next one?
c) Suppose you live 25 minutes from the theatre.
You are going to the 4:20 show.
What time should you leave home? Explain.
Show your work.

8. Write a story problem about elapsed time.
Trade problems with a classmate.
Solve your classmate's problem.

Reflect

Think about 2 things you do in one day.
Find the elapsed time between them.
Use words, pictures, or numbers
to explain.

At Home

Record the time you
go to bed tonight and the
time you get up tomorrow
morning.
How long did you sleep?

5 Estimating and Counting Money

Does Danielle have enough money to buy a chemistry set?

Wonders of Science
The store to explore!

ANT FARM	PULLEYS AND GEARS KIT	VOLCANO KIT	Chemistry Set	Kaleidoscope	ROCKS AND MINERALS
$19.95	$39.98	$24.75	$35.45	$5.95	$19.25

Explore

You will need play money.
➤ Choose a banker.
➤ The banker makes a collection of money behind a barrier.
➤ The banker lifts the barrier for a short time.
➤ Estimate how much money there is. Record your estimate.
➤ Count the money.
➤ The person with the closest estimate becomes the banker.

Show and Share

Share the strategies you used to estimate.
Compare the strategies you used to count the money.

Andrew earns money by walking the neighbours' dogs twice a day.

Andrew thinks he has earned enough money to buy a set of gel pens.

SAVE **24 Gel pen set   only $19.95**

Offer expires soon! See back of coupon for details.

Here's how Andrew counts his money.

➤ First he sorts the dollars.

He counts: "5, ...   7,   9,   11,   13,   ...14,   15 dollars",
                                                              or $15.00

➤ Then he makes as many one-dollar groups as he can.

He counts: " 1,   2,   3,   ... 4 dollars",
                                            or $4.00

➤ Finally he counts the rest of the coins.

"10,   20,   ...25,   30,   35,   ...36,   37,   38,   39,   40 cents",
                                                                      or $0.40

Andrew has $15.00 + $4.00 + $0.40.
He has $19.40. The gel pens cost $19.95.
Andrew doesn't have enough money for the pens.

214

1. Estimate, then count.
   Record each estimate and amount.

   a)

   b)

   c)

   d)

2. Use play money to show each amount.
   Draw pictures to record your work.
   a) $18.58   **b)** $45.21   **c)** $20.89
   d) $0.91   **e)** $31.31   **f)** $49.73

3. Show each amount using the least number of bills and coins.
   Use play money to help you.
   a) $15.35   **b)** $50   **c)** $37.28

4. Show three different ways to make each amount.
   a) $11.42   **b)** $25   **c)** $41.50

5. Suppose you have 5 bills in your wallet. They add up to $45.
   What bills are they?

Math Link

Social Studies

The loonie ($1 coin) was introduced
in Canada in 1987.
The toonie ($2 coin) was introduced in 1996.
Before that, $1 and $2 bills were used.

6. Explain how you could make $37.40 using only 3 bills and 4 coins.

7. Kiki has 6 bills and 4 coins.
She has between $40 and $50.
What bills and coins could Kiki have?
Give at least two different answers.
Show your work.

8. Here is the Wonders of Science ad from page 213.

a) Neil paid for the volcano kit with 1 bill and 5 coins.
He didn't get any change.
What bill and coins did Neil use?

b) Suppose you want to pay the exact amount for the ant farm.
What is the least number of bills and coins you could use?

c) Danielle has $32.96. She wants to buy the chemistry set.
Draw pictures to show how much more money
Danielle needs.

Reflect

Suppose you have a jar full of bills and coins.
How would you find the total amount of
money in the jar?
Use words and pictures to explain.

Making Change

Harry sells all kinds of novelty hats. Which one would you like to buy?

Explore

You will need play money.
Start with one $5 bill, one $10 bill,
and one $20 bill.

Take turns.
➤ Choose a hat you would like to buy.
➤ Pay for it.
➤ Have your partner make change.
➤ Keep buying hats until you run out
   of money.

Harry's HAT HUT

Joker's Hat - $12.99
Extra Long Stocking Hat - $10.50
"Cat in the Hat" Hat - $14.49
Propeller Beanie - $4.95
Umbrella Hat - $12.79
Sun Hat with Sunglasses - $9.29
Blinking Hat - $11.59
Alien Hat - $6.95
Water Bottle Hat - $8.89

Show and Share

What strategies did you use to make change?
How did you decide which bill to use to buy the first hat?
How did you decide which hats to buy?

Connect

Elizabeth bought a T-shirt for $12.69.
She used a $10 bill and a $5 bill to pay for it.

That's $2.31 in change.

Here is how the clerk made change for her:
"That's $12.69 …

$12.70   …$12.80   …$12.90   …$13.00   …$15.00"

Elizabeth got $2.31 in change.

Elizabeth estimated to make sure she got the correct change.

She thought: The T-shirt cost about $13.

Fifteen dollars minus $13 is $2.

This is the same as $2.31 rounded to the nearest dollar.

Practice

1. Use Harry's Hats price list.
   Model each problem
   with play money.
   Draw pictures to show the
   change for each purchase.
   a) Sargam bought a blinking hat.
      He paid with a $20 bill.
   b) Chelsey bought a joker's hat.
      She paid with 7 toonies.
   c) Emil bought a stocking hat.
      He paid with a $50 bill.

Harry's Hat Hut

Joker's Hat - $12.99
Extra Long Stocking Hat - $10.50
"Cat in the Hat" Hat - $14.49
Propeller Beanie - $4.95
Umbrella Hat - $12.79
Sun Hat with Sunglasses - $9.29
Blinking Hat - $11.59
Alien Hat - $6.95
Water Bottle Hat - $8.89

2. Oko bought a pair of shoes for $32.00
   and a pair of socks for $7.00.
   How much change did she get from a $50 bill?

3. How much change would each person get?
   Use play money to help you.
   a) Lily's meal cost $17.95. She paid with a $20 bill.
   b) Jordie's book cost $21.05.
      She paid with a $20 bill and a toonie.
   c) Jacob bought a new sweater for $41.60.
      He paid with two $20 bills and a $10 bill.

4. Casio paid for a $35.50 purchase with two $20 bills.
   He got 5 coins in change. What coins were they?

5. Julio paid $17.89 for a new CD. He paid with a $20 bill.
   What is the least number of coins Julio could get in change?
   Show your work.

6. Sookie has this money in his pocket.

   List three ways Sookie could pay for a $17.99 purchase.
   Tell how much change he would get each way.

7. Cassie bought a pogo stick for $27.29.
   She paid with a $50 bill. She got $23.71 change.
   Did Cassie get the right change? Explain.

8. Sybil bought a robot for $37.11.
   She gave the clerk $40.11.
   Why did Sybil do that?

Reflect

Suppose you bought a CD.
You think the clerk gave you the
wrong change. How would you check?
Use words, numbers, or pictures to explain.

Numbers Every Day

Number Strategies

Use related multiplication facts
to divide.

$49 \div 7$

$32 \div 4$

$45 \div 9$

$36 \div 6$

Strategies Toolkit

I could trade it for two 5-dollar bills.

Explore

You have $5 bills, loonies, and toonies.
How can you make change for a $10 bill?
You can make change using bills or coins, or both.
Try to make change using:
- 2 bills and coins
- 3 bills and coins
- 4 bills and coins, up to 10 bills and coins

Work together to solve this problem.
Use any materials you think will help.

Show *and* Share

Describe the strategy you used to solve the problem.

Connect

You have $20 bills, $10 bills, $5 bills, toonies, and loonies.
Try to make change for a $50 bill using:
3 bills and coins, 4 bills and coins, ..., 10 bills and coins.

Understand

What do you know?
- You can use $20 bills, $10 bills, $5 bills, toonies, and loonies.
- You must try to make change for $50 using 3, 4, 5, 6, 7, 8, 9, and 10 bills and coins.

Plan

Think of a strategy to help you solve the problem.
- You can **make an organized list**.
- Use play money.

Strategies

- **Make a table.**
- **Use a model.**
- **Draw a picture.**
- **Solve a simpler problem.**
- **Work backward.**
- **Guess and check.**
- **Make an organized list.**
- **Use a pattern.**

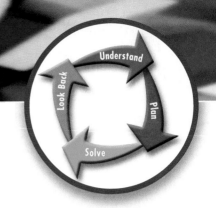

Make a table to record your list.
Show $50 in different ways.
Record each way in your list.
Can you make change using each number of bills and coins?

Bills and Coins Used				Number of Bills and Coins Used
$20	$20	$10		3
$20	$10	$10	$10	4

Check your list. Did you make $50 each time?
Did you make change using each number of bills and coins?
Could you make change more than one way for some numbers of bills and coins?

Practice

Choose one of the **Strategies**

1. Lulu emptied her piggy bank.
   She separated the loonies, quarters, and dimes into piles.
   One pile had 5 coins, one had 4 coins, and one had 3 coins.
   Altogether Lulu had $5.25. Which coins did she have?

2. There are 4 bills and 7 coins in this cash box.
   The total amount of money in the box is $48.38.
   Which bills and coins are in the box?

3. At the end of the bake sale, there were 9 bills in the cash box.
   Altogether there was $50. Which bills were in the cash box?

Reflect

Which other strategy could you use to solve the problem in *Connect*? Use words, pictures, or numbers to explain.

Measuring Capacity

Hanna is making Tropical Fruit Punch to serve at her party.
This recipe will make 1 glass of punch for each guest.

How many guests do you think will be at her party?

TROPICAL FRUIT PUNCH

500 mL orange juice
500 mL pineapple juice
75 mL Lemon juice
100 mL grenadine syrup
2 L ginger ale

Explore

You will need some containers and water.

➤ Choose a container.
➤ Estimate how much it holds in millilitres or litres.
Check your estimate.
Record your work in a table.
Repeat the activity with other containers.
➤ Use a 250-mL measuring cup and a 1-L container.
Find how many millilitres are in one litre.
Describe how you did it.

Show and Share

Share the strategies you used to make your estimates.
How does measuring how much one container holds help you to estimate how much another container holds?

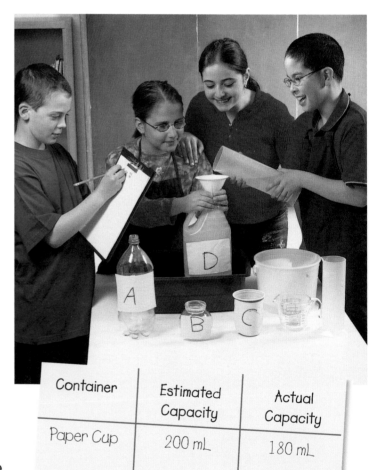

Container	Estimated Capacity	Actual Capacity
Paper Cup	200 mL	180 mL

The **capacity** of a container is the amount it can hold.

➤ The litre (L) and millilitre (mL) are units used to measure capacity.

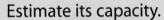
1000 mL = 1 L

This bottle has a capacity
of one litre.
It holds 1 L of green ketchup.

This bottle has a capacity of
four hundred millilitres.
It holds 400 mL of mustard.

➤ Here's how to estimate and measure the capacity of a sand pail.

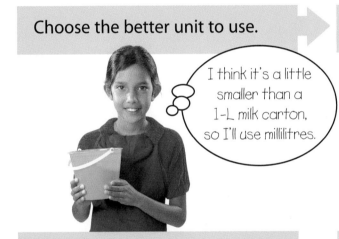

Choose the better unit to use.

I think it's a little smaller than a 1-L milk carton, so I'll use millilitres.

Estimate its capacity.

I'll guess 800 mL.

Fill the pail with water.
Empty the pail into a graduated
cylinder marked in millilitres.

Read the measurement.

It's about 900 mL.

The capacity of the pail is about 900 mL.

1. Which unit would you use to measure each capacity? Explain.

a)

b)

c)

d)

e)

f)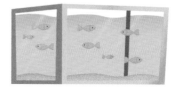

2. Choose the better estimate for each. Explain.

a) 4 mL or 4 L

b) 10 mL or 1 L

c) 15 mL or 2 L

d) 100 mL or 1 L

e) 4 mL or 4 L

f) 50 mL or 7 L

3. Copy and complete.

a) 1 L = ☐ mL

b) 2 L = ☐ mL

c) 3 L = ☐ mL

d) 4000 mL = ☐ L

e) 5000 mL = ☐ L

f) 6000 mL = ☐ L

4. Order these capacities from least to greatest.

a) 225 mL, 4 L, 75 mL, 640 mL

b) 2 L, 900 mL, 5 L, 990 mL

c) 38 mL, 40 L, 720 mL, 6 L

d) 24 L, 16 mL, 300 mL, 9 L

Numbers Every Day

Number Strategies

Add or multiply.

6×2 $2 + 2 + 2 + 2 + 2 + 2$
3×4 $4 + 4 + 4$
4×5 $5 + 5 + 5 + 5$

What do you notice? Explain.

Math Link

Science

The body of a human adult has about 5 L of blood. A mosquito's bite removes about $\frac{1}{200}$ of a millilitre of blood!

---

5. Manny drank 600 mL of water on the way to soccer practice.
He drank 400 mL on the way home.
How much water did Manny drink altogether?
Give your answer in two ways.

6. Josie drinks 500 mL of milk at each meal.
  a) How much milk does she drink each day?
  b) How many days would it take Josie
    to drink 6 L of milk?

7. Use the Tropical Fruit Punch recipe on page 222.
  a) How many millilitres of punch does the recipe make?
  b) Which ingredient do you use the most of?
    Which do you use the least of?
  c) Rewrite the recipe to make a double batch of punch.
  Show your work.

8. Ty plans to measure the capacity of a jug in litres and millilitres.
He says the number of litres will be greater than
the number of millilitres.
Do you agree? Explain.

Reflect

You have estimated and measured capacity.
When is an estimate good enough?
When do you need a precise measurement? Explain.

9 Measuring Mass

The bee hummingbird is the smallest bird in the world. It has a mass of about 2 g.

The North African ostrich is the world's largest bird. The mass of the male ostrich is about 140 kg.

Explore

You will need balance scales and items like those in the picture.

➤ Choose any object.
Estimate its mass to the nearest gram or kilogram.
Check your estimate.
Record your work in a table.
Repeat the activity with other objects.
Order the objects from least mass to greatest mass.

➤ Find how grams and kilograms are related. Tell how you found out.

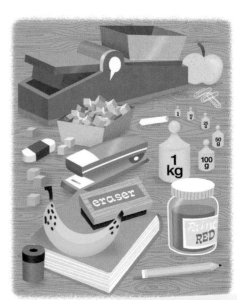

Object	Estimated Mass	Actual Mass
Pencil	6 g	4 g

Show and Share

Share the strategies you used to estimate. How did you decide whether to use grams or kilograms?

The mass of an object is a measure of how heavy the object is.

There are one thousand grams in one kilogram.

1000 g = 1 kg

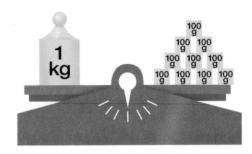

The gram (g) is a small unit of mass used to measure light objects.

The kilogram (kg) is a larger unit of mass used to measure heavier objects.

The mass of a paper clip is about 1 g.

The mass of one litre of milk is about 1 kg.

Use balance scales when they help.

1. Which unit would you use to measure each mass? Explain.

a)

b)

c)

d)

2. Copy and complete.

a) 1 kg = ☐ g

b) 2 kg = ☐ g

c) 3 kg = ☐ g

d) 4000 g = ☐ kg

e) 5000 g = ☐ kg

f) 6000 g = ☐ kg

Numbers Every Day

Number Strategies

Which of these show 657?

- 65 + 7
- 6 hundreds, 5 tens, and 7 ones
- 657 × 0
- 700 − 57
- 500 + 157

3. Choose the better estimate.

a) 5 g or 50 kg

b) 1 g or 100 g

c) 40 g or 2 kg

4. Match each object with one of these masses: 350 g, 2 kg, 5 g, 12 kg.

a)

b)

c)

d)

5. Order the objects in question 4 from heaviest to lightest.

6. Which unit is more appropriate: grams or kilograms?

a) The mass of a lobster is 690 ___.

b) Tangerines are on sale for $2.84 a ___.

c) Marty's cookie recipe calls for 150 ___ of chocolate chips.

7. There are about 40 marshmallows in a 250-g package.

a) What is the approximate mass of 1 marshmallow?

b) Suppose you need 10 marshmallows for a recipe.
About how many grams of marshmallows do you need?

8. Anna measured the mass of a box of books to be 7 kg.
Suppose she wants to know the mass in grams.
How will the mass in grams compare to the mass in kilograms? Explain.

9. Predict the mass of 500 loonies.
Compare your prediction with a classmate's prediction.
How could you check your prediction?

Reflect

When you look at an object, how can you tell if its mass
would be measured in grams or kilograms?

Meteorologist

Is it going to rain, snow, or thunder?

Everyone wants to know what the weather will be. Pilots use weather information to decide if they can fly safely. Farmers plant and harvest their crops based on the weather. The rest of us want to know if it will rain on the weekend.

Scientists who study weather are called meteorologists. A meteorologist measures temperature, wind speed and direction, rainfall, and the moisture in the air. Data are collected from around the world and even from space.

Weather balloons carry measuring instruments high in the atmosphere.

Weather satellites photograph weather systems from above Earth.

An *anemometer* measures wind speed.

A *rain gauge* measures the rainfall.

Weather satellites take photographs of Earth from above. These photographs show clouds, winds, and storms.

Meteorologists use their measurements and satellite photographs to make weather maps. They use these maps to predict when weather systems will arrive at different locations on Earth.

Meteorologists use measurements every day!

A *thermometer* measures temperature.

229

LESSON

1

1. Copy and complete.
  a) 1 decade = ☐ years   **b)** 1 century = ☐ years
  c) 1 millennium = ☐ years   **d)** 1 century = ☐ decades

2

2. Write each time in two ways.

a) 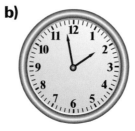   **b)** 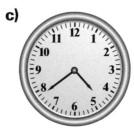   **c)**

3

3. Match each activity with its estimated time:
  1 minute, 10 hours, 1 hour, 5 minutes.
  a) get a good night's sleep
  b) eat an apple
  c) bake a pie
  d) put on your coat and hat

4

4. Keely started building a model at 3:23 p.m.
  She finished at 5:11 p.m.
  How long did it take Keely to build the model?

5. Ramesh practised the piano for 1 hour and 25 minutes.
  He started at 10:32 a.m. What time did Ramesh finish?

6. Count the money. Write each amount.
  a)

  b)

7. Draw pictures to show the change.
   a) Melody bought a can of 3 tennis balls for $1.79.
   She paid with a $20 bill.
   b) Tommy bought a bracelet for $13.00 and a necklace for $7.95.
   He gave the clerk a $20 bill and a $5 bill.

8. Choose the better estimate for each capacity.
   a) 15 mL or 500 mL   **b)** 50 mL or 4 L   **c)** 400 mL or 2 L

9. Choose the better estimate for each mass.
   a) 1 g or 50 g   **b)** 30 g or 1 kg   **c)** 500 g or 500 kg

10. Estimate the mass of each object.
   Order the objects from lightest
   to heaviest.

   a)

   b)

   c)

   d)

UNIT
6 Learning Goals

- ☑ relate units of time
- ☑ estimate and measure time intervals
- ☑ tell time to the nearest minute
- ☑ estimate and count money
- ☑ make purchases and make change
- ☑ estimate and measure capacity
- ☑ estimate and measure mass
- ☑ compare and order objects by mass

The Cooking Show

Part 1

- Here are the ingredients you bought
  for the show.
  How much change did you get
  from a $20 bill?

- The cooking show is today.
  You were told to arrive at the studio
  1 hour and 15 minutes before air time.
  It takes 20 minutes to get to the studio.
  What time should you leave home?

AIR TIME

Part 2

Here's the recipe you are using on the show.

Polka-Dotted Macaroni and Cheese

Elbow macaroni	500 g	
Olive oil	15 mL	• Cook macaroni in boiling water with oil and salt until tender. Drain and pour into baking dish.
Salt	10 mL	
Milk	250 mL	• Blend milk, cheese, and Worcestershire sauce. Mix with macaroni.
Grated cheese	250 g	
Worcestershire sauce	5 mL	• Top with sliced wieners.
4 wieners		• Bake at 180° C for 25 minutes.

- You do not have balance scales.
  You have a 1-kg package of macaroni.
  How can you measure 500 g of macaroni?
  Will your results be exact? Explain.
- You have a 1-L carton of milk.
  How much milk will be left over?
- There are 12 wieners in a 450 g-package.
  What is the approximate mass of
  1 wiener?
  About how many grams of wieners
  are used in the recipe?
- Suppose you put the macaroni
  in the oven at 7:52 p.m.
  What time will it be ready?

Show your work.

Your work should show
☑ how you calculated your
   answers
☑ your answers recorded
   correctly, including units
☑ a recipe that is easy to
   follow
☑ how you chose the
   amount (with unit) for
   each ingredient in your
   recipe

Part 3

Suppose you are to invent a new dish.
Write the recipe. Include:
- the ingredients and how much of
  each ingredient you will use
- instructions on how to make the dish
- the number of people it will serve

Reflect on the Unit

Tell one important thing you have learned about
time, money, mass, or capacity.
Use words, numbers, or pictures to explain.

Transformational

At the Fun House!

Learning Goals

- describe location and movement on a grid
- understand and use translations, reflections, and rotations
- discover patterns with translations, reflections, and rotations
- draw lines of symmetry

234

Geometry

Key Words

grid

coordinates

translation

translation arrow

image

reflection

decagon

rotation

turn centre

transformation

area pattern

Vivek is a designer.
He has designed the Fun House for a theme park.

Look at each room.
• What different kinds of movement are suggested?
• How do objects move or appear to move at the Fun House?

Grids and Coordinates

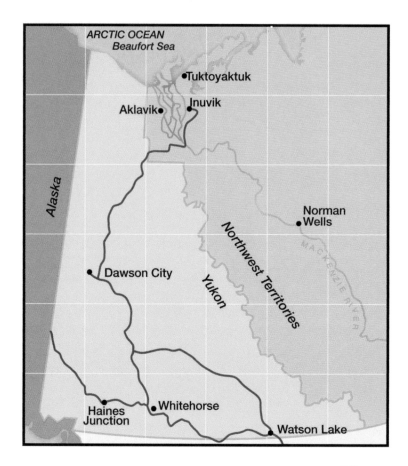

Here is a map of part of Yukon and Northwest Territories.

How would you describe where each place is on the map?

• Inuvik
• Mackenzie River
• Norman Wells

Explore

You will need 2-cm grid paper.
➤ With your partner, design a map of a town or region where you would like to live.
 Include at least 5 features or places on your map.
➤ Invent a way to describe the location of any place on your map.
➤ Trade maps with another pair of students.
 List 5 places on their map and where the places are located.

Show *and* Share

Share your strategy for locating a place on a map with another pair of students.
How did you describe the location when the place fills several squares? When the place is where two lines cross?

Here is a map of Pelee Island.
It is close to the southernmost point in Canada.

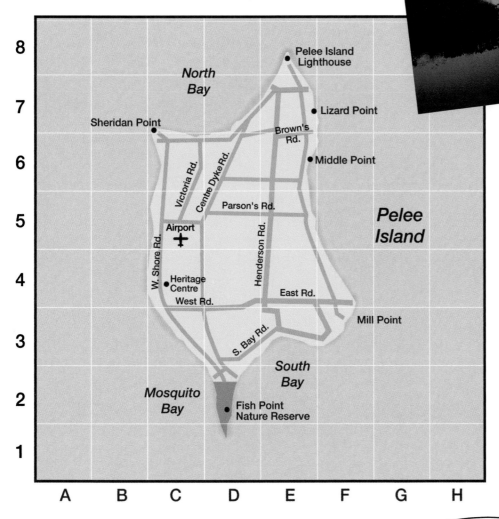

This map is drawn on a **grid**.

- Each square along the bottom
  of the grid is labelled with a letter.
- Each square along the side of the grid
  is labelled with a number.
- To locate any square, we use a letter
  and a number.
  These are called the **coordinates**.
  The lighthouse is at E8.
  Victoria Road goes from C5 to C6.

> The letter C and the number 5
> form the coordinates of the
> airport: C5. The first coordinate is
> the letter. The second coordinate
> is the number.

237

1. List the coordinates of each figure.

   a) green square

   b) red circle

   c) blue triangle

   d) purple rectangle

2. Describe the figure in each square.

   a) A6   **b)** C3

   c) E2   **d)** D4

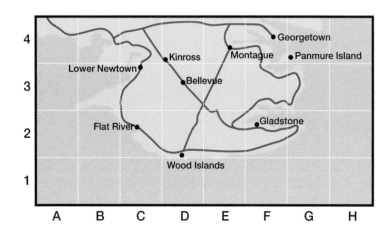

3. Here is a map of part of Prince Edward Island. Write the coordinates of each town.

4. Sandy found a coded message in a bottle.

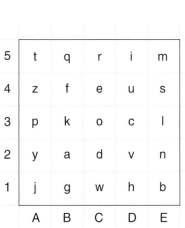

Use the coordinates of each letter to decode the message below.

	A	B	C	D	E
5	t	q	r	i	m
4	z	f	e	u	s
3	p	k	o	c	l
2	y	a	d	v	n
1	j	g	w	h	b

A5 C3 D4 B1 D1   E3 D4 D3 B3.

A5 D1 C4   B1 C4 E2 D5 C4   D5 E4   C3 E2

D2 B2 D3 B2 A5 D5 C3 E2.

238

5. Use the code in question 4. Write a message.
Trade messages with a classmate.
Decode your classmate's message.

6. Look at these two grids.
   a) How are the grids the same?
   How are they different?
   b) Suppose you planned to draw a town map on one of these grids. Which grid would you use?
   Show your work.

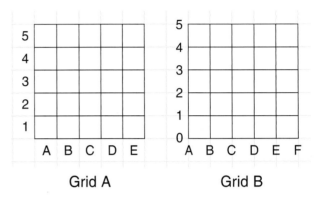

Grid A   Grid B

7. You will each need grid paper.
Play the game "Battleship."
Each person labels the squares on the grid
1 to 10 vertically and A to J horizontally.

Game

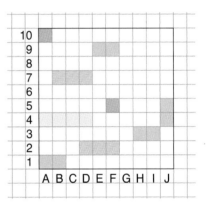

Shade: 4 squares for 1 battleship
         3 squares each for 2 cruisers
         2 squares each for 4 destroyers
         1 square each for 2 submarines

• Take turns to say the coordinates of a square.
  Record the coordinates.
• If your partner has a ship on that square,
  that ship is hit.
• When you hit all the squares of a ship,
  the ship sinks.
• The person who sinks all her
  partner's ships wins.

Reflect

Why do we use coordinates on a map?
Use words, pictures, or numbers to explain.

Numbers Every Day

Mental Math

Add.
    50 + 95
    75 + 98
    27 + 99

Which strategies
did you use?

Translations

You will need 1-cm grid paper, a 1-cm cube, and a ruler.

➤ Place the cube on a square.

- Trace the cube using a coloured pencil.
  Slide the cube along the ruler in a
  straight line to another square
  on the grid.
  Trace the cube in its new position.
- Your partner describes the slide
  by telling how many squares
  the cube moved right or left,
  and up or down.
- Take turns to slide the cube and
  tell how it slid.
  Record your work.

➤ Place the cube on a square.

Move the cube
3 squares right and
7 squares down.

- Trace the cube.
- Give your partner directions for a slide.
  Your partner follows your directions
  to move the cube.
  Trace the cube in its new position.
- Take turns to give the directions.
  Record your work.

Show *and* Share

Share your work with another pair of students.
How many different ways did you slide the cube?

When a figure moves along a straight line,
it is **translated** from one position to another.
The figure does not turn or flip.
The movement is a **translation**, or slide.
This figure has been translated 4 squares left and 3 squares down.

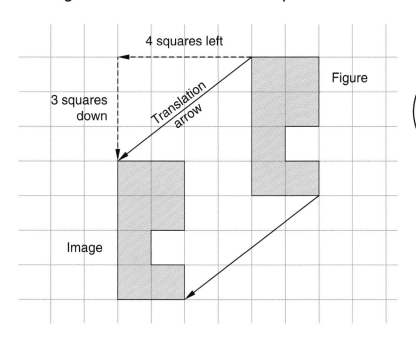

We say how many squares left or right before we say how many up or down.

The **translation arrow** joins matching points
on the figure and its **image**.
When a figure is translated, the figure and its image are congruent.

Math Link

Your World

Many patterns and designs show a figure and its translation images.
Identify a figure and its images in this design.

Practice ....

1. Which pictures show translations? How do you know?

a)

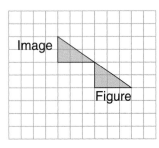

b)

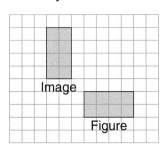

c)

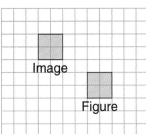

d)

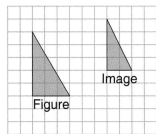

2. For each picture in question 1 that shows a translation:
   • Describe the translation.
   • Say what you know about the figure and its image.

3. Copy each figure on grid paper.
   Translate each figure using the translation given.
   Draw the image and the translation arrow.
   a) 6 squares right and 4 squares down

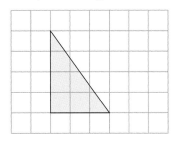

   b) 4 squares left and 5 squares up

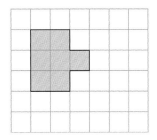

Numbers Every Day

Mental Math

Subtract.

$$20 - 9$$
$$85 - 9$$
$$37 - 9$$
$$42 - 9$$

Did you use the same
strategy each time?
Explain.

4. Write the translation that moved each figure to its image.

a)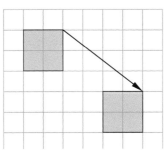

b)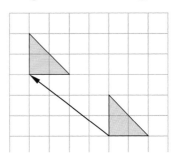

c)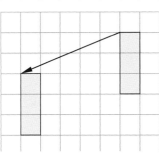

d)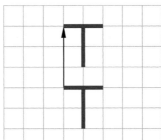

5. This figure has been translated twice.

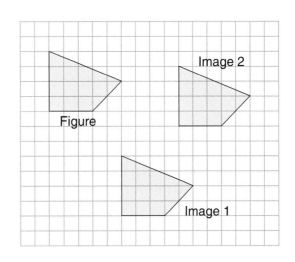

   a) Which translation moved the figure to Image 1?
   b) Which translation moved Image 1 to Image 2?
   c) Which translation would move the figure directly to Image 2?

Show your work. Explain your thinking.

6. Draw a figure on grid paper.
Translate it, then draw Image 1.
Translate Image 1, then draw Image 2.
Tell which translation moves the figure directly to Image 2.

Reflect

When you see a figure and its image, how can you tell if the figure has been translated? Use words, pictures, or numbers to explain.

Reflections

How is a **reflection** image of an object the same as the object?
How is it different?

Explore

You will need a ruler, a Mira, a 10 by 10 geoboard, geobands, and several sheets of dot paper.

➤ Use a band to divide the board into 2 congruent rectangles. Use this band as a mirror line.

• Make a figure on one side of the line.
  Have your partner make its image after a reflection in the line.

• Use a Mira to check if the image is correct. If the image is not correct, use the Mira to make it.

• Take turns to make the figure and its image. Record each figure and image on dot paper.

➤ Repeat the activity for other figures.
  Make figures that touch the line or lie across the line.

Show *and* Share

Share your pictures with another pair of students.
What do you notice about each figure, its image, and the mirror line?

Connect

When a figure is reflected
in a mirror line,
its image is congruent to
the figure.

The figure and its image
are the same distance
from the mirror line.

The figure and its image
face opposite ways.

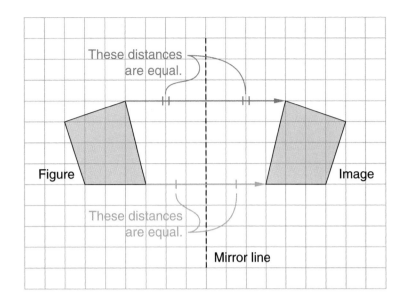

Practice

Use a Mira when it helps.

1. Which pictures show a reflection? How do you know?

a)

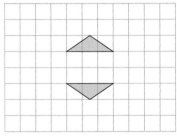

b)

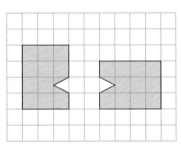

c)

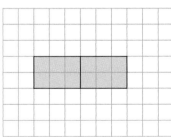

d)

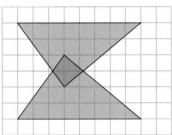

2. a) For each picture in question 1 that does not show a reflection,
explain why.

b) Which picture in question 1 shows a translation?
How do you know?

3. Copy each figure and mirror line on dot paper.
Draw each reflection image.

a)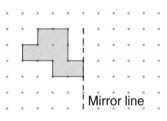
Mirror line

b)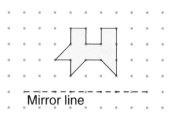
Mirror line

4. Suppose the letters of the alphabet are written as capital letters.
  a) A line is drawn above each letter.
    A Mira is placed on the line.
    Which letters look the same in the Mira?
  b) A line is drawn beside each letter.
    A Mira is placed on the line.
    Which letters look the same in the Mira?
  c) Create three words whose images read
    the same as the words when a Mira
    is placed above the letters.
    Show your work. Explain your thinking.

5. Draw a figure on dot paper. Draw a mirror line.
Draw the image of the figure using the mirror line you drew.
  a) Use a ruler. Join two matching points on the figure
    and the image.
  b) Use a ruler. Measure the distance between each point
    and the mirror line. What do you notice?
  c) Use a protractor. Measure the angle
    between the line you drew in part a
    and the mirror line. What do you notice?

Reflect

How are a translation and a
reflection alike? Draw a figure and
its image that could show both a
reflection and a translation.

Numbers Every Day

Number Strategies

Use the digits 2, 4, 6, and 8 to
make the sum that is closest
to 100.

Lines of Symmetry

A line of symmetry divides a figure into two congruent parts. When the figure is folded along its line of symmetry, the parts match exactly.

How can you tell that the two parts are congruent?

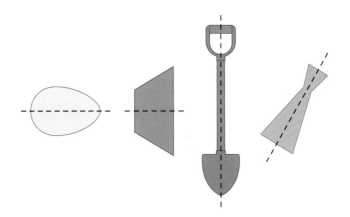

Explore

You will need a copy of the figures below and a Mira.

➤ Draw as many lines of symmetry on each figure as you can find.

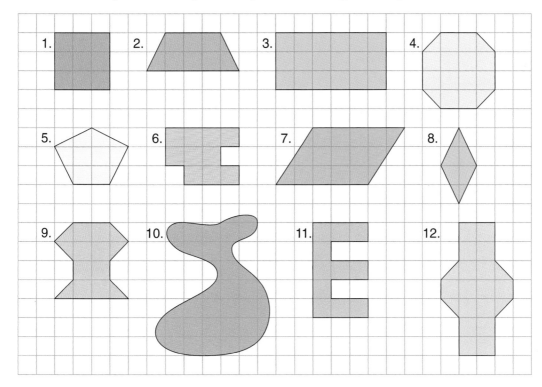

➤ Sort the figures by the numbers of lines of symmetry.

LESSON FOCUS | Draw lines of symmetry on figures.

247

Show *and* Share

Share your pictures with a classmate.
How can you check that you drew the lines of symmetry correctly?

Connect ....

A figure has symmetry when a line of symmetry can be drawn on it.
Some figures have no lines of symmetry.
Some figures have more than one line of symmetry.

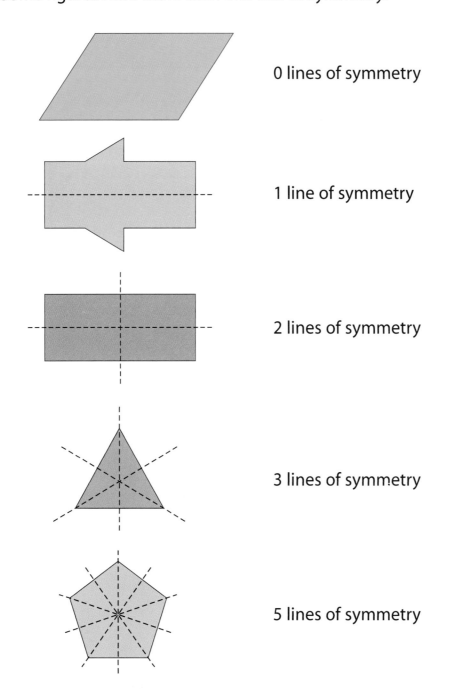

0 lines of symmetry

1 line of symmetry

2 lines of symmetry

3 lines of symmetry

5 lines of symmetry

Use a Mira when it helps.

1. Is each broken line a line of symmetry? How do you know?

   a) 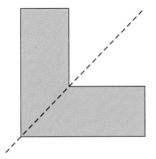   b) 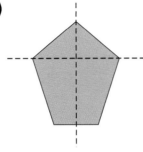   c)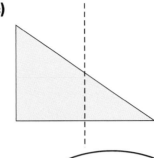

2. a) How many lines of symmetry
      does each regular figure have?

   A regular figure has
   all sides equal
   and all angles equal.

   b) How many sides does each regular figure have?
   c) Predict the number of lines of symmetry
      for a regular figure with 10 sides, a **decagon**.
      Explain your thinking.

3. Think about the quadrilaterals you know.
   Sketch and name all the quadrilaterals you know that have:
   a) no lines of symmetry
   b) 1 line of symmetry
   c) 2 lines of symmetry
   d) 4 lines of symmetry
   Explain your thinking.

Numbers Every Day

Number Strategies

Name the fewest coins
needed to make each amount.

$6.59

$11.76

$33.99

4. Part of a figure is shown.
Copy the figure on dot paper.
Draw the rest of the figure so the broken line shown
is a line of symmetry.

a)

b)

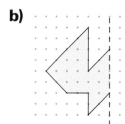

5. How would you change this design to make it symmetrical
about the line of symmetry shown?
Use coordinates to explain.

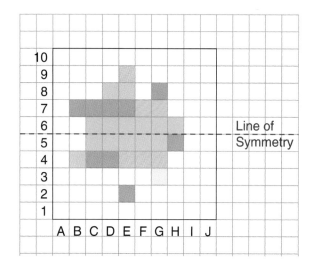

6. Look at questions 4 and 5 for ideas of puzzles.
Create your own symmetry puzzle or question for someone else
to try. Solve your puzzle before you give it to a classmate.

Reflect

How is a line of symmetry like a
mirror line?
Use words, pictures, or numbers
to explain.

At Home

Look through magazines to find
pictures with symmetry.
Cut out the pictures. Use a ruler
to draw each line of symmetry.

Rotations

A Ferris wheel rotates about its centre.

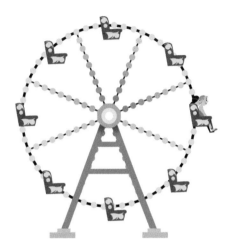

The children get on at
the bottom of this wheel.

What fraction of a turn has
the wheel rotated?

Explore

You will need Pattern Blocks and dot paper.
Use Pattern Blocks to show **rotations**.

➤ Circle a dot on the paper.
  This dot is the **turn centre**.

➤ Place a Pattern Block with one vertex
  at the turn centre.

➤ Take turns to trace the block and
  its image after each rotation:
  $\frac{1}{4}$ turn, $\frac{1}{2}$ turn, $\frac{3}{4}$ turn

Show *and* Share

Trade pictures with another pair of students.
Describe the rotation each picture shows.
Were there any pictures that could be described in two ways? Explain.

When a figure is rotated about a turn centre,
its image is congruent to the figure.

The rotation can be clockwise.

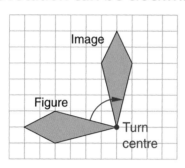

This kite has rotated $\frac{1}{4}$ of a turn
clockwise.

The rotation can be counterclockwise.

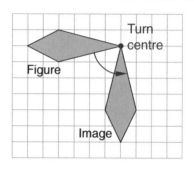

This kite has rotated $\frac{1}{4}$ of a turn
counterclockwise.

You can use tracing paper to identify a rotation.
➤ Trace the figure.
➤ Place a pencil point on the turn centre.
➤ Rotate the tracing paper.
    If the tracing of the figure matches
    the image, then the figure and its image
    show a rotation.

A translation, a reflection, and a rotation are
all **transformations**.

Practice

Use tracing paper.
1. Copy this kite on dot paper.
   Make a tile.
   Draw the image of the kite
   after each rotation about the turn centre:
   $\frac{1}{4}$ turn, $\frac{1}{2}$ turn, $\frac{3}{4}$ turn
   Colour your tile.

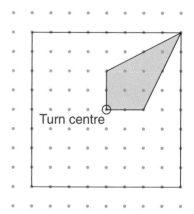

2. Design your own tile.
Use the method of question 1.
Start with a different quadrilateral.

3. Which pictures show a rotation? How do you know?
Describe each rotation.

a)

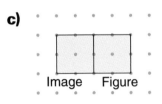

b)

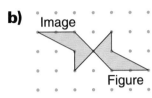

c)

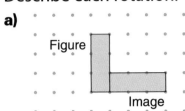

d)

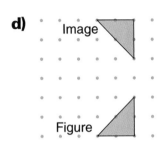

4. a) Which pictures in question 3 show a translation?
A reflection? How do you know?

b) Which picture in question 3 shows a translation,
a reflection, and a rotation?
Explain your thinking.

5. Sharif has a bowl of alphabet soup.
He decides to eat only the letters
that look the same after a rotation
of a $\frac{1}{2}$ turn about their centres.
Which letters does Sharif eat?
How do you know?

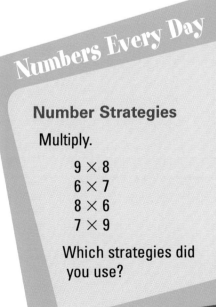

Numbers Every Day

Number Strategies

Multiply.

9×8
6×7
8×6
7×9

Which strategies did
you use?

253

6. Each picture shows a figure and its image after a transformation.
Say what the transformation is and how you know.
Which picture can you describe in two ways?

a)

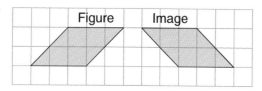

b)

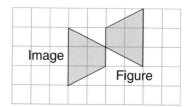

c)

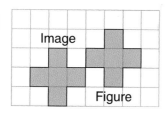

d)

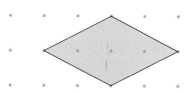

7. This rhombus has been rotated a $\frac{3}{4}$ turn.
Copy the rhombus on dot paper.
Show where the rhombus might have been
before it was rotated.
Include the turn centre in your drawing.
How many different ways can you do this?
Explain your work.

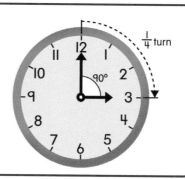

> **Math Link**
>
> **Measurement**
>
> A $\frac{1}{4}$ turn is also called a 90° turn.
> When the minute hand moves from 12 to 3,
> it turns through 90°.
> The minute hand makes a $\frac{1}{4}$ turn.

Reflect

Suppose you see a picture of a figure and its image.
How do you know which transformation the picture shows?
Use words, pictures, or numbers to explain.

Transformations on a Computer

TECHNOLOGY

You can use a computer to make a pattern with transformations.

Work with a partner.
Use AppleWorks. Follow these steps
to make a pattern with transformations.

1. Open a new document in
   AppleWorks.

   Click:
   Drawing

2. If a grid appears on the screen,
   go to Step 3.

   If not, click: `Options`

   then click: `Show Graphics Grid`

3. Check that Autogrid is on. Click: `Options`

   If **Turn Autogrid Off** appears in the menu, Autogrid is on.

   If not, click: `Turn Autogrid On    Ctrl+Y`

4. Check the ruler settings. Click: `Format`

   Click: `Rulers              ▶`   Click: `Ruler Settings...`

   Choose these settings:

   Click **OK**.

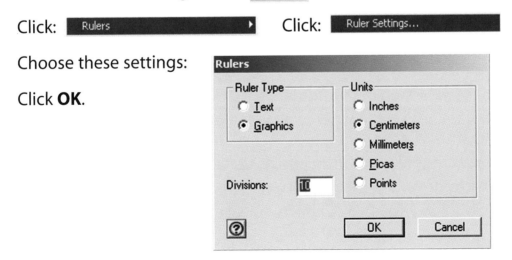

5. Use these tools to draw:

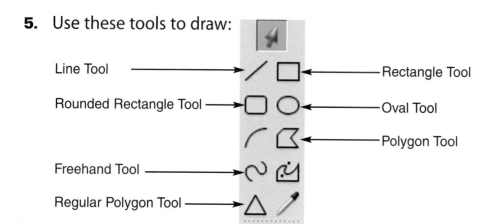

6. To draw, select the Tool you want.
The cursor will look like this: +

- Click and hold down the mouse button.
  Drag the cursor until the figure is the size and shape you want.
  Release the mouse button.
- If you are making a square or a circle, hold down the Shift key while you click and drag.
- To make an irregular polygon, select the Polygon Tool.
  Click and drag to make each side of the polygon.
  Double-click when you have finished.
- To make a regular polygon, select the Regular Polygon Tool.

Click: **Edit**   Click: Polygon Sides...

Type in the number of sides you want, then click **OK**.

7. To **copy a figure**, select the figure.

Click: **Edit**   Click: Copy   Ctrl+C

Click: **Edit**   Click: Paste   Ctrl+V

The copy shows on top of the figure.
Click and drag the copy to where you want it.

8. To **translate a figure**, put the cursor inside the figure.
Click and hold down the mouse button.
Drag the figure to where you want it. Release the mouse button.

9. To **rotate a figure**, select the figure.

Click: `Arrange`   Click: `Free Rotate        Shft+Ctrl+R`

The cursor will look like this: ✕
Put the cursor on one of the black dots on the edge of the figure.
Click, hold down the mouse button, and drag the figure
until it is where you want it.

10. To **reflect a figure**, select the figure. Click: `Arrange`

Click: `Flip Horizontally`

Or click: `Flip Vertically`

11. To **colour a figure**, click the figure to select it.

Click the Fill formatting button: ☐

Click the Color palette button: ▦ . Select a colour.

12. Use Steps 6 to 11 to create a pattern using transformations.

13. Save your pattern.

Click: `File`   Click: `Save As...        Shft+Ctrl+S`

Name your file. Then click **Save**.

14. Print your pattern.

Click: `File`   Click: `Print...        Ctrl+P`

Click **OK**.

Reflect

Compare your pattern with those of other students.
Which figure—a circle, a regular polygon, or an irregular
polygon—creates the most interesting transformation pattern?
Use pictures and words to explain.

6 Patterns with Transformations

Look at this pattern.

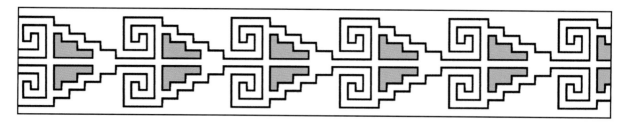

How can you use transformations to describe the pattern?

Explore

You will need Pattern Blocks, square grid
or dot paper, and triangular grid or dot paper.

➤ Choose one type of Pattern Block.
   Use one or more transformations to
   make a pattern in a line.
   Copy your pattern on grid paper.
   Colour your pattern.
   Write about the transformations
   you used to make the pattern.

➤ Choose a different Pattern Block.
   Use transformations to make a pattern
   that covers a region.
   Copy your pattern on grid paper. Colour your pattern.
   Write about the transformations you used.

Show and Share

Share your patterns with another pair of students.
Try to identify the transformations your classmates used.

258 LESSON FOCUS | Use transformations to make patterns.

Here is a pattern in a straight line.

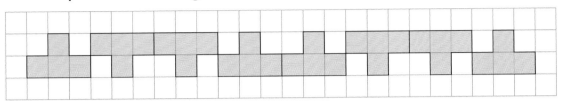

The octagon was rotated a $\frac{1}{2}$ turn, then reflected.

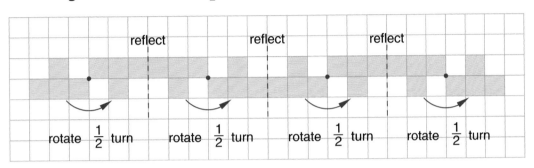

A pattern that covers a region is an **area pattern**.
Here is an area pattern.

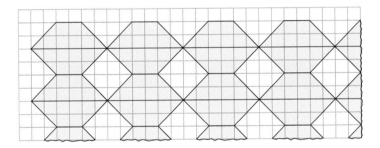

Start at A.
The trapezoid was:
- reflected to B
- translated to C
- reflected to D
- translated to E, and so on

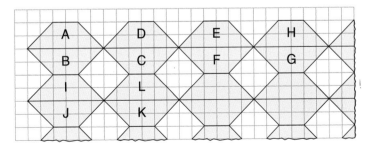

Then, from B, the trapezoid was:
- reflected to I
- reflected to J
- translated to K
- reflected to L, and so on

1. Use grid paper and this figure.

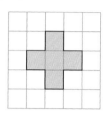

Numbers Every Day

Number Strategies
Divide.
$86 \div 4$
$77 \div 5$
$66 \div 6$
$99 \div 8$

   a) Use transformations to make a pattern in a line.
   b) Use transformations to make an area pattern.
   Describe the transformations you used.

2. Which transformations were used to make each pattern?
   Try to describe each pattern more than one way.

   a)

   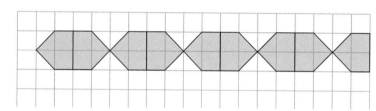

   b)

   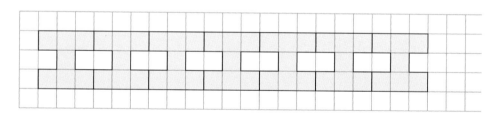

   c)

   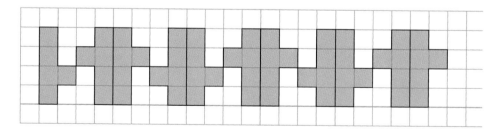

3. Anika made this pattern.
Suppose the pattern continues.
What will the 12th card be? Explain.

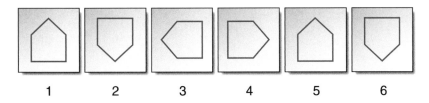

1   2   3   4   5   6

4. Copy this quilt pattern on grid paper.
Suppose you start with one purple triangle.
Write how you could use transformations
to make this pattern.

5. How many different area patterns
can you make using this hexagon?
Write about each pattern you make.
Include the transformations you used.
Show your work.

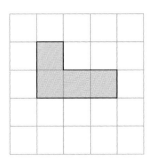

Reflect

How can transformations be used to make a pattern?
Use pictures and words to explain.

Strategies Toolkit

Explore

You will need grid paper and tracing paper.
This figure was translated, then rotated.
The final image is shown.
Copy the figure and its image on grid paper.
Where could the translation image be?
Show your work. Explain your reasoning.

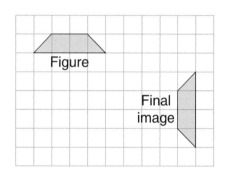

Show and Share

Describe the strategy you used to solve this problem.

Connect

A triangle was rotated,
then translated.
Here are the triangle
and its final image.

Where could the
rotation image be?

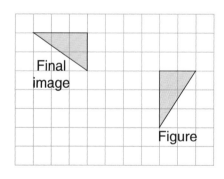

Strategies

- **Make a table.**
- **Use a model.**
- **Draw a picture.**
- **Solve a simpler problem.**
- **Work backward.**
- **Guess and check.**
- **Make an organized list.**
- **Use a pattern.**

Understand

What do you know?
- The triangle was rotated, then translated.
- The position of the triangle and its final image

Plan

Think of a strategy to help you solve the problem.
- You can **work backward** to find the rotation image.

Copy the picture on grid paper.
Work backward. Start with the final image.
Translate it. Then use tracing paper
to find a rotation that moves
the translation image
to the figure.
If the translation image
cannot be rotated to match
the figure, draw a different
translation image, then try again.

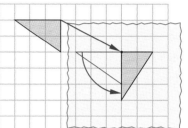

How many different rotation images can you find?

Practice

Choose one of the

Strategies

1. Draw a polygon at the centre of 1-cm grid paper.
   Assume this is the image after the polygon was translated
   4 squares left, 8 squares up, then rotated a $\frac{1}{4}$ turn clockwise.
   Draw the polygon in its start position.

2. Make up your own transformation problem.
   Draw a polygon.
   Reflect it, or translate it, or rotate it, two times.
   Draw the final image.
   Trade pictures with a classmate.
   Tell your classmate the two transformations you used.
   Draw the "in-between image" for your classmate's picture.

Reflect

Choose one problem from *Explore* or *Practice*.
Use words, pictures, or numbers to explain how you solved it.

LESSON

1

1. Here is a map of a zoo.

```
 7 |   | Polar Bear |   |   |   |   |   |   |   |   |
 6 |   | • Cave     |   |   | • Elephant House      |
 5 |   |            |   |   |   | • Ape and          |
 4 |   |            |   | • |   |   Monkey           |
 3 |   | Big Cat    | Aquarium |   House             |
   |   | Building   |   |   |   |   |   |   |   |   |
 2 |   | •          |   |   |   |   |   |   |   |   |
 1 |   |            |   | • Main Entrance            |
   | A | B | C | D | E | F | G | H | I | J | K |
```

a) Write the coordinates of each animal attraction.

b) Suppose you are at the Big Cat Building.
   How would you move to get to the Polar Bear Cave?
   How would you then move to get from the Polar Bear Cave
   to the Elephant House?

c) The Information Centre is 2 squares right and
   2 squares up from the Main Entrance.
   How would you get to the Information Centre from the Aquarium?

2
3
5

2. A figure has been translated, rotated, and reflected.
   Each image is labelled A to E.
   Describe the transformation that
   moves the figure to each image.
   a) image A
   b) image B
   c) image C
   d) image D
   e) image E
   Which movements can you
   describe in 2 ways? 3 ways?

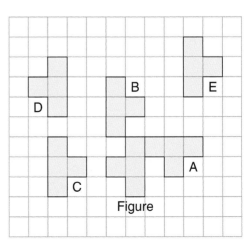

264

3. Copy each figure on 1-cm grid paper.
Draw all the lines of symmetry.

a)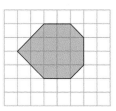

b)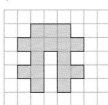

c)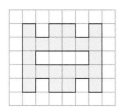

d)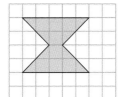

4. Which transformations were used to make each pattern?

a)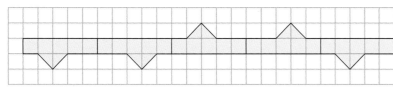

b)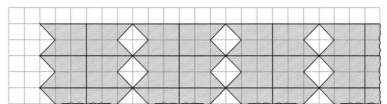

5. You will need grid paper.
Choose one figure from question 4.
  a) Use that figure to make a
     different pattern in a line.
  b) Use that figure to make a
     different area pattern.
Colour your patterns.
Write about the transformations you used.

UNIT

7 Learning Goals

☑ describe location and
   movement on a grid

☑ understand and use
   translations, reflections,
   and rotations

☑ discover patterns with
   translations, reflections,
   and rotations

☑ draw lines of symmetry

At the Fun House!

Suppose you have been asked to design a fun house.

Part 1
Create a pattern for the front wall of the fun house.
The pattern should use one or more transformations.
Colour your pattern.
Write about the transformations you used.
Identify any lines of symmetry.

Part 2
Your fun house will have 3 or more rooms.
Each room should use reflections, rotations, or translations
to make it fun for visitors.
Use 1-cm grid paper.
Draw a map that shows where each room is.
Choose a name for each room. Label the rooms on the map.
Use coordinates to describe where each room is.
Explain how a person could use the map to move
from one room to another.

Part 3

Use 1-cm grid paper.

Draw a plan of the inside of one room.

Explain how the room uses a transformation.

Draw a figure and its image to show the transformation.

Reflect on the Unit

What have you learned about transformations?

Use words and pictures to write about each transformation.

Circle Patterns

You will need a ruler and two copies of the sheet of circle diagrams below.

Part 1
- ➤ Write the first 12 multiples of 2.
- ➤ List the ones digit of each multiple. What do you notice?
- ➤ Use a circle diagram.
- ➤ On the circle, find the first number on your list. Draw a line from this number to the second number on the list, then from the second to the third, and so on.

Part 2

➤ Repeat Part 1 for multiples of 8.
➤ What do you notice about your diagrams?
➤ Write about the diagrams.

Part 3

➤ Repeat Part 1 and 2 for multiples of 3 and multiples of 7.
➤ How are your diagrams similar to those for multiples of 2 and multiples of 8?
How are they different?

Part 4

➤ Predict the patterns you will make for multiples of 4 and 6. Check your predictions.

Display Your Work

Make a poster display of your number patterns and circle diagrams.

Take It Further

➤ Predict other pairs of numbers whose multiples will produce the same diagrams. Explain your thinking.
➤ Check your predictions.

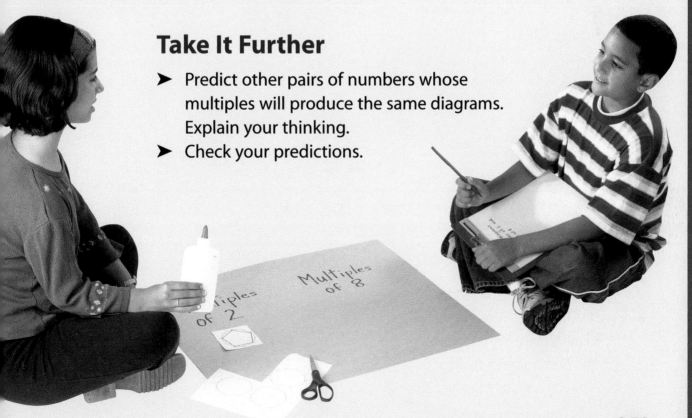

UNIT

8

Spring Activities Day

Learning Goals

- model, compare, and order fractions and mixed numbers
- explore and model tenths and hundredths as decimals
- compare and order decimals
- add and subtract decimals
- add and subtract money

Decimals

The Grade 4 students are holding an Activities Day to celebrate the arrival of spring.

In the Egg Race, the winner is the person who puts the most plastic eggs into the cartons. Here are some results.

Name	Carton Filled
Penny	$\frac{4}{12}$
Maria	$\frac{11}{12}$
Brady	$\frac{7}{12}$

- What does the fraction $\frac{4}{12}$ mean?
- Where have you seen fractions like those in the table? How were they used?
- What are some questions you can ask about the Egg Race?

Key Words

- tenths
- numerator
- denominator
- proper fraction
- equivalent fractions
- improper fraction
- mixed number
- decimal
- decimal point
- hundredths

1

Fractions of a Whole

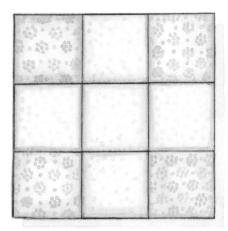

Pioneers made quilts from scraps of
material sewn together.
Square pieces are easy to fit together.

Explore

You will need Colour Tiles or congruent squares, and 1-cm grid paper.
Design a quilt that uses squares of at least 3 colours.
Record your quilt on grid paper.
Use fractions to describe your quilt.

Show *and* Share

Trade quilts with your partner.
Describe your partner's quilt using words
and fractions.
How did you know which fractions to use?

Numbers Every Day

Mental Math

Find each product.
Explain your thinking.

2×6 5×6

7×6 4×6

Fractions name equal parts of a whole.

2 equal parts are halves.
$\frac{1}{2}$ or one-half is blue.

4 equal parts are fourths.
$\frac{2}{4}$ or two-fourths are green.

10 equal parts are **tenths**.
$\frac{4}{10}$ or four-tenths are red.

$\frac{4}{10}$ of the rectangle are red.
$\frac{6}{10}$ of the rectangle are white.

10 is the **denominator**.
It tells how many
equal parts are in 1 whole. ⟶

$$\frac{4}{10}$$

← 4 is the **numerator**.
It tells how many
equal parts are counted.

A fraction is a number. $\frac{4}{10}$ is a **proper fraction**.
It represents an amount less than 1 whole.

Practice

1. Write a fraction to tell what part of each quilt is striped.

a)

b)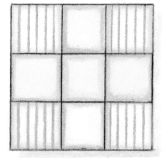

c)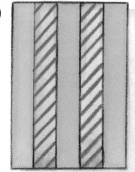

2. Use coloured squares to show each fraction.
   Record your work on grid paper.

   a) $\frac{2}{3}$　　　　**b)** $\frac{6}{10}$　　　　**c)** one-eighth　　　**d)** five-fifths

3. About what fraction is left?

   a) 　　　　**b)** 　　　　**c)**

4. Which pictures show thirds? How do you know?

   a) 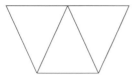　　　**b)** 　　　**c)**

5. Does this diagram show $\frac{3}{4}$? Explain.

   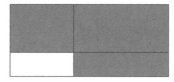

6. Use grid paper. Design a place mat by colouring squares in a rectangle.
   Use fractions to describe your place mat design.

7. Nadia shares her square brownie with Tran.
   Here are two ways to cut the brownie.
   Are the pieces the same size? Show your work.

Math Link

Physical Education

A volleyball court is divided into 2 equal parts. What other sports are played on an area that is divided into equal parts?

Reflect

Use pictures, words, or numbers to explain the fraction $\frac{5}{8}$.

Fraction Benchmarks

Explore

You will need 6 paper strips the same length as this strip.

0                  $\frac{1}{2}$ 1

➤ Fold and colour a paper strip to show $\frac{2}{3}$.
Line up your strip with the strip above.
Is $\frac{2}{3}$ closer to 0, $\frac{1}{2}$, or 1?

$\frac{2}{3}$	$\frac{3}{8}$	$\frac{7}{8}$
$\frac{1}{6}$	$\frac{5}{6}$	$\frac{1}{8}$

➤ Estimate if each fraction in the box is
closer to 0, $\frac{1}{2}$, or 1.
Use paper strips to check your estimates.
Record your findings in a table.

Closer to 0	Closer to $\frac{1}{2}$	Closer to 1

Show and Share

Talk with your partner about the fractions.
Which fraction is closest to 0? Closest to $\frac{1}{2}$? Closest to 1?

Connect

0             $\frac{1}{2}$ 1

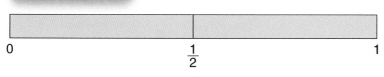   ← $\frac{4}{5}$ is closer to 1.

   ← $\frac{4}{10}$ is closer to $\frac{1}{2}$.
It is a little less than $\frac{1}{2}$.

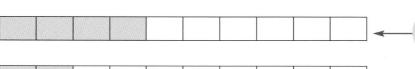   ← $\frac{2}{10}$ is closer to 0.

1. Is the fraction of juice left in each glass closer to 0, $\frac{1}{2}$, or 1?

   a)    b)   c)   d)

2. Is the fraction of eggs in each carton closer to 0, $\frac{1}{2}$, or 1?
   How do you know?

   a)    b)

   c)    d)

3. Name a fraction between $\frac{1}{2}$ and 1, but closer to 1.
   Draw a picture to show the fraction.
   Tell how you chose which fraction to draw.

4. Gary poured a little more than $\frac{1}{2}$ a glass of milk.
   Name a fraction that might tell how much milk that is.

Reflect

Write two different fractions close to 0.
Use paper strips to show which fraction
is closer to 0.

Numbers Every Day

Number Strategies

Estimate each sum.

59 + 72
24 + 86
373 + 109
281 + 410

Which strategies
did you use?

Fractions of a Set

$\frac{4}{5}$ of these kittens have collars.
What other fractions can you use
to describe the kittens?

Explore

You will need
- 25 two-colour counters
- 8 fraction cards

You will use the counters to model
a fraction of a set.

➤ Shuffle the cards.
  Put them face down in a pile.
➤ Take turns.
  One person takes a fraction card.
  Do not show the card.
➤ Count out the counters you need
  to match your card.
  Place all the counters red side up.
  Turn some groups of counters yellow side up
  to show your fraction.
➤ Have your partner tell you the fraction.
➤ Continue until you have used all the cards.

$\frac{3}{8}$ of 16

$\frac{4}{5}$ of 10

Show and Share

Talk to your partner about your strategy.
How did you know how many equal groups to make?

Connect

Fractions can show equal parts of a set.

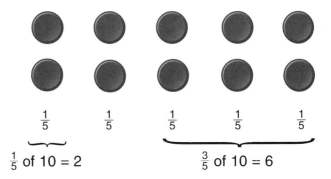

$\frac{1}{3}$ of 6 = 2

$\frac{2}{3}$ of 6 = 4

$\frac{3}{3}$ of 6 = 6

Here is a way to find $\frac{3}{5}$ of 10.

The denominator tells us we are counting fifths. Divide 10 counters into 5 equal groups to show fifths.

$\frac{1}{5}$ $\frac{1}{5}$ $\frac{1}{5}$ $\frac{1}{5}$ $\frac{1}{5}$

$\frac{1}{5}$ of 10 = 2 $\frac{3}{5}$ of 10 = 6

Practice

Use counters in questions 1 to 3.
Find the fraction of each set.

1. **a)** $\frac{1}{4}$ of 8   **b)** $\frac{2}{4}$ of 8   **c)** $\frac{3}{4}$ of 8

2. **a)** $\frac{1}{3}$ of 12   **b)** $\frac{2}{3}$ of 12   **c)** $\frac{3}{3}$ of 12

3. **a)** $\frac{2}{8}$ of 16   **b)** $\frac{4}{10}$ of 20   **c)** $\frac{3}{6}$ of 12

Math Link

Your World

Scientists say we spend $\frac{1}{3}$ of our lives sleeping.

About how many years have you spent sleeping?

4. Draw a picture to show the fraction of each set.

   a) $\frac{2}{5}$ of 10   **b)** $\frac{3}{4}$ of 16   **c)** $\frac{5}{5}$ of 10

5. Find:

   a) $\frac{1}{2}$ of 10   **b)** $\frac{3}{4}$ of 12   **c)** $\frac{1}{5}$ of 5

6. Print your first name.
   Use fractions to describe the letters in your name.

7. The pie shop sold 16 pies.
   One-half of them were apple pies.
   One-fourth of them were blueberry pies.
   How many pies were not apple or blueberry? Show your work.

8. 5 is $\frac{1}{4}$ of a set.
   How many are in the set?

9. There are 10 boys in a class.
   Two-fifths of the class are boys.
   How many students are in the class? How do you know?

Reflect

Explain why both pictures show $\frac{3}{10}$.

Numbers Every Day

Mental Math

Which numbers of markers can you share equally among 6 friends?

10 15 18 20 24

How do you know?

LESSON 4

Strategies Toolkit

Explore

Nawar had 24 stickers.
He kept $\frac{1}{6}$ of the stickers
and divided the rest equally among his 5 friends.
How many stickers did each friend receive?

Show *and* Share

Describe how you solved this problem.

Connect

Kalpana had 40 prizes to award at the school fair.
She put $\frac{1}{4}$ of the prizes in the raffle.
She divided the rest equally among the 6 races.
How many prizes were there for each race?

Understand

What do you know?
- There are 40 prizes.
- The raffle used $\frac{1}{4}$ of the 40 prizes.
- The rest of the prizes were for the winners of the 6 races.

Plan

Think of a strategy to help you solve the problem.
- You can **use a model**.
- Use counters to represent the prizes.

Strategies

- Make a table.
- Use a model.
- Draw a picture.
- Solve a simpler problem.
- Work backward.
- Guess and check.
- Make an organized list.
- Use a pattern.

LESSON FOCUS | Interpret a problem and select an appropriate strategy.

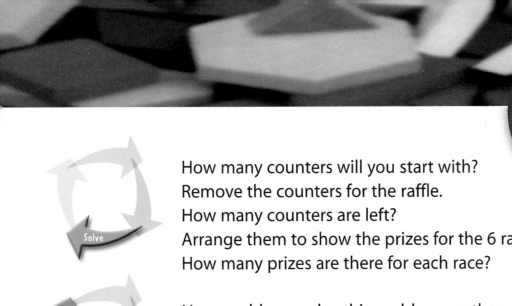

How many counters will you start with?
Remove the counters for the raffle.
How many counters are left?
Arrange them to show the prizes for the 6 races.
How many prizes are there for each race?

How could you solve this problem another way?
Try it, and use your answer to check your work.

Practice

Choose one of the
Strategies

1. Gabriella bought 20 batteries.
   She put 2 batteries in her radio.
   Her 3 brothers divided the rest equally.
   How many did each brother receive?

2. Ms. Logan had gel pens to award after BINGO.
   She gave 4 to Tip, and said that he had $\frac{2}{6}$ of them.
   How many gel pens did Ms. Logan have to start?

3. Mabel coloured a rectangular sheet of paper $\frac{1}{8}$ purple,
   $\frac{1}{2}$ blue, and the rest yellow.
   What fraction of the paper is yellow?

Reflect

How can counters help you solve fraction problems?
Use words, pictures, or numbers to explain.

5 Different Names for Fractions

Who is correct?

$\frac{3}{6}$ of the pie is left.

$\frac{1}{2}$ of the pie is left.

Explore

You will need Cuisenaire Rods or strips of coloured paper.

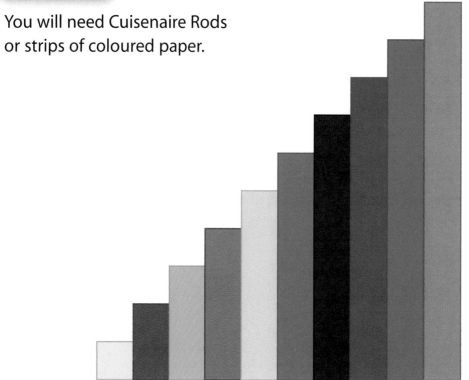

➤ Use the orange rod to represent 1 whole.
Line up other rods beneath the orange rod to show fractions of 1 whole.
Do this in as many ways as you can.
Draw a picture to record your work.

➤ Label the orange rod 1 whole.
Label each of the other rods with a fraction.
➤ Repeat the activity using the brown rod as 1 whole.

Show *and* Share

Share your pictures with another pair of students.
What fractions in your pictures name the same amount?

Connect

Fractions that name the same amount are called **equivalent fractions**.

1 Whole			
$\frac{1}{2}$		$\frac{1}{2}$	
$\frac{1}{4}$	$\frac{1}{4}$	$\frac{1}{4}$	$\frac{1}{4}$

$\frac{1}{2}$ and $\frac{2}{4}$ are equivalent fractions.

Here are some more equivalent fractions.

1 Whole								
$\frac{1}{3}$			$\frac{1}{3}$			$\frac{1}{3}$		
$\frac{1}{9}$	$\frac{1}{9}$	$\frac{1}{9}$	$\frac{1}{9}$	$\frac{1}{9}$	$\frac{1}{9}$	$\frac{1}{9}$	$\frac{1}{9}$	$\frac{1}{9}$

$\frac{1}{3}$ and $\frac{3}{9}$ are equivalent fractions.

$\frac{2}{3}$ and $\frac{6}{9}$ are equivalent fractions.

Practice

1. Use the dark green rod as 1 whole.
   Use other rods to find equivalent fractions.
   Draw a picture to record your work.

2. Use rods or paper strips.
   Find an equivalent fraction for each fraction.
   a) $\frac{1}{2}$ **b)** $\frac{1}{4}$ **c)** $\frac{1}{3}$ **d)** $\frac{2}{3}$ **e)** $\frac{4}{5}$ **f)** $\frac{3}{4}$

3. Write an equivalent fraction to name the coloured part of each figure.
   a)   **b)**   **c)**

4. Draw pictures to show that the fractions in each pair are equivalent.
   a) $\frac{1}{2}$ and $\frac{5}{10}$ **b)** $\frac{2}{3}$ and $\frac{4}{6}$ **c)** $\frac{2}{4}$ and $\frac{4}{8}$ **d)** $\frac{1}{2}$ and $\frac{3}{6}$

5. How many different ways can you show that
   $\frac{3}{4}$ and $\frac{6}{8}$ are equivalent fractions?
   Show your work.

6. Roxanne cut a pizza into 8 equal slices.
   She ate 2 slices.
   a) Write two equivalent fractions to describe
   how much pizza Roxanne ate.
   b) Write two equivalent fractions to
   describe how much pizza was left.

Numbers Every Day

Reflect

Write two equivalent fractions.
Use pictures to show how you know
the fractions are equivalent.

Number Strategies

Estimate each difference.

$87 - 36$
$81 - 38$
$352 - 148$
$351 - 152$

Which strategies did
you use?

6

More than One

There is more than 1 whole sandwich
on this plate.
There are 5 quarter pieces of sandwich.
How would you describe how much
sandwich there is?

Explore

You will need Pattern Blocks and triangular grid paper.
Use Pattern Blocks to show fractions
greater than 1 whole.
Use the yellow Pattern Block as 1 whole.

➤ Take a handful of another colour of
Pattern Blocks.
Arrange the blocks to show how many
yellow hexagons you could cover.
Name the amount in different ways.
Record your work on grid paper.

➤ Repeat the activity with another colour
of Pattern Blocks.

Show and Share

Share your work with another pair of students.
Did you draw the same pictures? Explain.
Which names did you use?

Connect

Brianna arranged 8 blue Pattern Blocks.

Her arrangement shows   It also shows two whole

thirds of : $\frac{8}{3}$ plus 2 thirds: $2\frac{2}{3}$

$\frac{8}{3}$ and $2\frac{2}{3}$ name the same amount.

$\frac{8}{3}$ is an **improper fraction**.

It shows an amount greater than 1 whole.

$2\frac{2}{3}$ is a **mixed number**.

It has a whole number part and a fraction part.

> I say two and two-thirds.

Practice

1. Describe each picture in two different ways.

    a)

    b)

    c)

    d)

286

2. Match each improper fraction with a mixed number.
   Use Pattern Blocks or draw pictures to show why each match is correct.

   $\frac{5}{4}$ $\frac{9}{4}$ $\frac{7}{4}$

          $1\frac{3}{4}$ $1\frac{1}{4}$ $2\frac{1}{4}$

3. The Fernandez family drank $3\frac{1}{2}$ bottles of juice on a picnic.
   Draw pictures to show the amount, and then
   write this mixed number as an improper fraction.
   Show your work.

4. Sarah and Brian used $4\frac{1}{4}$ sheets of paper to cover
   two boxes for a project.
   a) Write the mixed number as an improper fraction.
   b) What are some ways they may have divided the
          $4\frac{1}{4}$ sheets of paper for the two boxes?

5. Casey was making pancakes by the dozen.
   Casey's family ate $2\frac{1}{3}$ dozen pancakes.
   How many pancakes did they eat? Show your work.

6. Suppose you have only a $\frac{1}{2}$-cup measuring cup.
   How many times would you have to fill it to measure
   $2\frac{1}{2}$ cups of sugar? Explain how you know.

Reflect

Explain why $1\frac{1}{2}$ and $\frac{3}{2}$ show the same amount.

Comparing and Ordering Fractions

Use Pattern Blocks to explore ways to compare fractions.

Use the yellow Pattern Block as 1 whole.
Which number in each pair is greater?

$\frac{1}{6}$ and $\frac{3}{6}$ $\frac{7}{3}$ and $\frac{4}{3}$

$\frac{1}{3}$ and $\frac{1}{2}$ $\frac{1}{6}$ and $\frac{1}{3}$

$2\frac{1}{3}$ and $1\frac{2}{3}$ $1\frac{5}{6}$ and $2\frac{1}{6}$

Show and Share

With your partner, talk about the ideas you
used to choose your answers.
Record your work.

Numbers Every Day

Mental Math

There are 30 students and
4 different activity centres.

Can an equal number of
students go to each centre?

Explain how you know.

➤ When different fractions have the same denominator, the parts being counted have the same size.

$\frac{2}{10}$ ⟵ Tenths are counted.

$\frac{5}{10}$ ⟵ Tenths are counted.

The fewer the parts, the smaller the fraction. So, $\frac{2}{10} < \frac{5}{10}$

➤ Here is a way to order these mixed numbers from least to greatest:

$2\frac{7}{10}$, $1\frac{9}{10}$, and $2\frac{3}{10}$

• $1\frac{9}{10}$ is the least, because it is less than 2.

• Both $2\frac{7}{10}$ and $2\frac{3}{10}$ are between 2 and 3,

but $\frac{3}{10} < \frac{7}{10}$,

so, $2\frac{3}{10} < 2\frac{7}{10}$.

• From least to greatest: $1\frac{9}{10}$, $2\frac{3}{10}$, $2\frac{7}{10}$

You can make pictures to check your thinking.

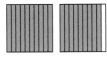

$1\frac{9}{10}$ $2\frac{3}{10}$ $2\frac{7}{10}$

➤ When different fractions have the same numerator, the parts have different sizes.

To compare $\frac{1}{4}$ and $\frac{1}{9}$, think about sharing 1 whole.

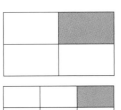

One-fourth gives you a bigger piece. So, $\frac{1}{4} > \frac{1}{9}$

 Practice

1. Look at each pair of figures. Compare the fraction parts that are shaded. Write a fraction sentence using <, >, or =.

a)   b)   c)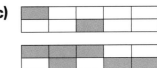

289

2. Make pictures to show which is greater.

a) $\frac{4}{6}$ or $\frac{7}{6}$ b) $2\frac{9}{10}$ or $1\frac{6}{10}$ c) $1\frac{1}{3}$ or $1\frac{2}{3}$

3. Make pictures to show which is greater.

a) $\frac{1}{2}$ or $\frac{1}{6}$ b) $\frac{1}{2}$ or $\frac{1}{4}$ c) $\frac{1}{3}$ or $\frac{1}{4}$

4. This number line is divided into tenths.

Which number below is closest to 1? Closest to 0?

Use the number line to help you.

$\frac{1}{10}$ $1\frac{5}{10}$ $\frac{8}{10}$ $\frac{17}{10}$ $\frac{21}{10}$ $2\frac{3}{10}$

Show how you know.

5. Which pair of students had the longest chess game?
Which had the shortest game?

6. Order these numbers from greatest to least.

a) $\frac{3}{9}, \frac{13}{9}, \frac{6}{9}$

b) $\frac{13}{15}, 2\frac{12}{15}, 1\frac{14}{15}$

c) $1\frac{3}{7}, \frac{4}{7}, 1\frac{5}{7}$

7. When can $\frac{1}{3}$ give you a bigger piece than $\frac{1}{2}$?
Draw diagrams to explain.

At Home

Reflect

Choose two different fractions.
Draw pictures to show a friend
how to compare them.

Look in the kitchen, the
bathroom, or the laundry
area. Where do you and
your family use fractions
at home?

8 Exploring Tenths

You have used Base Ten Blocks to model whole numbers.

What if you could use Base Ten Blocks to model fractions?

Explore

You will need Base Ten Blocks and grid paper.

Suppose a flat represents 1 whole.

What does a rod represent?

Use Base Ten Blocks to show these numbers.

$$1\frac{6}{10} \qquad 2\frac{9}{10} \qquad \frac{3}{10}$$

Record your work on grid paper.

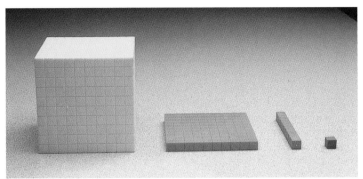

= 1

= ?

Show and Share

Share your work with another student.
Did you draw the same pictures for each number? Explain.
What do you think a rod represents?

Here is one way to model $2\frac{1}{10}$.

The number can be written as a **decimal** using a symbol, the **decimal point**.
The decimal point always comes right after the whole number.

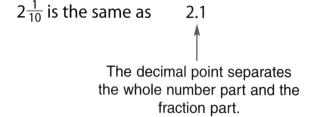

$2\frac{1}{10}$ is the same as   2.1

The decimal point separates
the whole number part and the
fraction part.

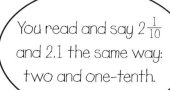

You read and say $2\frac{1}{10}$
and 2.1 the same way:
two and one-tenth.

You can use a place value chart to show a decimal.

Ones	Tenths
0	7

The decimal point is between
the ones place and the tenths place.

In the decimal 0.7 there are no whole number parts, only tenths.

Practice

1. Write a fraction or mixed number, and a decimal,
   for the coloured part of each picture.

   a)

   b)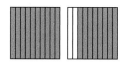

   c)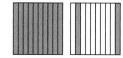

Numbers Every Day

Number Strategies

Estimate the sum:

19 + 9 + 13 + 12

Explain your estimation
strategy.

2. Write a fraction or mixed number, and a decimal, for the coloured part of each picture.

a)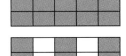

b)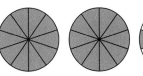

c)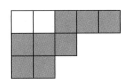

d)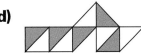

3. Draw a picture for each number. Write the number as a decimal.

  a) $1\frac{4}{10}$ **b)** $\frac{7}{10}$ **c)** $1\frac{9}{10}$

4. Draw a picture for each decimal.
Write the decimal as a fraction or mixed number.

  a) 4.1   **b)** 1.8   **c)** 0.2

5. Write as a decimal.

  a) one and nine-tenths   **b)** four and three-tenths

6. Alicia said 0.7 of the circle are red.
Is she correct? Explain.

7. The number line shows decimals from 0 to 3.0.
Write the decimal for each letter.

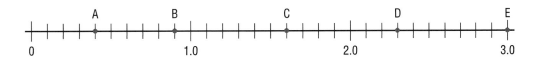

Reflect

Why is the decimal point important?
Use words, pictures, or numbers to explain.

Calculator Counting

You can use a calculator to explore counting by 0.1.
Model the counting with base-ten rods as you count
with the calculator.

➤ Press ⊕ 0.1 ⊜ ⊜
The calculator counts from 0.1 to 0.2.

➤ Continue pressing ⊜ until you reach 0.9.
The calculator continues to count by 0.1.

➤ Stop when you reach 0.9.

What do you think the calculator will display next?
Press ⊜ one more time to see if you are correct.

➤ Pressing ⊜ one more time is like
adding one more rod to your
model of base-ten rods.
Write down the next number the
calculator displays after 0.9.
Explain why this next number
makes sense.

Exploring Hundredths

Explore

You will need Base Ten Blocks and grid paper.

Suppose a flat represents 1 whole,
and a rod represents $\frac{1}{10}$.

What does a unit cube represent?
Use Base Ten Blocks to show these numbers.

$3\frac{10}{100}$ $2\frac{75}{100}$ $4\frac{3}{10}$ $\frac{21}{100}$

Record your work on grid paper.

Show *and* Share

Share your work with another pair of students.
How did you find out what a unit cube represents?

Connect ....

There are different ways to show numbers
with **hundredths**.
Decimals can represent hundredths.
Each of these represents the same amount:

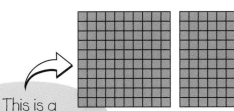

This is a
hundredths grid.

$1\frac{91}{100}$ **1.91**

one and ninety-one
hundredths

Numbers Every Day

Number Strategies

Is 27 × 3 greater than 60?

Explain how you know.

1. Write a fraction or mixed number, and a decimal
   for the coloured part of each picture.

   a)

   b)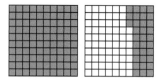

   c)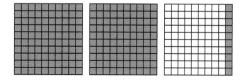

   d)

2. Colour hundredths grids to show each number.

   a) $2\frac{2}{100}$
   b) $1\frac{35}{100}$
   c) 0.05
   d) 1.18

3. Write each number as a decimal.

   a) $1\frac{17}{100}$
   b) $5\frac{60}{100}$
   c) $12\frac{39}{100}$
   d) $\frac{5}{100}$

4. Write as a decimal.
   a) six-hundredths
   b) seven and thirty-nine hundredths
   c) five-hundredths
   d) one and fourteen-hundredths

5. Write each decimal as a fraction or mixed number.
   a) 0.03
   b) 8.16
   c) 4.10
   d) 0.54

 6. Write a fraction and a decimal
   for the coloured part of each grid.
   What do you notice about
   the coloured parts? Explain.
   Show your work.

   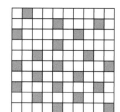 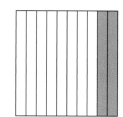

Reflect

Use words and pictures to explain the decimals 0.5 and 0.05.

Fractions and Decimals on a Calculator

You can use a calculator to change fractions to decimals.

➤ $\frac{1}{10}$ of this grid is shaded.

$\frac{1}{10} = 0.1$

$\frac{1}{10}$ means $1 \div 10$.
1 whole is divided into 10 equal parts.

Use a calculator. Press: $1 \div 10 =$ to display

➤ $\frac{3}{10}$ means $3 \div 10$.
Each of 3 wholes is divided into 10 equal parts.
Take one-tenth from each whole.

$\frac{3}{10} = 0.3$

Use a calculator. Press: $3 \div 10 =$ to display

Practice

Write each fraction as a decimal.

a) $\frac{7}{10}$ b) $\frac{9}{10}$ c) $\frac{23}{100}$ d) $\frac{40}{100}$ e) $\frac{7}{100}$

LESSON

10 Comparing and Ordering Decimals

Lakeside School had a track meet.
Here are the top 3 results of some of the events.

Girls' Shot Put	
Name	Distance
Lavita	4.98 m
Elke	5.86 m
Audra	4.12 m

Boys' Standing Long Jump	
Name	Distance
Bruce	1.04 m
Pedro	1.62 m
Hakim	1.53 m

Boys' 100-m Race	
Name	Time
Keon	14.51 s
Henri	15.09 s
Bram	13.96 s

For each event at the track meet, decide who came in 1st, 2nd, and 3rd.
Use any materials you need to help you.
Show your work.

Show *and* Share

Show your work to another pair of students.
Share how you know you put the results in the correct order.
Record the strategies you used to find the correct order.

LESSON FOCUS | Compare and order decimals to hundredths.

Connect

Here are the results for another event.
One way to put these results in order
is to colour hundredths grids.
Then, put the distances in order from
greatest to least.

Girls' Standing Long Jump

Name	Distance
Olga	0.89 m
Anita	0.86 m
Flo	0.91 m

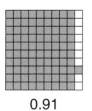

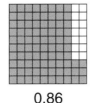

| 0.91 | 0.89 | 0.86 |

The best result is the longest jump.
So Flo had the best jump, then Olga, then Anita.

Practice

1. Which decimal is greater?
   a) 0.45 or 0.38
   b) 0.76 or 0.95
   c) 0.2 or 0.8
   d) 1.40 or 2.51
   e) 3.5 or 1.6
   f) 2.1 or 1.8

2. Put these decimals in order from
   least to greatest.
   a) 0.4, 1.3, 0.1
   b) 0.34, 0.19, 0.86
   c) 0.54, 1.02, 0.76
   d) 17.02, 17.40, 17.11
   e) 5.04, 5.91, 5.37
   f) 2.8, 1.9, 2.7

Numbers Every Day

Mental Math

What are the next 4 numbers in
each skip-counting pattern?

8, 12, 16, □, □, □, □

125, 250, 375, □, □, □, □

13, 11, 9, □, □, □, □

Tell how you know.

3. The table shows the Girls' Running Long Jump results.
   a) Whose jump was the longest?
   b) Whose jump was longer than Letisha's
      but shorter than Kim's?

Girls' Running Long Jump

Name	Distance
Letisha	1.45 m
Soon-yi	2.02 m
Kim	1.73 m
Maria	1.62 m

4. Grady is 1.35 m tall.
His sister is 1.78 m tall.
Grady's mother is 1.59 m tall.
   a) Who is the tallest?
   b) Who is the shortest?
   c) Do you think Grady is older or younger than his sister?
   Explain.

5. Write the items on the grocery receipt in order
from most expensive to least expensive.

```
THE GROCERY STORE

apple juice  $0.99
carrots      $1.20
bread        $1.10
milk         $4.39
oranges      $2.50
yogurt       $1.89
```

6. Copy then complete to make a true statement.
   a) 0.9 > ☐   **b)** 13.71 < ☐
   c) 0.21 > ☐   **d)** 0.99 < ☐

7. Write these numbers in order from least to greatest.

   0.01,   100.1,   0.1,   10,   1,   101.1,   1.01

   How do you know your answer is correct?
   Show your work.

8. Copy these decimals. Use <, >, or = to compare them.
   a) 0.1 ☐ 0.1   **b)** 0.7 ☐ 1.7   **c)** 4.96 ☐ 4.90
   d) 5.01 ☐ 5.10   **e)** 12.60 ☐ 1.26   **f)** 35.81 ☐ 35.80

9. Can a number with a 3 in the hundredths place be greater
than a number with a 9 in the hundredths place?
Explain.

Math Link

Measurement

You can use a metre stick to
represent tenths and hundredths.
If a metre stick represents
1 whole, then one decimetre
represents 0.1, and one
centimetre represents 0.01.

Reflect

Write two different decimals
greater than 1. How do you know
which decimal is greater?

11

Adding Decimals

Explore ··

Ty enjoys hiking.
He keeps track of his weekend hiking distances.

Hiking Log!

WEEKEND	SATURDAY	SUNDAY
1	3.9 km	4.4 km
2	4.9 km	3.3 km

Estimate how far Ty walked each weekend.
Find how far Ty walked each weekend.
Record your work.

Show *and* Share

Show how you solved the problem.
What strategies helped you?
Share your ideas to start a class list.

Numbers Every Day

Mental Math

What are the next 4 numbers in each pattern?

$\frac{1}{2}$, 1, $1\frac{1}{2}$, □, □, □, □

0.2, 0.4, 0.6, □, □, □, □

Tell how you know.

Another weekend, Ty hiked 2.7 km and 1.8 km.

To estimate Ty's total distance, start by rounding.

    2.7 is close to 3.

    1.8 is close to 2.

    $3 + 2 = 5$

    Ty hiked approximately 5 km.

To add $2.7 + 1.8$, use whole number strategies.

➤ Use mental math. Move tenths to make ones.

$$2.7 + 1.8 = \underbrace{2.7 + 0.3}_{} + 1.5$$
$$= \quad 3.0 \quad + 1.5$$
$$= 4.5$$

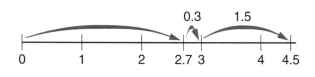

➤ Use Base Ten Blocks to add $2.7 + 1.8$.

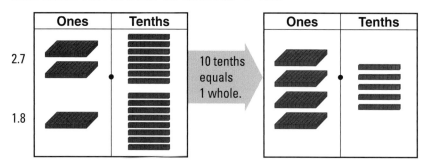

Ones	Tenths

2.7

1.8

10 tenths equals 1 whole.

Ones	Tenths

➤ Use place value to add $2.7 + 1.8$.

Add the tenths: 15 tenths	10 tenths equals 1 whole. 1 and 5 tenths	Add the ones.
2.**7**	^{1} 2.7	^{1} **2.**7
+ 1.**8**	+ 1.8	+ **1.**8
	.5	4.5

Ty hiked 4.5 km.

You can use a calculator to check: $2.7 + 1.8 = 4.5$

Practice •

1. Will each sum be greater or less than 3? How do you know?

   a) 2.1 + 0.4   b) 2.3 + 0.9   c) 1.3 + 1.6   d) 1.2 + 2.1

2. Estimate each sum.

   a) 0.4 + 0.3   b) 1.4 + 0.4   c) 2.6 + 1.1   d) 3.2 + 2.9

3. Add. Use Base Ten Blocks to help you.

   a) 1.8 + 2.1   b) 0.7 + 4.6   c) 3.6 + 1.2   d) 4.7 + 1.9

Use the map below for questions 4 to 6.

4. Use the map to find the shortest distances.

	From:	To:
a)	Miller's Landing	Jake's Point
b)	Elma	Pearl
c)	Greenville	Elma
d)	Jake's Point	Port Baker
e)	Port Baker	Pearl

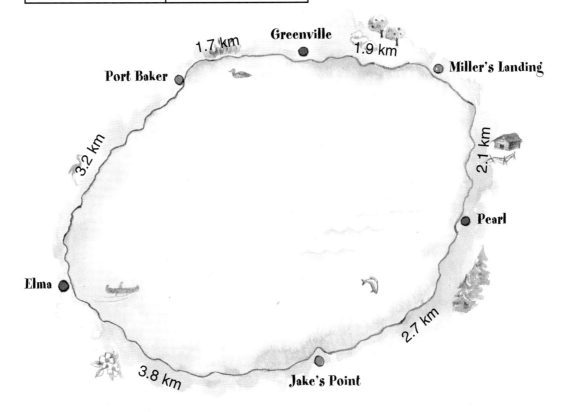

5. Franca travelled 6.8 km from one town to another town.
Where might Franca have travelled?
Show your work.

6. Make up a story problem that uses the map.
Solve your problem.

7. At 7:00 a.m., the temperature in Gander was 12.5°C.
By noon, the temperature had risen by 4.9°C.
What was the temperature at noon?

8. The Hon family buys fruit at the market.
Last Saturday, the family bought 2.6 kg of apples and
1.8 kg of bananas.
How much fruit did the family buy in total?

9. Alex's laptop computer has a mass of 2.3 kg.
The mass of the carrying case is 0.8 kg.
What is the total mass of the laptop and carrying case?

10. Marie-Claire rode her scooter
1.5 km to the store.
On the way home,
she took a different route that
was 0.7 km longer.
What was the total distance
Marie-Claire rode?
How do you know?

At Home

Reflect

Explain how adding decimals
is like adding whole numbers.
How is it different?

Look at the nutrition
information on a cereal box.
How are decimals used?
Write about what you notice.

LESSON 12

Subtracting Decimals

 **Explore**

Liak is a long distance swimmer.
Her coach keeps track of her progress.

Liak's Progress Chart		
Class	Tuesday	Thursday
Week 1	1.4 km	2.8 km
Week 2	3.9 km	5.7 km

For each week, estimate how much farther
Liak swam on the second day.
Then, find how much farther Liak swam.

Record your work.

Show and Share

Show how you solved the problem.
What strategies helped you?
Share your ideas to start a class list.

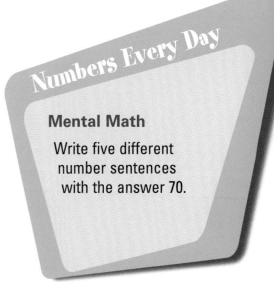

Numbers Every Day

Mental Math

Write five different
number sentences
with the answer 70.

LESSON FOCUS | Subtract decimals to tenths.

305

Suppose Liak swam 4.4 km on Thursday and 1.6 km on Tuesday.
How much farther did Liak swim on Thursday?

To estimate the distance:

4.4 is close to 4.

1.6 is close to 2.

$4 - 2 = 2$

Liak swam about 2 km farther on Thursday.

To subtract $4.4 - 1.6$, use whole number strategies.

➤ Use mental math. Think addition.

$1.6 + 0.4 = 2.0$
$2.0 + 2.4 = 4.4$
So, $4.4 - 1.6 = 0.4 + 2.4$
$4.4 - 1.6 = 2.8$

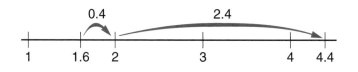

➤ Use Base Ten Blocks
  to subtract.

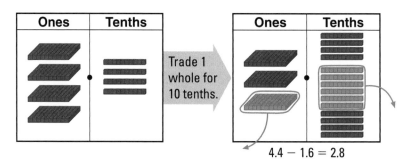

Trade 1 whole for 10 tenths.

$4.4 - 1.6 = 2.8$

➤ Use place value to subtract.
  Try to subtract the tenths.

You cannot take 6 tenths from 4 tenths.	Trade 1 whole for 10 tenths.	Subtract the tenths.	Subtract the ones.
	³ ¹⁴	³ ¹⁴	³ ¹⁴
4.**4**	4̷.4̷	4̷.4̷	4̷.4̷
− 1.**6**	− 1.6	− 1.**6**	− **1**.6
		.**8**	**2**.8

Liak swam 2.8 km farther on Thursday.

You can use a calculator to check: $4.4 - 1.6 = 2.8$

Practice

1. Subtract.
   a) 5.3 − 2.1   **b)** 4.9 − 0.7   **c)** 3.6 − 1.9   **d)** 7.4 − 4.8

2. Subtract.

   a)   52.7   **b)**   31.0   **c)**   9.6   **d)**   25.1
         − 45.8   − 5.7   − 2.7   − 12.2

3. Grant had 6.5 m of ribbon. He used 4.9 m to wrap up a gift.
   How much ribbon does Grant have left?
   How do you know your answer is reasonable?

4. Giorgio grew a 3.4-kg pumpkin, and Toni grew a 4.1-kg pumpkin.
   Whose pumpkin had the greater mass? How much greater was it?

5. The temperature at 9:00 p.m. was 15.4°C.
   At midnight, it was 12.5°C.
   What was the change in temperature?

6. Aimee adopted a puppy from the Humane Society.
   Its mass was 4.7 kg. At the first visit to the vet,
   the puppy had a mass of 5.4 kg.
   How much mass had the puppy gained?

7. Jan ran the 100-m dash in 14.8 s.
   The school record is 15.6 s.
   By how much did Jan beat the school record?

8. Use estimation.
   Is the difference between 1.8 and 0.5 greater than 1
   or less than 1? Show your work.

Reflect

You know several ways to subtract two decimals.
Which way do you prefer? Use words, pictures, or numbers to explain.

Adding and Subtracting Money

Money uses base ten with tenths and hundredths.

$1.00

$0.10
$\left(\frac{1}{10} \text{ of } \$1.00\right)$

$0.01
$\left(\frac{1}{100} \text{ of } \$1.00\right)$

Place value can help you read an amount of money.

Dollars (Ones)	Dimes (Tenths)	Pennies (Hundredths)

$2.54 or two dollars and fifty-four cents

Explore

Suppose you have $10.00 to spend.
What could you buy?
How much money would be left?

Fun Fair snack menu

Hot Dog — $1.25
Hamburger — $2.25
Onion Rings — $2.25
Pizza Slice — $0.99
Yogurt — $0.99
Fruit Cup — $1.25
Water — $0.49
Juice — $0.85
Milk — $0.75

Show and Share

Compare your answers with a classmate's answers.
How did you decide what to buy?

Lakshi had $5.
She bought a fruit cup for $1.25 and water for $0.49.

➤ How much did Lakshi spend?

Use a place-value mat to add $1.25 + $0.49.

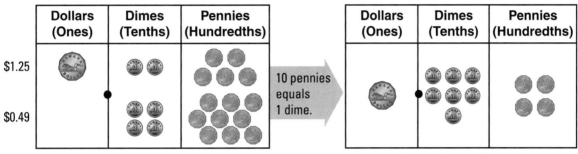

$1.25 + $0.49 = $1.74

The total cost is $1.74.

➤ What is Lakshi's change from $5?
  • You can count on.

$1.74,   ... $1.75,   ... $2.00,   ... $3.00   ... $5.00

The change is $3.26.

  • You can use place value and subtraction.

Line up the decimal points.	Trade $1 for 10 dimes. Trade 1 dime for 10 pennies.	Subtract the cents.	Subtract the dollars.
	9		
	4 10 10	4 9 10	4 9 10
$5.00	$5.00	$5.00	$5.00
− 1.74	− 1.74	− 1.**74**	− **1**.74
		.26	3.26

The change from a $5 bill is $3.26.

1. Find each sum.
   a) $2.86 + $3.61   **b)** $4.79 + $3.18
   c) $6.27 + $3.04   **d)** $7.29 + $0.49

2. Add.
   a) $5.31   **b)** $4.11   **c)** $6.23   **d)** $5.60
         + 2.03   + 1.66   + 5.34   + 4.78

3. Find each difference.
   a) $5.75 − $2.51   **b)** $7.37 − $4.29
   c) $8.25 − $5.62   **d)** $3.25 − $0.18

4. What is the change from $10 when you spend each amount?
   a) $5.42   **b)** $3.76   **c)** $8.22   **d)** $4.20

5. Look at the items below. Find the cost of each pair of items.

a)    **b)**

c)    **d)**

$5.95 $7.95 $2.79 $1.89 $4.75

6. Look at the items above.
   a) About how much will all 5 beach items cost?
   b) About how much change will you get from $25.00?
   c) Use a calculator to find the exact cost and your change.
       How close were your estimates?

7. Use the Ice Cold Drinks menu.
   a) Ira bought a milkshake. How much change did he get from $5.00?
   b) Suppose Ira bought water instead of a milkshake.
   How much money would he save?
   c) Jerry used a $5 bill to pay for one drink.
   His change was $2.21.
   What drink did Jerry buy?
   How do you know?

ICE COLD DRINKS

JUICE —————— $ 1.29
WATER —————— $ 1.10
MILKSHAKE —————— $ 2.95
ICE CREAM FLOAT— $ 2.79

8. Mei saved her allowance to go to the mall.
   She had $11.45 to spend.
   After two hours, Mei had spent $8.76.
   How much money did Mei have left?

9. Milo wants to buy some muffins.
   The cost is $5.85 plus tax. The tax is $0.41.
   Milo has $6.25.
   Does he have enough to buy the muffins?
   How do you know?

10. Hugh is a cashier.
   His cash register is out of pennies.
   Here is a customer's receipt.
   The customer pays with a $20 bill.
   Can Hugh make the correct change?
   Show your work.

THE GROCERY STORE

potatoes $2.87
bread $1.14
butter $2.99

Reflect

When you use place value
to subtract $3.56 from $5,
why do you write $5 as $5.00?
Do the subtraction.
Explain your work.

Numbers Every Day

Mental Math

Add or subtract.
Explain your strategy.

$$25 + 31$$
$$52 + 29$$
$$65 - 18$$
$$82 - 49$$

LESSON

1
3

8
9

6

7

10

1. Eighteen students from Kyle's class took part in Spring Activities Day.
   Draw a picture to show each fraction.
   a) One-half of the students helped to set up events.
   b) One-third of the students did the Beanbag Toss.
   c) One-sixth of the students did the Duck Waddle.

2. Write the fraction or mixed number, and decimal for each shaded part. Each grid represents 1 whole.

   a)

   b)

3. Use Pattern Blocks.
   Find an improper fraction that names the same amount as $2\frac{5}{6}$.
   Colour triangular grid paper to show your answer.

4. Write these numbers in order from least to greatest.
   Use any materials to help you.

   $\frac{7}{8}$ $1\frac{5}{8}$ $1\frac{3}{8}$ $\frac{9}{8}$

5. Colour a hundredths grid to show each decimal in the box.
   Order the decimals from greatest to least.
   Explain how you know the order is correct.

   | 0.45 | 0.09 | 0.80 |

6. Madhu is on the running team.
   Use a number line or a metre stick
   to show who came in 1st, 2nd, 3rd, and 4th.
   How do you know?

Madhu, 15.35 seconds
Keltie, 15.68 seconds
Sashana, 15.45 seconds
Kate, 15.52 seconds

2 5

7. Write a fraction equivalent to each fraction.
Say whether it is closer to 0, $\frac{1}{2}$, or 1.
   a) $\frac{1}{3}$ **b)** $\frac{5}{6}$

11 12

8. Kim started a sewing project with 2.6 m of blue fabric
and 1.6 m of yellow fabric.
How much fabric did Kim have altogether?
How much more blue fabric did Kim have?

9. Fill in each missing number. Use Base Ten Blocks to help you.
   a) $4.6 + 4.3 = \square$ **b)** $3.4 - 1.2 = \square$ **c)** $2.8 + 3.9 = \square$
   d) $1.7 - 1.5 = \square$ **e)** $5.1 + 0.9 = \square$ **f)** $1.3 - 0.8 = \square$

13

10. Imagine you have $10.00 to buy school supplies.

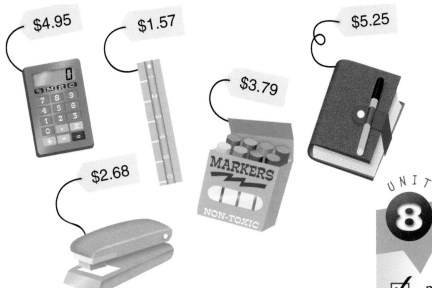

$4.95 $1.57 $5.25 $3.79 $2.68

a) Choose 2 items you want to buy.
About how much will they cost?
About how much money
would you have left?
b) Which two items could you *not* buy
with $10.00? Explain.

UNIT

8 **Learning Goals**

✓ model, compare, and
order fractions and
mixed numbers

✓ explore and model tenths
and hundredths as decimals

✓ compare and order decimals

✓ add and subtract decimals

✓ add and subtract money

Unit Problem

Spring Activities Day

You be the judge!

Here are the results for the top 3 students in each activity.

In the Egg Race, students had 5 minutes to carry the eggs, and fill the cartons. The winner was the person who filled the most egg cartons with the most eggs.

Egg Race

Name	Cartons Filled
Zachary	$1\frac{5}{12}$
Myles	$2\frac{1}{12}$
Wilma	$1\frac{7}{12}$

In the Beanbag Toss, students used an underhand throw to toss the beanbag as far as they could.

The winner was the person with the longest toss.

Beanbag Toss

Name	Distance
Percy	4.68 m
Misty	4.99 m
Joi	4.45 m

In the Duck Waddle, students walked like a duck around the playground. The fastest person was the winner.

Duck Waddle

Name	Time
Hunter	45.3 s
Maria	36.2 s
Thomas	29.8 s

314

Part 1

- Who won each activity?
  Who came second? Third?
  How do you know?
- The results for the Beanbag Toss
  were very close!
  What was the difference in the distances
  for 1st place and 2nd place?
  2nd place and 3rd place?
  How do you know?

Part 2

Make up a story problem about
the Spring Activities Day results.
Solve your problem.

Part 3

What event would you plan for a Spring Activities Day?
How would you award the prizes?
Make up some examples to show what might happen.
Use fractions or decimals in your activity.
Explain your work.

Reflect on the Unit

Explain how decimals are simply another way to write fractions.

UNIT

1 1. Start with 5. Multiply by 2 repeatedly.

   a) Record the first 10 numbers.

   b) Is there a pattern in the ones digits? The tens digits? Explain.

2 2. Pierre read one book with 356 pages.
   He read a second book with 275 pages.
   Use mental math.

   a) How many pages did Pierre read altogether?

   b) How many more pages are in the first book than the second book?

3 3. Find a triangular prism.
   Sketch the faces of the prism.
   Identify the equal sides on the faces.
   Identify the congruent faces.

4 4. How much greater is 8×36 than 6×36? Explain.

5 5. The table shows the number of people who like to hold each animal at the zoo.

Animal	Number of People
Banana slug	9
Gila monster	22
Koala	32
Macaw	14
Monkey	16
Rosy boa	6

   a) Draw a pictograph to display these data. What key will you use?

   b) How many more people prefer to hold a koala than a monkey?

   c) What is the range of the data?

   d) Which animal is most popular? Least popular?

   e) Write your own question about the pictograph.
   Answer the question.

UNIT

6

6. A racer drank a 1-L bottle of water during
a 10-km bike race.
She stopped at the 5000-m mark to drink
a 400-mL cup of water.
How much water did the racer drink in all?

7. A cookie recipe needs 500 g of chocolate chips.
Will two 225-g bags be enough? Explain.

7

8. Use dot paper. Draw a quadrilateral.
   a) Draw its translation image after a translation
      of 7 squares left and 3 squares up.
   b) Draw a vertical mirror line.
      Reflect the quadrilateral in the mirror line.
      Draw the reflection image.
   c) Choose a turn centre.
      Use tracing paper.
      Rotate the quadrilateral through a
      $\frac{1}{4}$ turn counterclockwise. Draw the rotation image.

9. For each transformation in question 8,
   how are the quadrilateral and its image the same?

8

10. Draw a picture for each number.
    a) 2.5   b) $\frac{3}{10}$ c) 0.6   d) $1\frac{1}{10}$

11. Order these numbers from least to greatest.
    a) $3\frac{7}{10}$, $2\frac{1}{10}$, $\frac{27}{10}$
    b) 2.13,   1.32,   1.23

12. What is the change from $50 when you spend each amount?
    a) $11.89   b) $2.05   c) $35.61   d) $0.47

UNIT

9 Length, Perimeter,

Design a Backyard

Learning Goals

- estimate and measure linear dimensions
- estimate and measure perimeter
- estimate and measure area
- relate units of measure
- relate area and perimeter

and Area

Key Words

linear dimensions

millimetre

decimetre

scale

square centimetre

square metre

- Which unit of length would you use to measure the perimeter of this yard? The depth of the pond? Could you use other units? Explain.

- Compare the areas of the deck and the playground. What do you notice?

- Which sections of the yard have about the same area? How do you know?

Measuring Linear Dimensions

You can measure how long, how wide, how tall, how deep, or how thick an object is.

Shannon measures the width of the blackboard in metres.

Danny measures Seveen's height in centimetres.

 **Explore** ·

You will need a 30-cm ruler and a metre stick or a measuring tape.
➤ Choose a classroom object.
➤ Estimate, then measure to the nearest unit.
➤ Record your work.

Repeat with other objects.
Include 2 objects you measure in centimetres and 2 in metres.

Show *and* Share

You can record your work in a table.

How did you use one measurement to help you estimate the next? How did you use your ruler to measure?

Object	What We measured	Estimate	Approximate measurement
Table	Length	100 cm	88 cm

Connect

Length, width, height, thickness, and depth are **linear dimensions**.

Width

This book is 22 cm wide.

Height

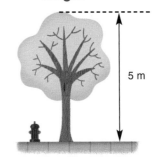

This tree is 5 m tall.

Thickness

This sandwich is 6 cm thick.

Depth

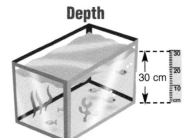

The water in the tank is 30 cm deep.

Length

King St. is 2 km long.

All the words wide, high, tall, thick, deep, describe how **long** something is.

Math Link

Literacy

The word *linear* contains the word *line*. Linear means "in a straight line." So, a linear dimension is a measure in a straight line.

321

Use a ruler or metre stick to help you.

1. Estimate each measure.
   Then measure each item to the nearest centimetre.
   a) the height of your chair
   b) the length of your pencil
   c) the width of your hand
   d) the thickness of your math book

2. Estimate each measure.
   Then measure each item to the nearest metre.
   a) the height of the classroom door
   b) the width of the classroom

3. Choose the better unit of length for measuring each object.
   a) centimetres or metres
   b) metres or kilometres
   c) centimetres or metres

   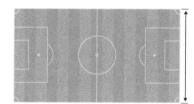   

4. Which unit would you use to measure each item?
   Explain your choice.
   a) the length of a highway
   b) the width of a pencil case
   c) the height of a building
   d) the depth of an ocean
   e) the length of a zipper on a jacket
   f) the thickness of a dictionary

5. Draw each item.
   Measure its length and width.
   a) a leaf   b) a feather

Numbers Every Day

Mental Math

Add or subtract.
Explain your thinking.

51 + 72 = ☐
83 + 25 = ☐
95 − 36 = ☐
67 − 29 = ☐

6. Use a ruler. Draw a picture of each item. Write its measure.
   a) a pencil 9 cm long   b) a book 14 cm wide
   Trade pictures with a classmate.
   Check your classmate's measures.

7. What is the length of each strip of paper? How do you know?
   a)

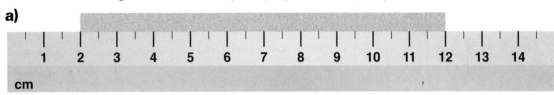

   b)

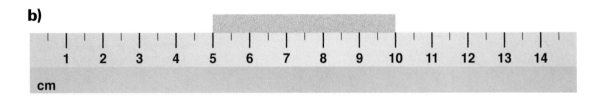

   c)

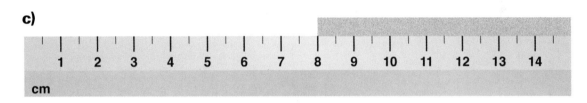

8. This box has dimensions 2 cm, 4 cm, and 6 cm.
   How would you name each dimension?

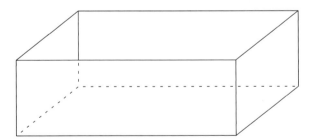

At Home

Reflect

Write a letter to a friend to explain the meaning of linear dimensions. Use words, pictures, or numbers to help your friend understand.

Name 2 items in your bedroom that would be measured in centimetres. Name 2 items you would measure in metres. Explain your choices.

Measuring in Millimetres

This ruler shows centimetres and **millimetres**.

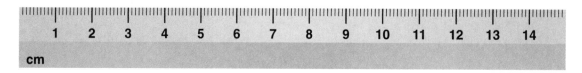

There are ten millimetres (10 mm) in 1 cm.

A dime is about 1 mm thick.

= 1 mm

Explore

You will need a 30-cm ruler.
Have a scavenger hunt.

➤ Estimate to find an object that has one dimension close to each measurement: 15 mm, 35 mm, 80 mm, 140 mm

➤ Measure to check your estimate.

➤ Record your results in a table.

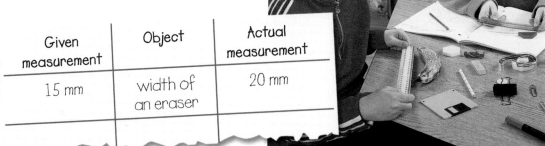

Given measurement	Object	Actual measurement
15 mm	width of an eraser	20 mm

Show *and* Share

Share your strategies for estimating with other students.
Record your strategies to start a class list.

Connect

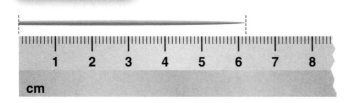

cm

This pine needle is about 6 cm long.
To be more precise,
you read the length in millimetres.
The pine needle is 62 mm long.

One millimetre is one-tenth of a centimetre.
So, you can also read the length of the
pine needle in centimetres.
The pine needle is 6.2 cm long.
You say: 6 and 2 tenths centimetres

Centimetres and millimetres are related.

Numbers Every Day

Mental Math

Skip count to make
each pattern.

10, 20, ☐, ☐, ☐, ☐

9, 18, ☐, ☐, ☐, ☐

8, 16, ☐, ☐, ☐, ☐

7, 14, ☐, ☐, ☐, ☐

10 mm = 1 cm
So, 1 mm = 0.1 cm

Practice

Use a ruler when it helps.

1. Copy and complete each table.

   a)
cm	1	2	3	4	5	6	7	8	9	10
mm	10	20								

   b)
mm	1	2	3	4	5	6	7	8	9	10
cm	0.1	0.2								

2. What patterns do you see in the tables in question 1?

3. Copy and complete. How can you use a ruler to help you?
   a) 8 cm = ☐ mm   b) 20 cm = ☐ mm   c) 63 cm = ☐ mm

4. Copy and complete.
   a) 60 mm = ☐ cm   b) 40 mm = ☐ cm   c) 100 mm = ☐ cm

5. Draw each item. Measure its length in millimetres.
   a) a pencil
   b) a needle

6. Use a ruler to draw each item.
   Write each measure.
   Trade pictures with a classmate.
   Check your classmate's measures.
   a) a worm 8.5 cm long
   b) a straw 13.8 cm long

7. Which is longer? How do you know?
   a) 6 cm or 80 mm
   b) 25 cm or 200 mm
   c) 9 cm or 70 mm

8. Suppose you found a leaf that was 88 mm long.
   a) Is its length closer to 8 cm or 9 cm?
       How do you know?
   b) How else could you write the length of the leaf?
   Show your work.

9. Which unit would you use to measure each item?
   Explain your choice.
   a) the height of a house
   b) the length of an eyelash
   c) the distance between your home and Arviat, Nunavut

10. Nicole drew a line longer than 8 cm but shorter than 99 mm.
   How long might the line be? How do you know?

11. Estimate the length of each line in millimetres. Then measure
   and record the actual length in millimetres and in centimetres.

   a) ――――――――――   **b)** ―――――――

Reflect

Name 2 items whose linear dimensions you would measure
in millimetres. Explain why you would use millimetres and
not any other unit.

Measuring in Decimetres

A Base Ten rod is 10 cm long.
An orange Cuisenaire Rod is also 10 cm long.

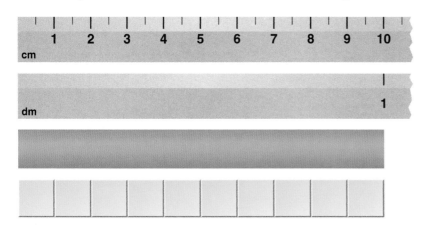

A length of 10 cm is **one decimetre (1 dm).**

Explore

You will need a metre stick.
➤ Choose a classroom object
  you can measure in decimetres.
➤ Estimate its measure.
➤ Measure the object to the nearest decimetre.
➤ Record your results in a table.

Repeat with other objects.

Show *and* Share

Which was the longest object
you measured? The shortest?
How do you know?
Share your strategy for rounding
to the nearest decimetre.

Object and dimension	Estimate	Approximate measurement
height of desk	6 dm	7 dm

Connect

You can read the height of this seedling in 3 ways.

The seedling is 3 dm tall.
The seedling is 30 cm tall.
The seedling is 300 mm tall.

1 dm = 10 cm
1 dm = 100 mm

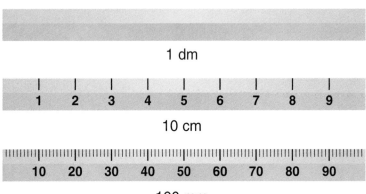

1 dm

10 cm

100 mm

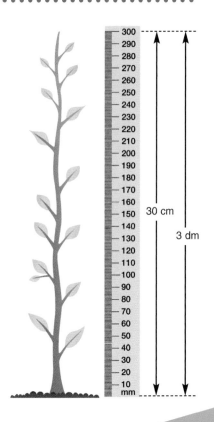

Practice

Use a ruler or metre stick to help you.

1. Copy and complete this table.
What patterns do you see? Explain.

dm	1	2	3	4	5	6	7	8	9	10
cm	10									
mm	100									

2. Copy and complete.
   a) 8 dm = ☐ cm   **b)** 9 dm = ☐ cm   **c)** 70 dm = ☐ cm

3. Copy and complete.
   a) 40 cm = ☐ dm   **b)** 70 cm = ☐ dm   **c)** 100 cm = ☐ dm

328

4. Which is shorter? How do you know?
  a) 5 dm or 45 cm   **b)** 700 mm or 8 dm   **c)** 26 cm or 200 mm

5. Match each item below with an estimate of its measure:
  2 mm, 19 cm, 7 dm, 1 dm
  a) the width of your hand   **b)** the length of a new pencil
  c) the thickness of a loonie   **d)** the height of a dog house

6. Name 2 objects that are about 1 dm long.

7. How could you measure something in decimetres
  if your ruler was marked in centimetres?
  Use words, pictures, or numbers to explain.

8. Oscar found an interesting plant in the woods.
  When he measured it, he said it was 3 dm tall.
  a) What is this height in centimetres? In millimetres?
  b) Which unit is best for measuring this plant?
  Explain.

9. Which unit would you use to measure each item?
  Explain your choice.
  a) the height of a flagpole
  b) the height of a bookcase
  c) the width of your fingernail
  d) your height
  e) the distance between Earth and the moon

Reflect

You have estimated and measured in 4 units.
When do you think a precise
measurement would be needed?
When would an estimate
be good enough?
Write about your ideas.

At Home

Measure the height of a relative.
Draw a picture.
Write the height using as many
different units as you can.
Round when you need to.

LESSON 4 — Strategies Toolkit

Explore

Norton lives 6 km from the park. After riding half way home, he realized he had left his tennis racquet on a park bench. He rode back to the park to get it and then rode home. How far did Norton travel altogether?

Work together to solve this problem.

Show *and* Share

Describe the strategy you used to solve the problem.

Connect

Abby, Bart, Carmen, and Dee live on the same street.
Abby and Dee live 10 km apart.
Bart and Carmen live between Abby and Dee.
It is 4 km from Abby's house to Bart's house.
It is 2 km from Carmen's house to Dee's house.
How far is it from Bart's house to Carmen's house?

Strategies

- Make a table.
- Use a model.
- Draw a picture.
- Solve a simpler problem.
- Work backward.
- Guess and check.
- Make an organized list.
- Use a pattern.

What do you know?
- It's 10 km from Abby's to Dee's.
- It's 4 km from Abby's to Bart's.
- It's 2 km from Carmen's to Dee's.

Think of a strategy to help you solve the problem.
- You can **draw a picture** of the street.
- Show each person's house on the street.

Find how far it is from Bart's to Dee's.
Find how far it is from Carmen's to Bart's.

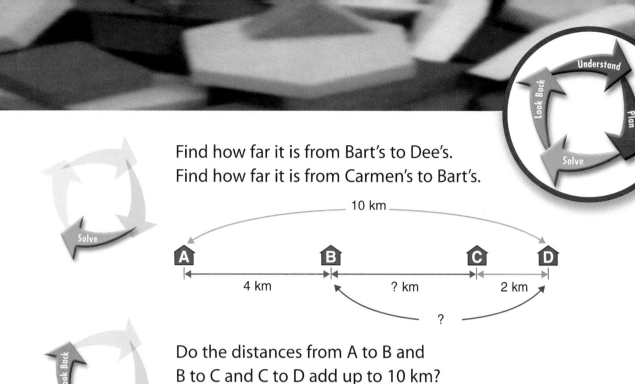

Do the distances from A to B and
B to C and C to D add up to 10 km?
How could you have solved this
problem a different way?

Practice

Choose one of the

Strategies

1. Shivani used 60 m of fencing to fence her
   rectangular garden.
   The length of the garden is 4 m longer than the width.
   What are the length and width of Shivani's garden?

2. A ball was dropped from a height of 8 m.
   It bounced half the distance it fell.
   After each bounce, it travelled half as high as it had on the last bounce.
   The ball bounced 3 times before it was caught.
   How far did it travel?

3. Zenia's garden is 5 m long and 3 m wide.
   She planted zinnias 1 m apart around the perimeter of the garden.
   How many zinnias did Zenia plant?

Reflect

Explain how drawing a picture helps you solve a problem.

5

Relating Units of Measure

Every year, Leila enters the
soapbox derby in her town.
So far, she has won 2 trophies.

Leila built a shelf for her trophies.
The shelf is 1 m 15 cm long.
The shelf is also 115 cm long.

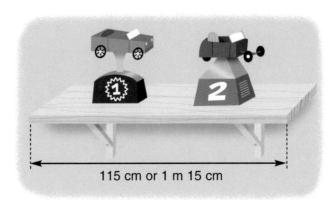

115 cm or 1 m 15 cm

Explore

You will need some toy cars
and materials to build a ramp.

➤ Build a ramp.
Test some cars on the ramp
to see how far they travel.
Experiment with the height of the
ramp until you find the height
that makes the cars go farthest.

➤ Take turns.
Choose a car and let it
roll down the ramp.
Estimate the distance the car
travels beyond the ramp.
Measure the distance to the
nearest centimetre.
Record the distance using 2 units.

➤ Take 3 turns each.

➤ On your table, circle your
greatest distance.

Turn	Estimated distance	Approximate Distance	
		cm	m and cm
1			

Show and Share

How can you use a measured distance to estimate the next distance?
Whose car went the farthest? The shortest?
How do you know?

Connect •••

One metre equals 100 cm.

This soapbox racer is 190 cm long.
You can write this as 1 m 90 cm.

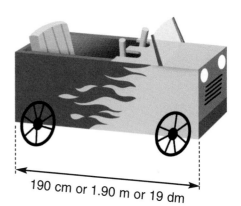

190 cm or 1.90 m or 19 dm

Since 1 cm is
$\frac{1}{100}$ of a metre, you can also say
the racer is 1 and 90 hundredths
of a metre long, or 1.90 m.

This helmet is 20 cm wide.
The helmet is also 0.20 m wide or 2 dm wide.

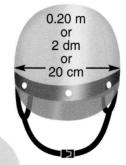

0.20 m
or
2 dm
or
20 cm

1 m = 10 dm	1 dm = 10 cm	1 cm = 10 mm
1 m = 100 cm	1 dm = 100 mm	
1 m = 1000 mm		
1 mm = 0.1 cm	1 cm = 0.01 m	10 cm = 0.10 m

Practice ••••••••••••••••••••••••••••••••••

Use a ruler or metre stick when it helps.

1. Copy and complete.
   a) 1 m = ☐ cm
   b) 2 m = ☐ cm
   c) 0.30 m = ☐ cm
   d) 100 cm = ☐ m
   e) 200 cm = ☐ m
   f) 50 cm = ☐ m

Math Link

Number Sense

To change centimetres to millimetres, multiply by 10.
To change metres to centimetres, multiply by 100.

2. Copy and complete.
  a) 30 cm = ☐ mm   **b)** 80 cm = ☐ mm   **c)** 26 cm = ☐ mm
  d) 60 mm = ☐ cm   **e)** 80 mm = ☐ cm   **f)** 81 mm = ☐ cm

3. In the track and field meet,
  Selma jumped 2.7 m in the running long jump.
  Write this measurement in decimetres and in centimetres.

4. Copy and complete. Use =, >, or <.
  a) 5 dm ☐ 2 m   **b)** 300 cm ☐ 2 m   **c)** 3 m ☐ 44 cm
  d) 600 cm ☐ 9 m   **e)** 4 m ☐ 400 cm   **f)** 7 dm ☐ 70 cm

5. Draw a line of each length.
  Trade lines with a classmate.
  Check the lengths of your classmate's lines.
  a) 0.09 m   **b)** 0.1 m   **c)** 0.12 m

6. Which unit would you use to measure the length of each object?
  Explain your choice.
  a) a baseball bat   **b)** a fence
  c) a ladybug   **d)** a licorice stick

7. Tristan said he grew 0.3 m this year.
  His brother Aaron said this was impossible.
  Do you agree with Aaron?
  Explain your thinking.

Reflect

You have used 4 units to measure length. Use words, pictures, or numbers to explain how to change a measurement from one unit to another.

Numbers Every Day

Number Strategies

Which numbers below are divisible by 2? By 5? By 10?

8, 18, 20, 35, 40, 55, 95

Explain your strategy.

Measuring Perimeter

You will need a 30-cm ruler.
➤ Choose a classroom object.
➤ Estimate the perimeter of the object in units of your choice.
➤ Measure to find the perimeter. Use a calculator if you need it.
➤ Record your work.

Repeat with 4 more objects.

Show *and* Share

You could record your work in a table.

Object	Estimated perimeter	Actual perimeter
Yellow pattern block	12 cm	2.4 cm + 2.4 cm + 2.4 cm + 2.4 cm + 2.4 cm + 2.4 cm = 14.4 cm

What strategies did you use to estimate perimeter?
Which object had the least perimeter?
Which object had the greatest perimeter?

➤ You can find the perimeter of an object by measuring the lengths of its sides, then adding.

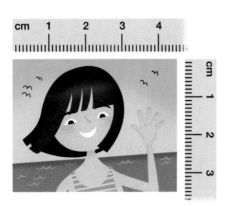

Perimeter = 3.5 cm + 4.5 cm + 3.5 cm + 4.5 cm
Perimeter = 16 cm

➤ When the lengths of the sides are given, add to find the perimeter.
This figure is drawn to **scale** of the measures given.
That is, each side represents the given length.

Perimeter = 27 cm + 36 cm + 21 cm
Perimeter = 84 cm

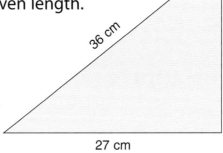

36 cm

21 cm

27 cm

Practice

1. Find the perimeter of each object.

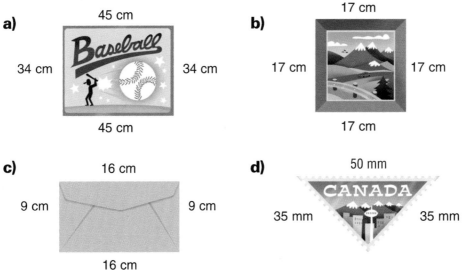

a)
45 cm
34 cm   34 cm
45 cm

b)
17 cm
17 cm   17 cm
17 cm

c)
16 cm
9 cm   9 cm
16 cm

d)
50 mm
CANADA
35 mm   35 mm

2. Estimate which figure has the greatest perimeter
and which has the least perimeter.
Then measure to check your estimates.

a)

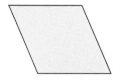

b)

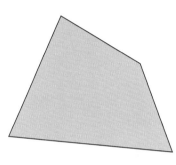

c)

d)

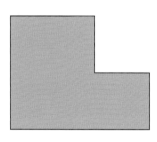

3. Order the figures in question 2 from least to greatest perimeter.

4. Trace around each Pattern Block.
Estimate which block has the greatest perimeter. The least perimeter.
Measure each perimeter.
Order the blocks from least perimeter to greatest perimeter.

5. Write the length of the unmarked side of each regular figure.
How do you know you are correct?

a)

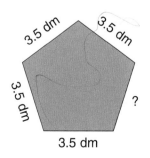

3.5 dm   3.5 dm

3.5 dm

?

3.5 dm

b)

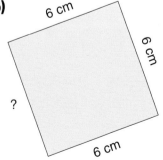

6 cm

6 cm

?

6 cm

c)

20 mm   20 mm

?   20 mm

20 mm

20 mm   20 mm   20 mm

6. Find the perimeter of each figure in question 5.

7. Write the length of each unmarked side of each rectangle.
How do you know you are correct?

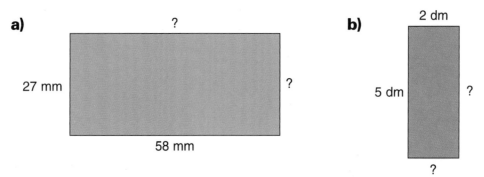

a)

?

27 mm

?

58 mm

b)

2 dm

5 dm

?

?

8. Find the perimeter of each rectangle in question 7.
Find 2 ways to do this.

9. The perimeter of a square is 8 dm.
How long is each side? How do you know?

10. The perimeter of a rectangle is 10 cm.
How long might its sides be?
How do you know? Show your work.

11. Which unit of length would be best to find
the perimeter of each object? Explain your choice.
  a) the teacher's desk   **b)** a calculator
  c) a pencil case   **d)** a calculator key

12. Is each a precise measurement or an estimate? Explain.
  a) The perimeter of my book is 96.2 cm.
  b) The postage stamp is 23 mm long and 20 mm wide.
  c) The perimeter of the table is about 4 m.

Reflect

What does it mean to find the perimeter of an object or a figure?
When might you need to find the perimeter of an object?
Use words, pictures, or numbers to explain.

Finding the Perimeter of a Large Region

Explore ·

Both Peta and Marc run every morning.
Peta runs once around the perimeter
of Silver Springs Park.
Marc runs once around the perimeter
of Shady Pines Park.
Who runs the farthest?

Solve this problem.
Show your work.

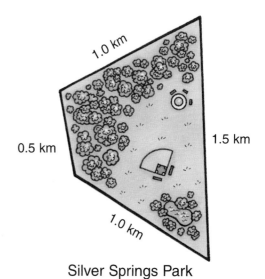

1.0 km

0.5 km

1.5 km

1.0 km

Silver Springs Park

Show *and* Share

Tell how you found each perimeter.
How did you compare perimeters in
metres and in kilometres?

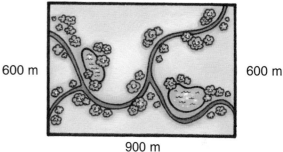

900 m

600 m

600 m

900 m

Shady Pines Park

Connect ·

To measure the perimeter of a large region,
you use metres or kilometres as the unit of length.

The perimeter of this cornfield
= 500 m + 500 m + 500 m + 500 m
= 2000 m

Since 1000 m = 1 km, then 2000 m = 2 km

The perimeter of the cornfield is 2 km.

> **1 km = 1000 m**

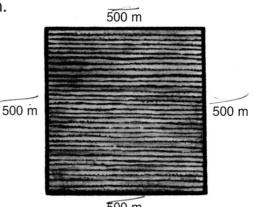

500 m

500 m

500 m

500 m

1. Find the perimeter of each region.

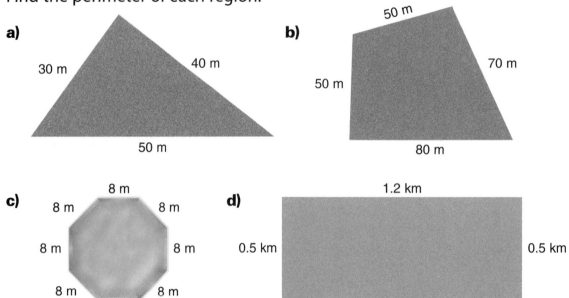

a)

30 m   40 m

50 m

b)

50 m

50 m   70 m

80 m

c)

8 m

8 m   8 m

8 m   8 m

8 m   8 m

8 m

d)

1.2 km

0.5 km   0.5 km

1.2 km

2. Copy and complete this table.
   What patterns do you see? Explain.

km	1	2	3	4	5	6	7	8	9	10
m	1000									

3. Which figure in each pair has the greater perimeter? How do you know?

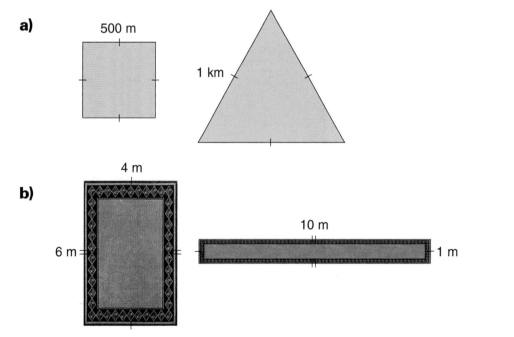

a)

500 m

1 km

b)

4 m

6 m

10 m

1 m

4. Which garden will take the most fencing to surround it?
How do you know?

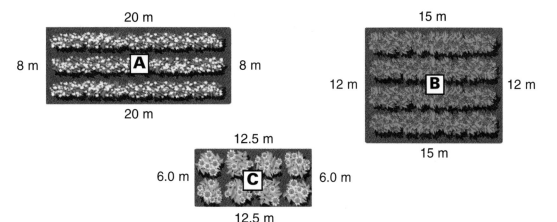

20 m

8 m **A** 8 m

20 m

15 m

12 m **B** 12 m

15 m

12.5 m

6.0 m **C** 6.0 m

12.5 m

5. The perimeter of a square field is 1 km.
How long is each side? How do you know?

6. The perimeter of a rectangular field is 8 km.
How long might its sides be?

7. Which unit of length would you use to find
the perimeter of each item? Explain your choice.
  a) a playing card **b)** the province of Alberta
  c) a school gym **d)** a flower garden

8. Is each a precise measurement or an estimate? Explain.
  a) The coastline of Prince Edward Island is about 1110 km long.
  b) Ms. Diaz bought 20 m of fencing for her garden.

Reflect

To find the perimeter of a figure, you
need to know the lengths of its sides.
For which figures do you need to know
only 1 side? 2 sides? More than 2 sides?
Use words, pictures, or numbers to
explain your ideas.

Numbers Every Day

Number Strategies

Write each fraction as a
decimal.

$\frac{1}{10}$, $\frac{1}{100}$, $\frac{3}{10}$, $\frac{55}{100}$

Write each decimal as a
fraction.

0.5, 0.02, 0.75, 0.4

LESSON

8 Exploring Area

You will need Colour Tiles or congruent cardboard squares.

Object	Estimated number of squares	Area
book	50	64 square units

➤ Estimate how many squares will cover the surface of a book.
➤ Cover the book. Find its area in square units.
➤ Record your work in a table.

Repeat this activity with 5 other objects.

Show and Share

After you covered a surface, how could you find the area
without counting every square?
Share your ideas with your partner.

Connect

➤ To find the area of a figure,
you can count the number of square units.

The area of this patio is 6 square units.

➤ To find the area of a rectangle,
you can count the square units or multiply.
There are 4 rows of 3 squares.
$4 \times 3 = 12$

The area of this rectangular patio is 12 square units.

Practice

1. Estimate which figure has the greatest area.
Then find the area of each figure in square units.

a)   b) c) 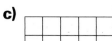 d)

2. Order the figures in question 1 from least to greatest area.

3. Write a multiplication sentence to find
the area of each rectangle.

a) 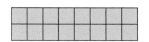 b)

c)  d)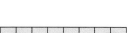

Numbers Every Day

Number Strategies

Multiply.

$6 \times 7 = \square$

$5 \times 3 = \square$

$9 \times 4 = \square$

$2 \times 8 = \square$

4. Find the area of each game board in square units.
   Write a multiplication sentence for each area.

   a) Checkers

   b) Snakes and Ladders

5. The area of a rectangle is 32 square units.
   The rectangle has 8 rows of squares.
   How many squares are in each row? How do you know?

6. Estimate which figure has the greatest area.
   Then find each area in square units.
   How can you do this by multiplying, then adding?

   a) 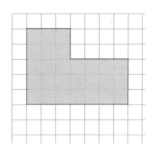   b) 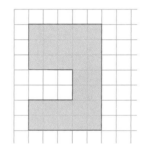   c)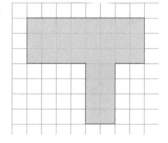

7. Use grid paper. Draw a rectangle with each area.
   a) 12 square units   b) 7 square units
   c) 15 square units   d) 9 square units
   For which areas can you draw more than 1 rectangle?
   How many more? Explain.

8. Kelly drew a figure with an area of 48 square units.
   What might the figure look like?
   Use words, pictures, or numbers to show your ideas.

Reflect

Draw a rectangle on grid paper. Cut it out. Use the rectangle
as part of a poster to explain how to find area in square units.

Measuring Area in Square Centimetres

Explore

You will need cardboard rectangles and a transparent 1-cm grid.

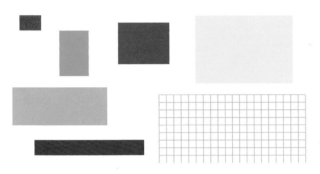

➤ Choose a rectangle. Estimate its area in centimetre squares.
➤ Place the transparent grid over the rectangle.
  Make sure you line up the sides of the rectangle with the lines on the grid.
➤ Find the area of the rectangle.
➤ Record your work in a table.
➤ Repeat the activity with the other rectangles.
➤ Order the rectangles from least to greatest area.

Rectangle	Estimated area	Actual area
Red	8 squares	

Show and Share

How could you use the area of one rectangle to estimate the area of another? Why must the grid lines line up with the sides of the rectangle?

Numbers Every Day

Calculator Skills

Write each number as the product of two numbers.
20, 24, 30, 36

(For example, $12 = 2 \times 6$)

How many different ways can you do this?

LESSON FOCUS | Use a 1-cm grid to measure area in square centimetres.

345

Each side of every square on this grid paper is 1 cm long.

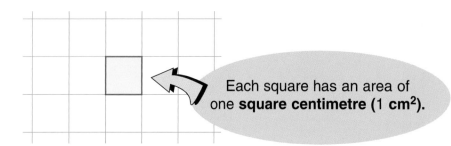

Each square has an area of one **square centimetre (1 cm²).**

You can use square centimetres to measure area.
This rectangle is drawn on 1-cm grid paper.
It has 2 rows of 3 squares.
2 × 3 = 6
The area of the rectangle is 6 cm².

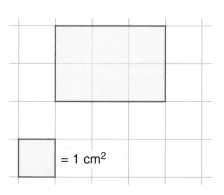

= 1 cm²

One face of a Base Ten unit cube has an area of 1 cm².
You can fill a figure with unit cubes,
then count the cubes to find the area in square centimetres.

Practice

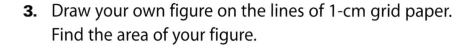

1. Estimate the area of each object in square centimetres.
    Then use a transparent 1-cm grid to find the approximate area.
    a) the top of a calculator
    b) the cover of a small book

2. Roland drew this robot's head on 1-cm grid paper.
    a) What is the area of the head?
    b) What is the area of one robot eye?
        Its nose? Its mouth?

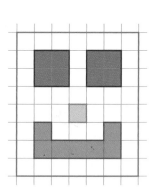

3. Draw your own figure on the lines of 1-cm grid paper.
    Find the area of your figure.

4. Use 1-cm grid paper. Draw 2 different rectangles with each area.

 a) 8 cm^2 **b)** 24 cm^2 **c)** 16 cm^2 **d)** 18 cm^2

5. Look at this rectangle. Use 1-cm grid paper.

 a) Draw a rectangle with a greater area.

 b) Draw a rectangle with a lesser area.

 c) Draw a different rectangle with the same area.

 d) Double the length and the width of the rectangle. Draw a rectangle with these new dimensions. Record its area.

 Show your work.

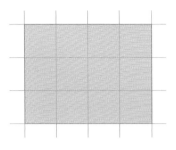

6. You will need 1-cm grid paper, a number cube, and 2 different colour crayons.

Game

Outline a 10 by 10 square on the grid paper.

Take turns to roll the number cube.

The number you get is the area in square centimetres you colour on the grid.

For example, if you roll a 3, you colour in:

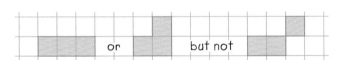

Continue to play until you have filled the 10 by 10 square.

Count the squares to find who coloured in the greater area.

7. The area of a rectangle is 20 cm^2.
The length of the rectangle is 10 cm. What is its width?

8. The area of a square is 16 cm^2. What are its linear dimensions?

Reflect

Draw a rectangle on 1-cm grid paper.
Find its area. Find its perimeter.
How are area and perimeter different?

Estimating and Measuring Area

Explore

You will need cardboard or plastic polygons and 1-cm grid paper.

Choose 3 polygons.
➤ Trace each polygon onto 1-cm grid paper.
➤ Estimate the area of each tracing.
➤ Count squares and parts of squares to find an approximate area.
Record the approximate area of each tracing.

Show and Share

Share your strategies for counting part squares.
What do you do when part of a square is
greater than one-half a square?
Less than one-half a square?

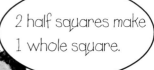

2 half squares make
1 whole square.

Social Studies

Patchwork quilts were an early form of recycling.
They were made from leftover fabric and pieces cut
from old clothing.
How many squares are on this patchwork quilt?
How can you find out without counting every square?

This triangle is drawn on 1-cm grid paper.

Here is one way to find the
approximate area of this triangle.

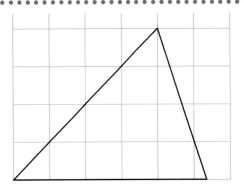

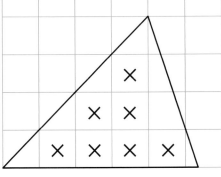

Count the whole squares.
There are 7 whole squares.

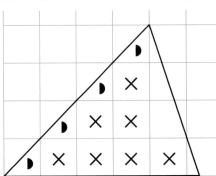

Put half squares together to count
as whole squares.
There are 4 half squares.
4 half squares = 2 whole squares

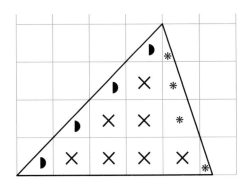

For parts of squares that are not half squares:
If the part is greater than $\frac{1}{2}$ a square,
count it as 1 square.
If the part is less than $\frac{1}{2}$ a square, ignore it.
There are about 2 more squares.

Find the total number of squares:
7 + 2 + 2 = 11
The area of the triangle is about 11 cm^2.

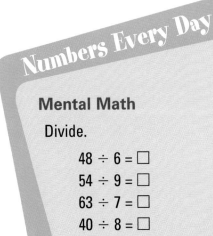

Numbers Every Day

Mental Math

Divide.

$48 \div 6 = \square$

$54 \div 9 = \square$

$63 \div 7 = \square$

$40 \div 8 = \square$

1. Find the approximate area of each figure.

   a)
   b)
   c)

2. Order the figures in question 1 from greatest to least area.

3. Use 1-cm grid paper. Draw a polygon with each area.
   a) about 10 cm^2 b) about 12 cm^2 c) about 19 cm^2

4. Use 1-cm grid paper.
   Draw 3 different polygons with an area of about 15 cm^2.

5. Draw this face on 1-cm grid paper.
   Find the area of each part of the face.
   a) one eye
   b) the nose
   c) the mouth
   d) the whole face

   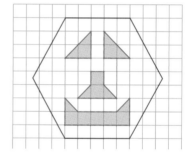

6. Copy this figure onto 1-cm grid paper.
   Explain how you would find the
   approximate area of this figure.
   Show your work.

   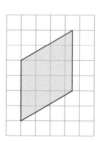

Reflect

You have estimated and measured area in square centimetres.
When might an estimate be good enough?
When might you need to know the area precisely?
Write about your ideas.

Finding Area in Square Metres

You will need newspapers, tape, scissors, and a metre stick.

➤ Use the materials above to make a square with side length 1 m for each group member.

➤ Use your metre squares to find the areas of different parts of your classroom or school.

➤ Record your results.

Show *and* Share

What did you do when the area was not an exact number of metre squares? Show how you can order the areas you measured from least to greatest.

Connect

Each square you made has an area of one **square metre**. You write one square metre as 1 **m²**.

You can use grid paper to model a large area. On this grid, the area of 1 small square represents 1 m².

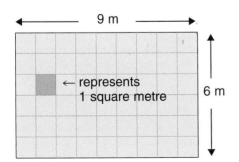

← represents 1 square metre

This is a model of a gymnastics centre. It is 6 m wide and 9 m long. The model has 6 rows of 9 squares. $6 \times 9 = 54$

The area of the gymnastics centre is 54 m².

LESSON FOCUS | Use a square metre to find the area of a region.

351

Practice

1. Find the area of each rectangle.

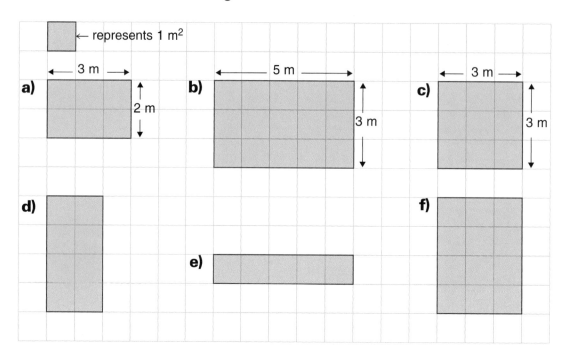

2. In question 1, which rectangle would need the most paint to cover it? The least paint to cover it?

3. The area of a rectangular garden is 24 m². The garden is 6 m long.
   a) How wide is the garden?
   b) Draw a model of the garden on 1-cm grid paper.

4. Louie's patio is rectangular.
   It has a perimeter of 18 m. The patio is 5 m long.
   a) How wide is the patio?
   b) What is its area?
   c) Draw a model of the patio on 1-cm grid paper.

5. Which unit would you use to find the area of each region?
   Explain your choice.
   a) a classroom wall
   b) a page of your math book
   c) a photograph
   d) a flower garden
   e) a kitchen floor
   f) a table tennis table

6. Here is a map of the playground at Peekaboo Day Care Centre.

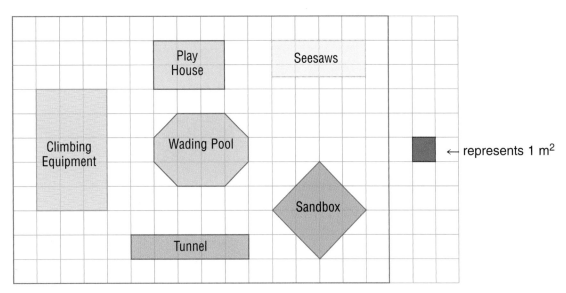

←— represents 1 m²

a) Find the area of each section of the playground.
Record your work in a table.

b) Which section of the playground has the least area?
The greatest area? How do you know?

c) Find the area of the playground.
Show your work.

7. Would you need to measure perimeter
or area?
Explain your choice.
a) You want to seed your lawn.
b) You want to fence your garden.
c) You want to paint your ceiling.
d) Your bedroom needs a rug.

Reflect

How can you use the linear dimensions
of a rectangle to find its area?
Use numbers, pictures, or words to explain.

Exploring Figures with Equal Perimeters

Explore

You will need a geoboard, geobands, and 1-cm grid paper.

Simon wants to build a rectangular pen in
his backyard for his potbelly pig, Smiley.
Simon has 22 m of wire mesh to enclose the pen.
Simon wants the greatest possible area for the pen.

➤ Use a geoboard to make models of all possible
  rectangles. Draw each model on grid paper.
➤ Find the area of each pen.
➤ Write the perimeter of each pen.
➤ Record your work.
➤ Find the pen with the greatest area.

Show *and* Share

One way to record your work is in a table.
How many different areas did you find?
What is true about each perimeter?

Length	Width	Area	Perimeter

Connect

Figures with different areas can have equal perimeters.
Each figure below has perimeter 10 cm.

☐ = 1 cm²

6 cm²   4 cm²   5 cm²   4 cm²

1. Use 1-cm grid paper. Draw all possible rectangles with each perimeter.
   Find the area of each rectangle.
   a) 16 cm   **b)** 20 cm   **c)** 14 cm

2. Copy each figure onto 1-cm grid paper.
   • Find the perimeter of each figure.
   • Draw a rectangle with the same perimeter as the figure.
   • Find the area of each rectangle you draw.

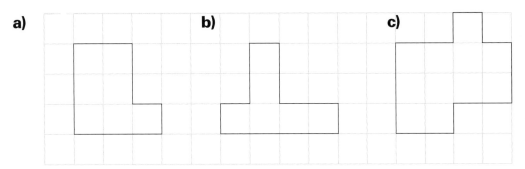

3. Draw 2 different figures with each perimeter.
   Find the area of each figure you draw. Use a geoboard to help you.
   a) 18 cm   **b)** 10 cm   **c)** 12 cm   **d)** 8 cm

4. Suppose you want to make a rectangular garden
   with a perimeter of 24 m.
   a) The garden must have the greatest possible area.
   What should the dimensions of the garden be?
   b) Which garden would you design
   if you do not like garden work?
   Explain your design.
   Show your work.

Numbers Every Day

Number Strategies

Write each number as the sum of 2 pairs of equal numbers.
16, 20, 24, 36

(For example,
12 = 1 + 1 + 5 + 5)

How many different ways can you do this?

Reflect

Write a letter to a friend to explain the
difference between area and perimeter.

Exploring Figures with Equal Areas

You will need 48 Colour Tiles or congruent squares, and grid paper.
Each tile or square represents 1 m².

Ms. Daisy is planning a rectangular garden for her backyard.
The garden will have an area of 48 m².
Ms. Daisy will put a fence around the garden.

➤ Use the tiles or squares to find all the
possible rectangles that Ms. Daisy can make.
➤ Draw each rectangle on grid paper.
➤ Find and record the perimeter of each rectangle.

Show *and* Share

Tell what you know about the area of each rectangle.
Which garden needs the most fencing? The least fencing?
Which rectangle would you recommend to Ms. Daisy?
Explain your choice.

Connect

Figures with different perimeters can have equal areas.
Each figure below has area 12 m².

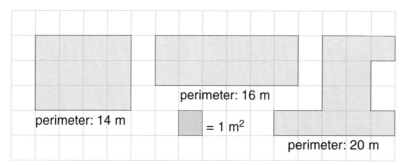

perimeter: 16 m

= 1 m²

perimeter: 14 m

perimeter: 20 m

Use Colour Tiles or congruent squares when they help.

1. Use 1-cm grid paper.
   • Draw all possible rectangles with each area.
   • Find the perimeter of each rectangle you draw.
   a) 1 cm²
   b) 18 cm²
   c) 12 cm²
   d) 16 cm²

2. Copy each figure onto 1-cm grid paper.
   • Find the area of each figure.
   • Draw a rectangle with the same area as the figure.
   • Find the perimeter of each rectangle.

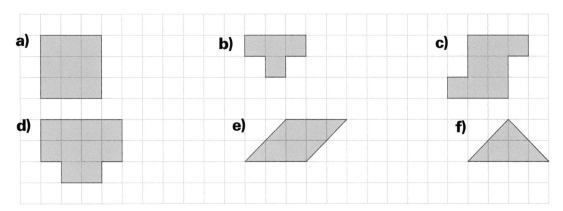

3. Use 1-cm grid paper. Draw 2 different figures with each area.
   a) 14 cm²
   b) 11 cm²
   c) 18 cm²
   d) 9 cm²

4. The area of a rectangular garden is 36 m².
   What is the greatest perimeter the
   garden could have?
   Show your work.

Numbers Every Day

Calculator Skills

Divide.
$$124 \div 2 = \square$$
$$248 \div 4 = \square$$
$$372 \div 6 = \square$$
$$496 \div 8 = \square$$

What patterns do you see?
Explain the patterns.

Reflect

Explain what you learned about the
perimeters of different figures with
equal areas.

Show What You Know

1. Estimate, then measure the width, length, and height of your desk or table.
   Record each measurement in 4 different units.

2. Which unit would you use to measure each item?
   Explain your choice.
   a) the distance between your knee and your foot
   b) the distance between your home and school
   c) the width of the toenail on your smallest toe
   d) the height of the tallest tree on your street

3. For each measurement in question 2:
   • When might you need to know it precisely?
   • When might an estimate be good enough?

4. Use a ruler. Draw each item.
   a) a stick 9 cm long   **b)** a pencil 0.08 m long
   c) a pen 1 dm long   **d)** a pin 15 mm long

5. Copy and complete.
   a) 600 cm = ☐ m   **b)** 6 cm = ☐ mm   **c)** 60 cm = ☐ dm
   d) 3 m = ☐ cm   **e)** 3 m = ☐ mm   **f)** 3 m = ☐ dm

6. Find the perimeter and area of each item.

   a)

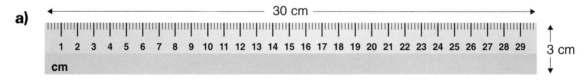

30 cm

1 2 3 4 5 6 7 8 9 10 11 12 13 14 15 16 17 18 19 20 21 22 23 24 25 26 27 28 29

cm

3 cm

   b)

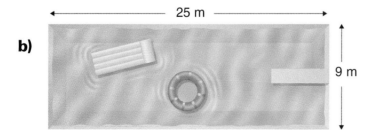

25 m

9 m

10

7. Draw each polygon on 1-cm grid paper.
Estimate the area of each polygon, then find the area.
Approximate when you need to.

a)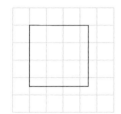

b)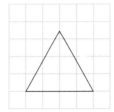

c)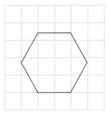

6

8. Estimate, then measure the perimeter of each polygon
in question 7.

5

9. Joe measured his room and found it was 360 cm long.
What unit could Joe use instead of centimetres?
What would the measure be in that unit?

7
11

10. Would you need to measure perimeter or area?
Explain your choice.
a) You want a wallpaper border for your bedroom.
b) You want framing material to make a photo frame.
c) You want wall-to-wall carpeting for a room.

6
9

11. Use 1-cm grid paper. Draw:
a) a rectangle with perimeter 10 cm
b) a square with area 9 cm^2
c) a figure with area 12 cm^2
d) a figure with perimeter 12 cm

12
13

12. Use 1-cm grid paper.
a) Draw 3 different figures with
area 20 cm^2.
b) Draw 3 different figures with
perimeter 20 cm.

UNIT

9 Learning Goals

☑ estimate and measure
linear dimensions
☑ estimate and measure
perimeter
☑ estimate and measure area
☑ relate units of measure
☑ relate area and perimeter

Design a Backyard

Design a backyard for the Rizvi family.

Here are some guidelines.

- The yard is a rectangle 20 m long and 16 m wide.
- It must have:
  - flower beds
  - a vegetable garden
  - a patio
  - a toolshed
  - space for a trampoline and climbing equipment

- You may include other features in the yard.
- Your plan must show all dimensions.

Reflect on the Unit

You have learned about linear dimensions, perimeter, and area.
Use words, pictures, or numbers to explain how they are related.

Fun and Games

Learning Goals

- describe and extend a pattern
- find pattern rules
- use a rule to make a pattern
- use models, drawings, and pictures to create patterns
- use patterns to solve problems
- identify patterns in multiplication and division
- multiply and divide a 3-digit number by a 1-digit number
- use a computer to explore patterns

and Geometry

- What kinds of patterns do you see?
- How could you describe the patterns?
- How could you extend any of the patterns?

Repeating Patterns

Look at this **repeating pattern**.

In this pattern, three attributes change: size, shape, and colour.
What other attributes can you think of?
What is the core of the pattern?

Explore

You will need Attribute Blocks.
➤ Create a repeating pattern in which
  three attributes change.
  Show three repeats of the core.
➤ Your partner looks at the pattern and:
  • continues the pattern for one more core.
  • predicts what the 20th block will be.
  • extends the pattern to check the
    prediction.
➤ Write about your pattern and record
  your partner's prediction.
➤ Switch roles. Repeat the activity.

Show *and* Share

Show your patterns to another pair of students.
Compare how you predicted what the 20th block would be.

Connect

Here is a pattern with Attribute Blocks.

This is the core.

What is the 24th block?

There are 3 blocks in the core.
To predict the 24th block in this pattern,
you can use a hundred chart.
Start at 1 and count on by 3s until you get close to 24.
The closest is 22.

1	2	3	4	5	6	7	8	9	10
11	12	13	14	15	16	17	18	19	20
21	22	23	(24)	25	26	27	28	29	30
31	32	33	34	35	36	37	38	39	40

- The 22nd block is the same as the 1st block.
- The 23rd block is the same as the 2nd block.
- So, the 24th block is the same as the 3rd block.

The 24th block is ◯,
a small, thin, yellow circle.

Numbers Every Day

Calculator Skills

Find each product.

16 × 14
26 × 34
76 × 54

What do you notice about the ones digits of the factors and the products? Explain.

Practice

1. Predict the 20th figure in this pattern.
How did you make your prediction?

Extend the pattern to check your prediction.

2. Use Pattern Blocks.

   a) Create a repeating pattern with four blocks in the core.
Sketch two repeats of the core.

   b) What will the 18th block be?

3. Darren and his friends plan to share a 29-scoop sundae!
There is a pattern in the scoops of ice cream.
The core of the pattern is: chocolate, strawberry, vanilla.

   a) What flavour will the 21st scoop be?

   b) How many scoops of vanilla ice cream will be in the sundae?

 4. Here is the beginning of a repeating pattern.
The core of the pattern is five squares.

Use congruent blue, red, and yellow squares.
How many different ways can you make a pattern?
Sketch all the different ways. Show your work.

5. Predict the 20th coin in this pattern.

How many coins do you need in the pattern for the total to be 49¢?

Reflect

How can you use skip counting to predict with repeating patterns?
Use words, pictures, and numbers to explain.

366   **ASSESSMENT FOCUS** | Question 4

Patterns in Multiplication

You will need a copy of this multiplication chart.
Use patterns to complete the chart.

Show *and* Share

Show your completed chart to
another pair of students.
Talk about the patterns you used,
and the patterns in the chart.
Describe the pattern in the
products that have 11 as a factor.

x	1	2	3	4	5	6	7	8	9
10	10	20	30	40	50	60	70	80	90
11	11	22	33	44	55				
12	12	24	36	48	60				
13	13	26	39	52	65				
14	14	28	42	56	70				
15	15	30	45	60	75				
16	16	32	48	64	80				
17	17	34	51	68	85				
18	18	36	54	72	90				
19	19	38	57	76	95				
20									

Connect

In Unit 4, Lesson 6, you learned three ways to multiply a 2-digit number
by a 1-digit number.
Here is another pattern you can use.

You can use multiples of 10.

➤ Multiply: 6×79

Think: 79 is 1 less than 80.
So, 6×79 is
6 less than 6×80.
$6 \times 80 = 480$
Subtract 6.
$480 - 6 = 474$
So, $6 \times 79 = 474$

➤ Multiply: 8×42

Think: 42 is 2 more than 40.
So, 8×42 is
8×40 plus 8×2.
$8 \times 40 = 320$
Add 8×2, or 16.
$320 + 16 = 336$
So, $8 \times 42 = 336$

LESSON FOCUS | Use patterns to multiply a 2-digit number by a 1-digit number.

367

Practice

1. Multiply. What pattern do you see?
   a) 2 × 99   b) 3 × 99   c) 4 × 99   d) 5 × 99   e) 6 × 99

2. Multiply.
   a) 43 × 8   b) 9 × 37   c) 5 × 72   d) 36 × 6   e) 7 × 17

3. Stickers cost 68¢ a sheet.
   How much money do you need for 6 sheets?

4. How can you tell what the ones digit of the product of 53 × 7 will be without solving the whole problem?

5. These numbers are from one row of a multiplication chart:

117	126	135	144	153	162

   What number is being multiplied?
   How do you know? Show your work.

6. Copy and complete this multiplication chart. What patterns did you use?

×				
	130	135		145
	156		168	
		189		
		216	224	232
			252	

Reflect

How do patterns help you to multiply?
Use words and numbers to explain.

Numbers Every Day

Number Strategies

Write each number in expanded form.

3148
2496
1024
4901

What does the digit 4 represent in each number?

Multiplying a 3-Digit Number by a 1-Digit Number

Explore

Serena bought 2 packages of counters.
Each package contains 136 counters.
How many counters did Serena buy?

Use Base Ten Blocks to model the problem.
Write a multiplication fact for your model.
Record your work.

Show *and* Share

Share your work with another pair of students.
How is multiplying a 3-digit number by a 1-digit number
like multiplying a 2-digit number by a 1-digit number?
How is it different?

Mr. Soares arranged his class into 3 groups for an activity.
Each group needs a piece of string 145 cm long.
What length of string does Mr. Soares need?

The total length of string is 3 × 145 cm.

Here are two ways to multiply.

➤ Use Base Ten Blocks to model the problem.

 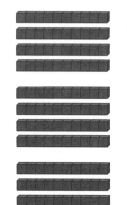 

Multiply the hundreds.	Multiply the tens.	Multiply the ones.
3 × 100	3 × 40	3 × 5
300	120	15

Add. 300 + 120 + 15 = 435
So, 3 × 145 = 435

➤ Break a number apart to multiply.

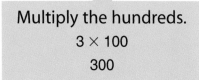

$$
\begin{array}{r}
145 \\
\times\ 3 \\
\hline
15 \\
120 \\
+\ 300 \\
\hline
435
\end{array}
$$

Multiply the ones: 3 × 5 ⟶ 15
Multiply the tens: 3 × 40 ⟶ 120
Multiply the hundreds: 3 × 100 ⟶ + 300
Add.

Mr. Soares needs 435 cm of string.

Use Base Ten Blocks when they help.

1. Multiply.

   a) 121
       × 3

   b) 216
       × 4

   c) 171
       × 5

   d) 412
       × 3

   e) 210
       × 6

2. Multiply.

   a) 3 × 492   b) 152 × 7   c) 5 × 215   d) 124 × 6   e) 2 × 198

3. A large box of crayons holds 128 crayons.
   How many crayons are in 4 large boxes?

4. Write a story problem that can be solved by
   multiplying a 3-digit number by a 1-digit number.
   Solve your problem. Show your work.

5. Each seat on a roller coaster holds 3 people.
   There are 42 seats.
   The roller coaster completes 6 rides every hour.
   Could 800 people ride the roller coaster
   in one hour? Explain.

6. Copy and complete
   this multiplication
   chart.
   Explain your
   thinking.

×				
	600	603		
	800			812
			1010	1015
	1200		1212	1218

Numbers Every Day

Calculator Skills

Use the digits from 2 to 9
to make the least sum.
You may only use each
digit once.

☐☐☐☐
+ ☐☐☐☐
‾‾‾‾‾‾

Reflect

Is the product of a 3-digit number and a
1-digit number always a 3-digit number?
Use words and numbers to explain.

Growing Patterns

Explore

You will need congruent squares
and grid paper.
Build this growing pattern.

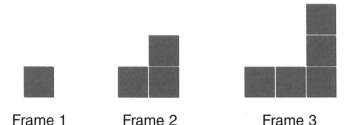

Frame 1   Frame 2   Frame 3

➤ Think about what Frame 4
   will look like, then build it.
   Build Frames 5 and 6.
   Sketch the pattern on
   grid paper.
   Show the squares you
   added in each frame.
➤ Make a table.
   Record the number of squares
   you add each time and
   the number of squares in
   each frame.
➤ Describe the patterns in the
   frames and in the table.

How many squares will you need
to build Frame 12?

Show *and* Share

Show your work to another pair
of students.
Talk about the number patterns you found.
Write a pattern rule for each pattern.
How did you find the number of squares needed for Frame 12?

Frame	Squares Added	Squares in a Frame
1	–	1
2	2	3

Here is a growing pattern with circles.

  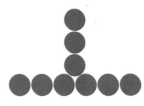

Frame 1   Frame 2   Frame 3

Numbers Every Day

Number Strategies

What is the fewest coins needed to make change?

Cost	Amount Given
$3.49	$4.00
$3.04	$5.04
$24.85	$25.10

How do you know?

What does Frame 4 look like?
What is the pattern rule for the number of circles in a frame?
How can you predict the number of circles in Frame 10?

➤ Each frame has 3 more circles than the frame before.
You can record this pattern in a table.
From the table, 3 circles are added each time.
Add 3 circles to Frame 3 to make Frame 4.

There are 12 circles in Frame 4.

Frame	Circles Added	Circles in a Frame
1	–	3
2	3	6
3	3	9

Frame 4

➤ The pattern rule for the number of circles in a frame is:
Start at 3. Add 3 each time.

➤ Extend the pattern to predict the number of circles in Frame 10:
3, 6, 9, 12, 15, 18, 21, 24, 27, 30

There will be 30 circles in Frame 10.

Frame	Circles Added	Circles in a Frame
1	–	3
2	3	6
3	3	9
4	3	12

1. Use congruent squares to build this growing pattern.

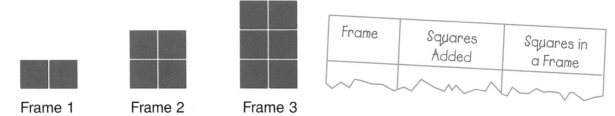

Frame 1   Frame 2   Frame 3

Frame	Squares Added	Squares in a Frame

a) Copy and complete the table.
b) Build Frame 4 and Frame 5.
c) What is the pattern rule for the number of squares in a frame?
d) Predict the number of squares needed to build Frame 12. How did you make your prediction?

2. Here is a growing pattern made with pennies.

Frame 1   Frame 2   Frame 3

a) Draw Frame 4 and Frame 5.
b) What is the pattern rule for the number of pennies in a frame?
c) What sum of money is in Frame 7?
d) What is the total sum of money in the first seven frames?

3. Use Pattern Blocks to build this pattern.

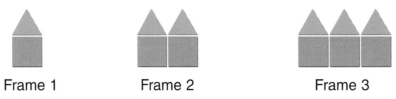

Frame 1   Frame 2   Frame 3

a) Build the next three frames of the pattern.
b) Copy and complete the table.

Frame	Triangles Added	Triangles in a Frame	Squares Added	Squares in a Frame

c) How many of each type of block do you need to build Frame 14? How do you know?

4. This growing pattern was made with Pattern Blocks.

Frame 1   Frame 2   Frame 3

How many of each type of block do you need to build Frame 10?
How do you know?

5. Nicole has congruent squares.
She makes 4 frames of a growing pattern.
Frame 1 has 1 square. Frame 4 has 10 squares.
What might Nicole's pattern look like?
Draw the first four frames.
Can you find more than one growing pattern?
Explain. Show your work.

6. Build a growing pattern to match each table.
Extend each pattern to Frame 6.

a)

Frame	Triangles Added	Triangles in a Frame
1	—	2
2	4	6
3	4	10

b)

Frame	Squares Added	Squares in a Frame	Circles Added	Circles in a Frame
1	—	1	—	2
2	1	2	2	4
3	1	3	2	6

Reflect

How does recording a growing pattern in a table help you make
predictions? Use words, pictures, or numbers to explain.

Changing-Step Growing Patterns

You will need congruent squares and grid paper.

➤ Build these growing patterns.

Pattern A

Frame 1   Frame 2   Frame 3   Frame 4

Pattern B

Frame 1 Frame 2   Frame 3   Frame 4

Frame	Squares Added	Squares in a Frame

For each pattern:

- Record the pattern on grid paper and in a table.
- Write the pattern rule for the number of squares added and for the number of squares in a frame.
- Build Frame 5 and Frame 6.
  How many squares do you need for each frame?

➤ How are Patterns A and B the same? How are they different?

Show *and* Share

Share your work with another pair of students.
How did you find out how many squares you needed?

➤ Here is a pattern with Attribute Blocks.

Frame 1   Frame 2   Frame 3   Frame 4

From the table or picture,
2 blocks are added each time.

The pattern rule for the
number of blocks in a frame is:

Frame	Blocks Added	Blocks in a Frame
1	–	1
2	2	3
3	2	5
4	2	7

Start at 1. Add 2 each time.
This pattern is a **same-step growing pattern**.

➤ Look at this pattern of growing squares.

Frame 1   Frame 2   Frame 3   Frame 4

From the table or picture, the number
of blocks added changes each time.
The number of blocks added increases
by 2 each time.

Frame	Blocks Added	Blocks in a Frame
1	–	1
2	3	4
3	5	9
4	7	16

The pattern rule for the
number of blocks added is:

Start at 3. Add 2 each time.

Look at the pattern for the number of blocks in a frame: 1   4   9   16

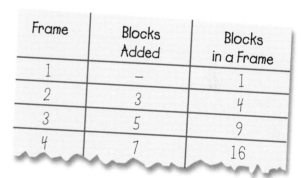

+3   +5   +7

The pattern rule for the
number of blocks in a frame is:

Start at 1. Add 3. Increase the number you add by 2 each time.
This pattern is a **changing-step growing pattern**.

1. Use Pattern Blocks to build this pattern.

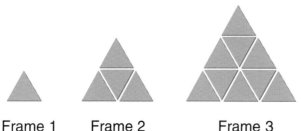

Frame 1   Frame 2   Frame 3

a) Copy and complete the table.
b) What kind of growing pattern is this? How do you know?
c) Build Frame 4.
d) What is the pattern rule for the number of blocks in a frame?
e) Predict the number of blocks needed to build Frame 10. How did you make your prediction?

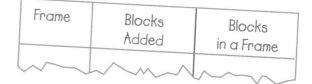

Frame	Blocks Added	Blocks in a Frame

2. Use congruent squares.
   Make a changing-step growing pattern.
   Record your pattern in a table.
   How many squares will there be in Frame 8?

3. Look at the second pattern in *Connect*.

a) Each block has side length 1 unit. Find the perimeter of each frame.
b) Copy and complete the table.

Frame	Perimeter

c) Describe any patterns in the perimeters.

Numbers Every Day

Mental Math

Which pairs of facts are related? Explain how you know.

- $5 \times 7 = 35$ $25 \div 5 = 5$
- $2 \times 3 = 6$ $6 \div 3 = 2$
- $4 \times 4 = 16$ $16 \div 4 = 4$

4. Jon made a growing pattern with congruent squares.

Frame 1   Frame 2   Frame 3

He said, "When I double the length of the side
of a square, the area of the square doubles."
Do you agree with Jon's statement?
Use congruent squares or 1-cm grid paper to support
your answer. Show your work.

5. A grocery clerk has 36 cereal boxes.
She continues this pattern.
The clerk uses all the boxes.
How many boxes will be in the bottom row?
How do you know?
Sketch the display.

6. Use question 5 as a guide.
Make up a problem that can be solved
by making a growing pattern.
Trade problems with
a classmate.
Solve your classmate's
problem.

Math Link

History

The ancient Egyptians multiplied by
doubling, then adding.
To multiply 7×12, make a doubling table.

Groups of 7	Total
1	7
2	14
4	28
8	56

The sum of 4 and 8 is 12,
so 7×12 is the sum: $28 + 56 = 84$
$7 \times 12 = 84$

Reflect

Describe two different kinds of
growing patterns. Use words,
pictures, or numbers to explain.

Strategies Toolkit

Explore

Mrs. Chan has triangular tables in her library.
She arranges the tables into one long row.
The tables fit together as shown.
One person can sit at each side of a table.
Mrs. Chan needs to seat 25 people.
How many tables does she need?

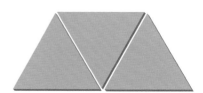

Show *and* Share

Describe the strategy you used to solve the problem.

Connect

Mr. Pasma has to seat 32 people at square tables.
He arranges the tables into one long row.
One person can sit at each side of a table.
How many tables does Mr. Pasma need?

Strategies

- **Make a table.**
- **Use a model.**
- **Draw a picture.**
- **Solve a simpler problem.**
- **Work backward.**
- **Guess and check.**
- **Make an organized list.**
- **Use a pattern.**

Understand

What do you know?
- The tables are square.
- There is a maximum of 4 seats at each table.
- The tables are arranged in a row.

Plan

Think of a strategy to help you solve the problem.
- You can **use a pattern**.
- Use orange Pattern Blocks to model the tables.
- List the numbers of tables and the numbers of seats.

Record your list.

Number of Square Tables	Number of Seats
1	4
2	6

Look for patterns.
Continue the patterns to find
the number of tables needed to seat 32 people.

Check your work.
Does your answer make sense?

Practice

Choose one of the

Strategies

1. Suppose you have regular hexagonal tables.
   You want to seat 42 people.
   The tables will be joined in a row.
   How many tables do you need?

2. Pool decks come in many shapes and sizes.
   Use grid paper to model this growing pattern for a deck.
   How many blue tiles are there in the frame that has 20 red tiles?

Frame 1

Frame 2

Frame 3

Reflect

How can you use a pattern to solve a problem?
Use words and numbers to explain.

Patterns in Division with Remainders

The Remainder Game

You will need a deck of cards with the 10s and face cards removed.

Choose a dealer.

➤ The dealer deals three cards to each player.
➤ Use the numbers from your three cards to make a division statement.
  You may use the numbers in any order.
➤ Divide. Record your work.
  The remainder is your score.
  If the remainder is 0, you score 10 points.
➤ The first person to get 30 points wins.

Show and Share

Compare your division sentences with those of your group members.
How did you decide how to arrange the numbers?

Connect

In Unit 4, you used arrays, related multiplication facts, and Base Ten Blocks to divide.

Numbers Every Day

Number Strategies

Arrange the digits 2, 4, 6, and 8 to make the greatest difference.

$$\begin{array}{r} \square\square \\ -\ \square\square \\ \hline \end{array}$$

Explain your strategy.

You can also use skip counting.

Divide: 61 ÷ 8
Start at 8 and count on by 8s:
8, 16, 24, 32, 40, 48, 56
There are 7 eights in 61
and 5 left over.
So, 61 ÷ 8 = 7 R 5

I like to use a number line to skip count.

Practice

1. Divide. What patterns do you see?
   a) 96 ÷ 8   **b)** 95 ÷ 8   **c)** 94 ÷ 8   **d)** 93 ÷ 8   **e)** 92 ÷ 8
   f) 91 ÷ 8   **g)** 90 ÷ 8   **h)** 89 ÷ 8   **i)** 88 ÷ 8   **j)** 87 ÷ 8

2. Mrs. Oliveira needs tables in her library.
   Eight students can sit at each table.
   Seventy-three students will be in the library.
   How many tables are needed? How do you know?

3. Write a story problem that can be solved using 83 ÷ 9.
   Solve the problem.
   How did you deal with the remainder?

4. Ben has to learn 60 spelling words in 7 days.
   He says that means he needs to learn 8 words
   each day. Is Ben correct?
   Explain. Show your work.

Reflect

Explain how you can use skip counting to help you divide.
Use words and numbers to explain.

LESSON

8

Dividing a 3-Digit Number by a 1-Digit Number

Explore

Each sheet of this photo album holds 8 photos.
Evan has 325 photos.
How many sheets does he need?
Show your work.

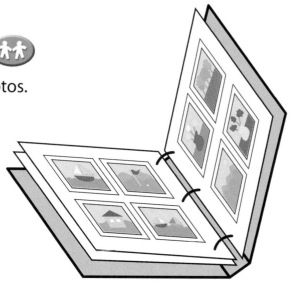

Show *and* Share

What strategies did you use to solve this problem?

Connect

There are 125 campers at Adventure Camp.
Each tent at the camp sleeps 3 campers.
How many tents are needed?

Divide: 125 ÷ 3

➤ You can use Base Ten Blocks.

Trade the hundred flat for 10 rods.

Arrange the 12 rods and 5 unit cubes into 3 equal rows.

So, 125 ÷ 3 = 41 R 2

Each row is 41.

384 LESSON FOCUS | Use different strategies to divide a 3-digit number by a 1-digit number.

➤ You can subtract multiples of the divisor.
For 125 ÷ 3, the divisor is 3.
Multiples of 3 are: 3, 6, 9, 12, 15, 18, 21, 24, 27, 30, 33, …

Write 125 ÷ 3 as 3)125.

Choose any multiple of 3 less than 125.
Start with 30.

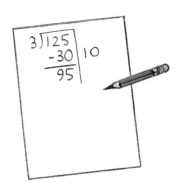

30 is a multiple of 3.
I subtract 30 from 125.
3 × 10 = 30, so I write
10 at the side.

Then subtract 90.

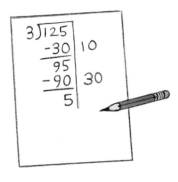

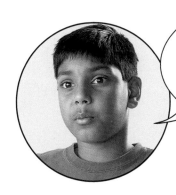

90 is a multiple of 3.
I subtract 90 from 95.
3 × 30 = 90, so I write
30 at the side.

Then subtract 3.

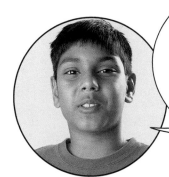

3 is a multiple of 3.
I subtract 3 from 5.
3 × 1 = 3, so I write 1 at the side.
I add the numbers at the side.
3)125 is 41 with 2 left over.

Forty-two tents will be needed. One tent will have only 2 campers.

1. Divide.
   a) $794 \div 2$ b) $263 \div 9$ c) $410 \div 4$ d) $314 \div 6$

2. Divide.
   a) $4\overline{)484}$ b) $3\overline{)651}$ c) $6\overline{)670}$ d) $5\overline{)715}$
   e) $375 \div 8$ f) $274 \div 6$ g) $434 \div 7$ h) $853 \div 4$

3. A baker made 615 loaves of bread in 5 days.
   She made the same number of loaves each day.
   How many loaves did she make each day?

4. Write a story problem that can be solved
   by finding $342 \div 3$.
   Trade problems with a classmate.
   Solve your classmate's problem.

5. Without dividing, how can you tell if $415 \div 5$
   has a 3-digit answer or a 2-digit answer?
   Show your work.

6. Kendra has twice as many building blocks as Janet.
   Janet has twice as many as Fariah.
   Fariah has 57 blocks.
   The girls use all the blocks to build 3 identical towers.
   How many blocks are in each tower?
   How do you know?

Numbers Every Day

Reflect

When you divide a 3-digit number
by a 1-digit number, will the
answer ever be a 1-digit number?
Explain.

Mental Math

Write all the related facts
for each set of numbers.

- 8, 8, 16
- 6, 7, 13
- 8, 4, 12
- 9, 8, 17

9 Area Patterns

Explore

You will need Pattern Blocks.

Choose more than one type of Pattern Block.
Make an area pattern.
Draw a picture to record your pattern.

Show *and* Share

Show your pattern to another pair of students.
Talk about how you made the pattern.

Connect

Christina is covering this floor with carpet tiles.
She continues this pattern.

How many of each tile does Christina need
to cover the floor?

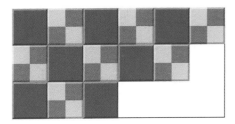

There are two sizes of square tiles in three colours.
All the large tiles are blue.
The small tiles are either purple or yellow.
Four small tiles fit the same space as one large tile.

Complete the pattern.
Count the tiles.

Christina needs 9 blue tiles,
18 purple tiles, and 18 yellow tiles.

LESSON FOCUS | Model and extend area patterns.

387

Practice

1. Describe each pattern.

a)

b)

c)

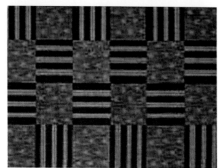

d)

2. Describe the pattern on this quilt.
   Use grid paper to model the pattern.

3. Use Pattern Blocks.
   Begin an area pattern.
   Trade patterns with a classmate.
   Complete your classmate's pattern.
   How did you know how to complete
   the pattern?

Numbers Every Day

Mental Math

Write the related division facts
for each multiplication fact.

$7 \times 8 = 56$

$8 \times 9 = 72$

$10 \times 10 = 100$

$9 \times 4 = 36$

388

4. Use Pattern Blocks to model this pattern.
Extend the pattern.
There are 8 yellow hexagons in the
complete pattern.
How many of each type of
Pattern Block do you need?

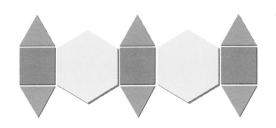

5. Rick is beading a bracelet.

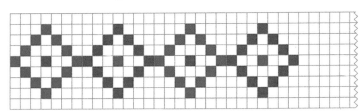

He plans to continue until there are
five red diamonds and five blue diamonds.
How many red beads will the finished bracelet have?
How do you know? Show your work.

6. Kendra is tiling the counter in her bathroom.
The counter is L-shaped.
Kendra is using black and white square tiles.
How many tiles of each colour does Kendra need?

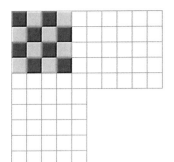

Reflect

Draw and colour an area pattern
on grid paper.
Write about how you
made your pattern.

At Home

Look around your home.
What area patterns can you find?
Sketch one area pattern and
describe it.

Creating Patterns on a Computer

Work with a partner.

Use AppleWorks.
Follow these steps to create a growing pattern on a computer.

1. Open a new document. Click:
   Drawing

2. If a grid appears on the screen, go to Step 3.
   If not, click: Options

   Click: Show Graphics Grid

3. Check the ruler units are centimetres.
   Click: Format

   then click: Rulers ▶

   then click: Ruler Settings...

   Choose these settings:

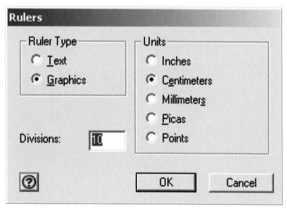

   Click **OK**.

4. Use these tools to draw:

Line Tool ⟶ / 　□ ◀⟵ Rectangle Tool

Rounded Rectangle Tool ⟶ ▢　◯ ◀⟵ Oval Tool

⟋　◁ ◀⟵ Polygon Tool

Freehand Tool ⟶ ∿　✍

Regular Polygon Tool ⟶ △　✎

5. To draw, select the Tool you want.
The cursor will look like this: **+**

➤ Click and hold down the mouse button.
Drag the cursor until the figure is the size and shape you want.
Release the mouse button.

➤ If you are making a square or a circle, hold down the Shift key while you click and drag.

➤ To make an irregular polygon, select the Polygon Tool.
Click and drag to make each side of the polygon.
Double-click when you have finished.

➤ To make a regular polygon, select the Regular Polygon Tool.

Click: **Edit**　then **Polygon Sides...**

Type in the number of sides you want, then click **OK**.

6. To **move a figure**, put the cursor inside the figure.
Click and hold down the mouse button.
Drag your figure to where you want it. Release the mouse button.

7. To **colour a figure**, click the figure to select it.

Click the Fill formatting button: □

Click the Color palette button: ▦
and select a colour.

8. To **flip or turn a figure**, select the figure.

   Click: `Arrange`

   then click `Free Rotate          Shft+Ctrl+R`

   The cursor will look like this: ✕
   Put the cursor on one of the black dots on the edge of the figure.
   Click, hold down the mouse button, and drag the figure
   until it is in the position you want.

9. To **copy a figure**, select the figure.

   Click: `Edit`

   then click: `Copy          Ctrl+C`

   Click: `Edit` then click: `Paste          Ctrl+V`

   The copy shows on top of the figure.
   Click and drag the copy where you want it.

10. Use Steps 5 to 9 to create a growing pattern or an area pattern.

11. Save your pattern.

    Click: `File` then click: `Save As...          Shft+Ctrl+S`
    Name your file. Then click **Save**.

12. Print your pattern.

    Click: `File` then click: `Print...          Ctrl+P`
    Click **OK**.

Reflect

Which is easier, making a pattern by hand or with a computer?
Write about your ideas.

Graphic Designer

A graphic designer usually uses a computer to create the "look" of a magazine, a book, or a web page. The designer's job is to provide information on an attractive page.

A designer begins by creating one or more page *templates*. A template is an empty form. In this template, the designer arranges the *type* (words and letters) and *images* (pictures). The template usually has a number of vertical columns.

For a magazine, a designer may use several templates: one for a feature page, one for general pages, one for a table of contents, and one for an index. These templates are ordered in a pattern. For example, a feature page (A) might be followed by several general pages (B and C) like this: A, B, C, B, C, B; A, B, C, B, C, B; A ...

The size of the type is measured in *points*. A type size of 36 points is about 1 cm high.

This sentence is in 36-point type.

The number of words, the pictures, and the blank spaces all affect how readable a page is.

Show What You Know

1 **1.** This pattern was made with Attribute Blocks.

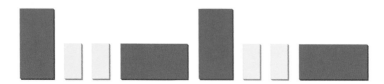

    a) Predict what the 16th block will look like.
How did you make your prediction?

    b) How could you check your prediction? Explain.

2 **2.** Copy and complete this multiplication chart.
Explain how you used patterns to do this.

×	85	86	87	88	89
5	425	430	435		
6	510	516			
7	595				
8					
9					

3 **3.** Multiply.

    a) 178
       × 6

    b) 319
       × 3

    c) 164
       × 2

    d) 462
       × 5

3 8 **4.** There are 365 days in one year.

    a) How many days are there in 3 years?

    b) Suppose a person is 3000 days old.
About how many years is that?
How do you know?

5. You will need Pattern Blocks.
Here are the first 3 frames of a growing pattern.

    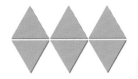

Frame 1   Frame 2   Frame 3

Frame	Blocks Added	Blocks in a Frame

a) Build Frame 4 and Frame 5.
b) Copy and complete the table.
c) How many blocks are needed to build Frame 15?
d) Which frame needs 20 blocks? How do you know?

6. Use 34 congruent squares.
Build the first four frames of a changing-step growing pattern.
Frame 1 has 2 squares. Frame 4 has 17 squares.
How many different patterns can you build?
Record your work.

7. Divide. What patterns do you see?
    a) 99 ÷ 3   **b)** 98 ÷ 3
    c) 97 ÷ 3   **d)** 96 ÷ 3
    e) 95 ÷ 3   **f)** 94 ÷ 3

8. Divide.
    a) $3\overline{)681}$ **b)** $8\overline{)212}$ **c)** $9\overline{)737}$

9. There are 187 congruent squares.
Each student needs 9 squares
to make a larger square.
Are there enough congruent squares
for 25 students? How do you know?

10. Create an area pattern.
Describe your pattern.

UNIT

10 Learning Goals

☑ describe and extend a pattern
☑ find pattern rules
☑ use a rule to make a pattern
☑ use models, drawings, and pictures to create patterns
☑ use patterns to solve problems
☑ identify patterns in multiplication and division
☑ multiply and divide a 3-digit number by a 1-digit number
☑ use a computer to explore patterns

Unit Problem

Fun and Games

Part 1

Create your own game.
- Your game must use patterns in some way.
- You can use number patterns, geometry patterns, or both.

Check List

Your work should show
- ☑ how you used patterns to create a game
- ☑ the types of patterns you used and their rules
- ☑ a clear description of the game
- ☑ your thinking in words, pictures, or numbers

Part 2

Describe your game. Include:
- the patterns you used and their pattern rules
- a sketch of the game board, if there is one
- a list of the materials needed to play the game
- instructions on how to play the game
- the number of players

Be creative and have fun!

Reflect on the Unit

Write about some different kinds of patterns.
Use words, pictures, or numbers to explain what you know.

Probability

ORANGE: WIN NOTHING
PURPLE: WIN A SMALL STUFFED ANIMAL
GREEN: WIN A LARGE STUFFED ANIMAL

DRAW the **ACE** of spades and **WIN** a **PRIZE!**

Learning Goals

- use the language of probability
- conduct experiments
- predict the results of experiments
- draw tree diagrams
- compare actual results with predicted results
- use probability to solve and pose problems

You can WIN up to 4 prizes.
Just HIT the bull's-eye.

1 2 3 4 3 2 1

Key Words

probable

improbable

prediction

experiment

outcome

probability

equally probable

tree diagram

predicted results

Look at the different carnival games.

- Which games would you play? Why?

- Which game would you likely win? Explain.

- Which game would you likely lose? Explain.

- What else do you know from looking at this picture?

399

The Language of Probability

Can you find a flower that talks?

HEY,
HOW'S
IT
GROWING?

Is the month after June always July?

Some events are impossible.

Some events are certain.

Events that could happen are possible.

Make a table with these headings.
Write 5 events under each heading.

Impossible	Possible but Unlikely	Possible and Likely	Certain

Show and Share

Share your events with another pair of students.
Do you agree about the likelihood of each event? Explain.

If an event is likely to happen, it is **probable**.
If an event is unlikely to happen,
it is **improbable**.

Luis has these coins in his pocket.

9 pennies   2 nickels   2 dimes

One coin falls out.
How likely is it that this coin is:

a ?   a ?   a ?   a ?

- It is impossible for the coin to be a because Luis doesn't have any quarters.

- It is probable that the coin is a because most of Luis' coins are pennies.

The coin is most likely to be a .

- It is improbable that the coin is a or a because Luis has only 2 of each coin.

The coin is equally likely to be a or a .

You can use a line to show how likely it is an event will happen.

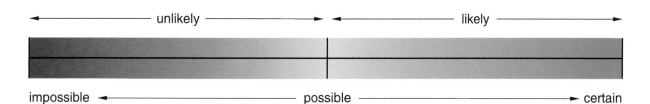

1. Use the words "impossible," "possible," "certain," "unlikely," or "likely" to describe each event.
   a) It will snow tomorrow.
   b) You will have orange juice with your lunch today.
   c) You will see a whale next week.
   d) You will go camping in the spring.
   e) Tomorrow is Friday.
   f) The sun will rise tomorrow.

Numbers Every Day

Number Strategies

Find the fewest coins that would make each amount.
- 49¢
- $1.67
- $3.99

2. This spinner is from a board game.

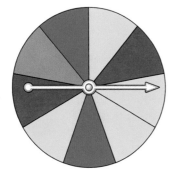

   The pointer is spun.
   a) Which colour is the pointer most likely to stop on? How do you know?
   b) It is equally likely that the pointer will stop on one of two colours. What are the two colours? How do you know?
   c) Write a statement about the pointer using the word "impossible."

3. Fatima is playing this game for the first time.
   She throws a dart at the target.
   a) Is it likely Fatima will hit the bull's-eye?
      Explain your answer.
   b) Explain why the chances of hitting
      white or red are *not* equally likely.
   c) Design a target so the chances of hitting
      red or white are equally likely.
   Show your work.

4. Suppose you close your eyes, then pick one marble from this bag.

   Say which colour:
   a) You are most likely to pick.
   b) You are least likely to pick.
   c) You will never pick.

5. Draw a bag of marbles for which:
   a) Picking a pink marble is a likely event.
   b) Picking a green marble is an unlikely event.
   c) Picking an orange marble is possible.
   d) Picking a black marble is impossible.

At Home

Reflect

Which event is likely to happen
at school today?
Which event is unlikely
to happen at school today?
Explain.

What are two likely events
and two unlikely events that
could happen at home this
week?

Identifying Outcomes and Predicting Results

A meteorologist predicts the weather.

When you decide the likelihood of an event, you make a **prediction**.

Explore

You will need a blank spinner and an open paper clip as a pointer.
➤ Design your own spinner.
  Use four colours.
➤ List the possible outcomes of a spin.
➤ Predict which colour the pointer is most likely to stop on.
  Test your prediction by spinning the pointer.
  Record your results in a tally chart.
➤ Repeat this until you have the results from 20 trials.

  How do your results compare with your prediction?

Show *and* Share

Compare your spinner with that of another pair of students.
How are the spinners alike? Different?
How are the results alike? Different?

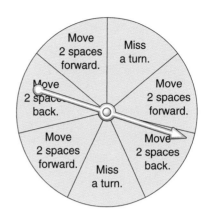

Connect

This is a spinner from a game board.
There are 7 equal sectors.
There are 7 possible **outcomes**,
but only 3 different outcomes.

Spinning the pointer is an **experiment**.
To predict the results of the experiment,
you find how likely each outcome is.
This is called the **probability** of the outcome.

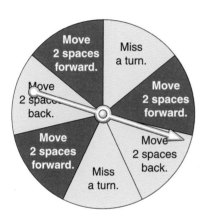

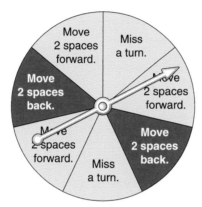

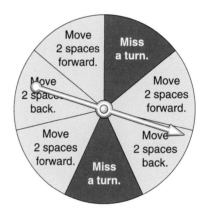

• Three sectors show "Move 2 spaces forward."
The probability of "Move 2 spaces forward" is 3 out of 7.

You write this as a fraction: $\frac{3}{7}$

• The probability of "Move 2 spaces back" is 2 out of 7.

You write: $\frac{2}{7}$

• The probability of "Miss a turn" is 2 out of 7.
You write: $\frac{2}{7}$

"Move 2 spaces forward" is **most probable**.
"Move 2 spaces back" and "Miss a turn" are **equally probable**.

You can show probabilities on a line.

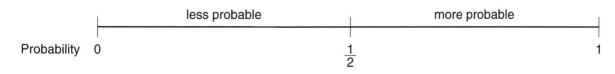

1. List the possible outcomes for each experiment.
   a) tossing a coin
   b) rolling a number cube

2. Use the words "more probable," "less probable," or "equally probable" to compare each pair of events.
   a) It will rain today.
      It will snow today.
   b) You will eat dinner today.
      You will eat breakfast tomorrow.
   c) You will sleep for 1 hour tonight.
      You will sleep for 8 hours tonight.
   d) The pointer on each spinner will land on red.

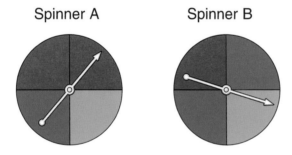

Spinner A   Spinner B

3. Use question 2 to give you ideas.
   Make up two events.
   Use the words "more probable," "less probable," or "equally probable" to compare the events.

4. The pointer on this spinner is spun.
   a) What are the possible outcomes?
   b) What is the probability of the pointer landing on each fruit?
      • banana
      • apple
      • orange
      • pear
   c) Describe the likelihood of each outcome.
      Use the words "most probable," "equally probable," or "less probable."

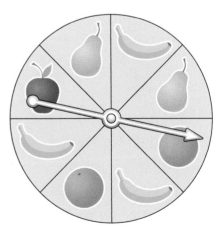

5. Suppose you close your eyes, then pick a marble from this jar.

a) What are the possible outcomes?

b) What is the probability that you pick each marble?
• a red marble
• a yellow marble
• a black marble

c) Which outcome is most probable? Least probable?

d) Which outcomes are equally probable?

6. Design a spinner so that when the pointer is spun:
• Landing on red is most probable.
• Landing on blue is impossible.
• Landing on green and landing on yellow are equally probable.
• Landing on purple is least probable.
Explain your work.

7. Todd and Anna disagree on the probabilities of the outcomes for this spinner.
Todd thinks that the pointer landing on 1 is more probable than the pointer landing on any other number.
Anna thinks that the pointer landing on 2 is more probable because it has two spaces on the spinner.
Who is correct? Why?

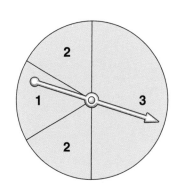

Reflect

Suppose you have a spinner with equal sectors and different colours. What do you know about the probability of landing on each colour? Use words, pictures, or numbers to explain.

Numbers Every Day

Number Strategies

Estimate each product.
• 52×3
• 71×8
• 327×5
• 415×2

Strategies Toolkit

Explore

Jolene has a nickel, a dime, and a loonie in one pocket.
She has a $5 bill, a $10 bill, and a $20 bill in another pocket.
Without looking, Jolene picks one coin and one bill.
What is the probability that Jolene picks a $10 bill and a dime?

Show *and* Share

Describe the strategy you used to solve the problem.

Connect

Strategies

- **Make a table.**
- **Use a model.**
- **Draw a picture.**
- **Solve a simpler problem.**
- **Work backward.**
- **Guess and check.**
- **Make an organized list.**
- **Use a pattern.**

Scott has 4 pairs of pants: red, blue, black, green
Scott has 3 T-shirts: white, blue, purple
Scott dresses in the dark.
What is the probability that he chooses the
blue pants and blue T-shirt?

What do you know?
- Scott has 4 pairs of pants and
  3 T-shirts.
- He chooses 1 pair of pants and
  1 T-shirt.

Think of a strategy to help you solve the problem.
- You need to find out how many possible outfits
  there are.
- You can **draw a picture**.

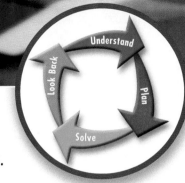

Draw a **tree diagram**. List the pants.
Next to each pair of pants, list the T-shirts.
Then list all possible outfits.

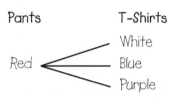

Pants	T-Shirts	Possible Outfits
Red	White	Red Pants, White T-shirt
	Blue	Red Pants, Blue T-shirt
	Purple	Red Pants, Purple T-shirt

Copy and complete the tree diagram.
How many outfits does Scott have?
What is the probability that Scott chooses the blue pants
and blue T-shirt?

How could you solve this problem a different way?

Practice

Choose one of the

Strategies

1. There are four types of sandwiches on
   white or brown bread: cheese, tuna, tomato, egg
   Suppose you pick a sandwich without looking.
   What is the probability that you pick a tuna on brown bread?

2. Students' names are put in two bags.
   The teacher, without looking, picks one name from each bag.
   Bag A has Amy, Alice, Jan, and Joline.
   Bag B has Brock, Brady, Tran, and Kim.
   What is the probability that Jan and Tran are picked?

Reflect

When can you use a tree diagram to solve a problem?

Exploring Predictions

Explore

You will need an envelope, 10 paper clips of one colour, and 10 paper clips of another colour.

➤ Close your eyes while your partner puts at least 10 paper clips in the envelope.
Your partner tells how many there are in total.
There must be two colours of paper clips in the envelope.

➤ Without looking, take 1 paper clip from the envelope.
Record the colour, then put the paper clip back.
Repeat the experiment until you have the results of 20 trials.

➤ Use the results to predict how many paper clips of each colour are in the envelope.

➤ Take the paper clips from the envelope and compare the numbers of paper clips with your prediction.

➤ Trade roles and repeat the experiment.

Show *and* Share

How close was your estimate of the numbers of paper clips to the actual numbers?
Suppose you carried out only 5 trials.
Would your predictions have been the same? Explain.

Sue and Tim conducted an experiment with
2 colours of tiles in a paper bag.
Sue put 2 red tiles and 8 blue tiles in the bag.
Tim picked a tile, recorded its colour,
then returned the tile to the bag.
Here are the results.

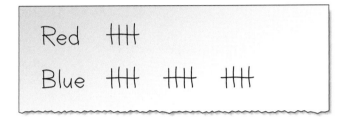

The experiment suggests that there are about
3 times as many blue tiles as red tiles.
Tim knows there are 10 tiles in the bag.
So, Tim estimates 3 red tiles and 7 blue tiles.

Numbers Every Day

Calculator Skills

Order from least to greatest.

0.72 $\frac{3}{4}$ $\frac{7}{10}$ 0.77 $\frac{80}{100}$

Describe the strategies
you used.

Practice

1. Work with a partner.
    One student puts paper clips of 3 colours in an envelope,
    then tells how many in total.
    The other student conducts an experiment to find
    how many of each colour.
    a) Decide how many trials you will conduct.
    b) Conduct the trials, then make a prediction.
    c) Count the number of paper clips of each colour.
       How close was your prediction?

2. Use a coin.
    a) Predict how many times heads and tails will show
       when you toss the coin 30 times.
    b) Conduct the experiment.
    c) How do the results compare with your predictions?

Math Link

Your World

A company that makes potato chips offers a prize to any person who finds a game piece in a bag of chips.

The probability of winning each prize is written on the bag.

The probability of winning a free packet of chips is 1 out of 20, or $\frac{1}{20}$.

3. Use a copy of this spinner.

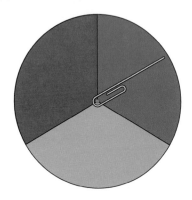

   a) Predict how many times the pointer will land on each colour in 25 spins.
   b) Conduct the experiment.
   c) How do the results compare with your predictions?

4. Use a number cube.
   a) Predict how many times each number will show when you roll the cube 25 times.
   b) Conduct the experiment.
   c) How do the results compare with your predictions?
   Explain your work.

Reflect

Describe an experiment you conducted, and how you used it to check your predictions.

Predicted and Actual Results

Explore

You will need a number cube.

➤ Suppose you roll the number cube 30 times.
Predict how often each outcome will occur.
  - You roll a 6.
  - You roll an even number.
  - You roll an odd number.

➤ What is the probability of each outcome?
Are the outcomes equally probable? Explain.
Record your predictions.

➤ Roll a number cube 30 times.
Record your results on a tally chart.

1	2	3	4	5	6

Show and Share

How do your results compare with your predictions?
Combine your results with those of another pair
of students.
What do you notice about the
combined results?
Combine your results with those of
all your classmates. What do you notice?

Numbers Every Day

Number Strategies

Estimate each sum.
  - 136 + 251
  - 478 + 223
  - 1211 + 2326
  - 1235 + 2145

Here are the results of another experiment.
The spinner has 8 equal parts.
Milly will spin the pointer 50 times.

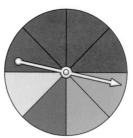

Since $\frac{1}{2}$ of the spinner is red,
Milly predicts red will come up 25 times.

Since $\frac{1}{4}$ of the spinner is green,
Milly predicts green will come up about 12 or 13 times.

Since $\frac{1}{8}$ of the spinner is yellow and $\frac{1}{8}$ is blue,
Milly predicts yellow and blue will each come up about 6 or 7 times.

The probability that the pointer lands:

- on red is 4 out of 8, or $\frac{4}{8}$
- on green is 2 out of 8, or $\frac{2}{8}$
- on yellow is 1 out of 8, or $\frac{1}{8}$
- on blue is 1 out of 8, or $\frac{1}{8}$

Milly spun the pointer 50 times.
Here are her results.

Red	Green	Yellow	Blue
22	15	7	6

Milly's results are close to her predictions.

Milly combined her results with the results
of 3 classmates, for a total of 200 spins.

Milly now predicted that:

- Red should show 100 times.
- Green should show 50 times.
- Each of yellow and blue should show 25 times.

Here are the combined results.

Red	Green	Yellow	Blue
99	51	26	24

The combined results suggest that the more trials
you conduct, the closer the **predicted results** are
to the actual results.

1. Work with a partner.
   a) Suppose you spin the pointer on this spinner 100 times.
      • Predict how many times the pointer will land on each colour.
      • What is the probability of the pointer landing on each colour?
   b) Use a copy of this spinner.
      Spin the pointer 100 times. Record your results.
      How do your predicted results compare with your actual results?

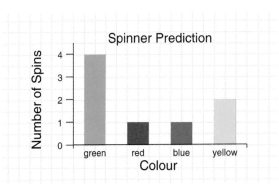

2. Work with a partner.
   Suppose you roll a number cube 100 times.
   • Predict how many times each outcome below occurs.
   • What is the probability of each outcome?
   • Roll the number cube 100 times. Record your results.
   • How do your predicted results compare with your actual results?
   • Combine your results with those of another pair of students.
     What are your new predicted results?
     How do they compare with the actual results?
   a) You roll a 2.
   b) You roll a number greater than 2.

3. This graph shows the predicted results for a spinner. Draw a spinner that corresponds to the bar graph. Explain your work.

Spinner Prediction

Number of Spins / Colour

green 4, red 1, blue 1, yellow 2

How do predicted results and actual results compare when you repeat an experiment many times?
Use your results from *Explore* and *Practice* to explain.

1

1. Use the words "likely," "unlikely," "impossible," "possible," or "certain" to describe each event.
   a) It will rain tomorrow.
   b) You will be in school this afternoon.
   c) You will go canoeing in January.
   d) You will travel to the moon in the future.

2

2. The Grade 4 class cannot agree on a name for its new goldfish: Drew or Jamie.
   One student says:

   > Let's roll a number cube to decide. If 3 or higher comes up, we'll choose Drew. If not, we'll choose Jamie.

   Is this a fair way to choose? Explain.

3

3. Dezi packed these clothes for a trip:
   red shirt, green shirt, blue shirt, yellow shirt, brown pants, black pants

   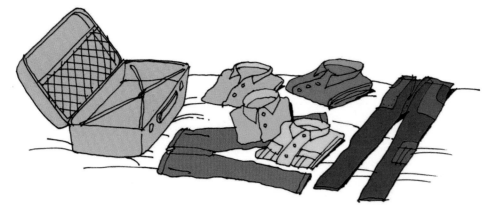

   Dezi takes a shirt and a pair of pants from her suitcase, without looking.
   What is the probability Dezi picks a yellow shirt and brown pants?

4. Which spinner below most likely has these results after 100 spins?
60 blue and 40 red

Spinner A

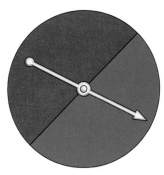

Spinner B

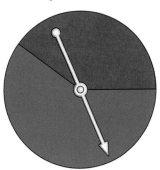

Explain your thinking.

5. These paper clips are put in an envelope.

a) Suppose you pick a paper clip, without looking.
What is the probability the paper clip is red?

b) Suppose you conducted the
experiment 50 times.
Predict how many times
you would pick a red paper clip.

c) Conduct the experiment 50 times.
Record your results.

d) How do your predicted results
compare with the actual results?

e) Combine your results with the
results of 3 classmates.
What are your new predicted results?
How do they compare with the
actual results?

UNIT

11 **Learning Goals**

☑ use the language of
probability
☑ conduct experiments
☑ predict the results of
experiments
☑ draw tree diagrams
☑ compare actual results with
predicted results
☑ use probability to solve and
pose problems

Unit Problem

At the Carnival

Think about the carnival games on pages 398, 399.

Design 3 new carnival games.
- one game in which winning is not probable
- one game in which winning and losing are equally probable
- one game in which the probability of winning is 1 out of 5

Write about each game you design.

WINS
$2.00 PER PLAY
3 PLAYS FOR $5.00

Check List

Your work should show

- [x] your designs for 3 games
- [x] a description of each game, using probability
- [x] how you found the probability of winning each game
- [x] appropriate language to explain the games

Reflect on the Unit

Write about a way you could use probability to help you make decisions.

Fair Game?

You will need a number cube and a shoebox lid.

The game board is a shoebox lid. It is divided into 4 different coloured sections.
Here are the rules.

➤ Each player chooses a different section.
➤ Take turns to drop a number cube onto the middle of the board.
➤ If the number cube lands on your section, you score the number shown
   on the cube. If the cube lands on a diagonal, nobody scores.
➤ The first player to score 25 points wins.

David lost the first game. He said:

> The game board is not fair.
> My area is not one quarter of the
> board. I'm not as likely to win a point
> as Maria or Lindsay.

➤ Investigate David's statement.
  Does this game board show fourths? Explain

➤ Test the game board. Use a shoebox.
  Draw the diagonals of the base.
  Make each section a different colour. Record the results.
  Does the game board seem fair? How do you know?

Lindsay suggested changing the shape of the board.

➤ Investigate other 4-sided game boards.
  Which shapes give a fair game board?
  How do you know?
  How are the fair game boards alike?

 Display Your Work

Report your findings using
words and pictures.

Take It Further

Design a game board that would be fair for 6 players.
Explain why your game board is fair.

UNIT

1

1. On a hundred chart:
   • Shade all the multiples of 3 in one colour.
   • Shade all the multiples of 5 in a different colour.
   a) Describe the position pattern for each set of multiples.
   b) Write the pattern rule for each set of multiples.
   c) Look at the numbers shaded in both colours.
      Write the pattern rule for these numbers.
      Describe the position pattern for these numbers.

2. Write 15 as the sum of three numbers.
   15 = ☐ + ☐ + ☐
   How many different ways can you do it?

2

3. Write a low estimate and a high estimate for each sum.
   a) 713 + 126   b) 235 + 418   c) 436 + 96
   Tell about the strategies you used.

4. Halifax is 4975 km from Calgary.
   Calgary is 1050 km from Vancouver.
   a) How much closer is Calgary to Vancouver than to Halifax?
   b) Suppose you drove from Halifax to Calgary to Vancouver.
      How far would you go?

3

5. Use 20 Snap cubes.
   How many different rectangular prisms can you make with
   a volume of 20 Snap cubes?
   Describe each prism you make.

6. Which figures are similar? How do you know?

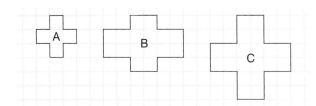

7. Use Plasticine and straws.
Make a skeleton of a square pyramid.
How many edges and how many vertices does it have?

4

8. There are 8 nickels and 7 dimes in a change purse.
How many cents is that?

9. Estimate each product.
a) 5 × 52   **b)** 68 × 6   **c)** 4 × 44   **d)** 9 × 32

10. There are 85 counters.
They are to be shared equally among 6 students.
Each student needs 14 counters.
Are there enough counters? Explain.

11. The tally chart shows the favourite animals
for students in Grades 4 and 5.

Favourite Animal	Number of Students
Bird	|||
Cat	₩₩ ₩₩ ₩₩ ₩₩ ₩₩ ||||
Hamster	₩₩ ||||
Horse	₩₩ ₩₩ ₩₩ ₩₩ ||||
Rabbit	₩₩ ₩₩ ||

a) Draw a bar graph to display these data.
What scale will you use?
b) Which animal is twice as popular as the rabbit?
c) What is the range of the data?
d) How many more students chose a cat over a hamster?
e) Suppose students in Grades 1 and 2 were asked about
their favourite animals. Would the data change? Explain.
f) Write a question about the tally chart or bar graph.
Answer your question.

5

12. This circle graph shows the weather every day
for the month of April in one Alberta town.

a) About what fraction of the month
was it rainy? Cloudy? Sunny?

b) About how many days was it rainy?
Explain.

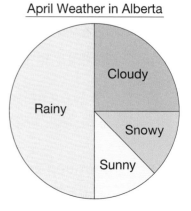

April Weather in Alberta

6

13. Danny and Laurie met for lunch.
Danny arrived at quarter past 1.
Laurie arrived at 1:05 p.m.

a) Who arrived second?
How many minutes later was this person?

b) Draw a digital clock and an analog clock
to show the time each person arrived.

7

14. Use dot paper.
Draw each figure and its lines of symmetry.

a) square   **b)** rectangle   **c)** parallelogram

Which figure has the most lines of symmetry?
The fewest lines of symmetry?

8

15. Fill in each missing number.

a) $1.8 + 3.6 = \square$ **b)** $4.5 - 1.7 = \square$

c) $5.9 + 2.3 = \square$ **d)** $8.4 - 3.6 = \square$

9

16. The tallest known giraffe was about 6.10 m tall.
The tallest human was about 272 cm tall.
Which was taller? How much taller?
Give your answer in centimetres.

17. Use 1-cm grid paper.

    a) Draw 2 different figures with area 18 cm².

    b) Draw 2 different figures with perimeter 30 cm.

18. Multiply.

    a) 2×198 **b)** 4×136 **c)** 333×3 **d)** 164×5

19. This growing pattern is made with rhombuses.
The pattern continues.
The length of each side of a rhombus is 1 unit.

Frame 1   Frame 2   Frame 3

    a) Look at the first three frames.
       What is the perimeter of each frame?

    b) What is the perimeter of frame 4? Frame 7? Frame 10?

    c) Which frame has a perimeter of 30 units? Explain.

20. Divide.

    a) $368 \div 4$ **b)** $229 \div 5$ **c)** $136 \div 6$

21. Use a copy of this spinner.

    a) Predict how many times
       the pointer will land on each colour
       in 30 spins.

    b) Conduct this experiment.

    c) How do the results compare
       with your prediction?

    d) What is the probability of the spinner
       landing on each colour?

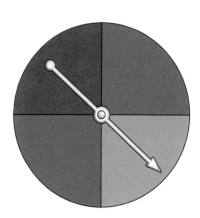

Illustrated Glossary

a.m.: A time between midnight and just before noon.

Angle: Two straight lines cross to form an angle. Each side of an angle is called an *arm*. We show an angle by drawing an arc.

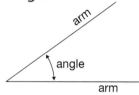

Area: The amount of surface a figure or region covers. We measure area in square units, such as square centimetres and square metres.

Arm: See Angle.

Axis (plural: axes): A number line along the edge of a graph. We label each axis of a graph to tell what data it displays.

Bar graph: Displays data by using bars of equal width on a grid. The bars may be vertical or horizontal.

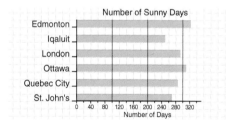

Base: The face that names a solid.

Capacity: A measure of how much a container holds. We measure capacity in litres or millilitres.

Centimetre: A unit to measure length. We write one centimetre as 1 cm.
1 cm = 0.01 m

Century: A unit of time equal to 100 years.

Changing-step growing pattern: A number pattern where the number added increases.

Circle graph: Displays data using a circle divided into sectors. We use a circle graph to show data about one whole or one group.

Favourite Subjects in Grade 4

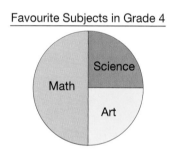

Clockwise / Counterclockwise: The hands on a clock turn in a clockwise direction. The opposite direction is called counterclockwise.

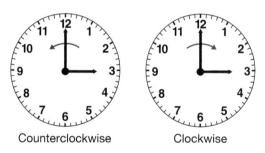

Counterclockwise   Clockwise

Cone: A solid with a circular base, curved surface, and a vertex.

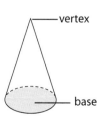

Congruent figures: Two figures that have the same size and shape are congruent.

Coordinates: Describe a location on a grid. Coordinates use a letter and a number to label a column and a row on the grid. The coordinates D2 show the location of the airport on this map:

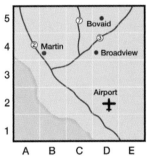

Core: See Repeating pattern.

Cube: A solid with 6 faces that are congruent squares. Two faces meet at an edge.

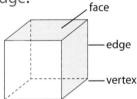

Cylinder: A solid with 2 congruent circular bases joined by a curved surface.

Decade: A unit of time equal to 10 years.

Decagon: A polygon with 10 sides.

Decimal: A way to write a fraction or mixed number. The mixed number $3\frac{2}{10}$ can be written as the decimal 3.2.

Decimal point: Separates the whole number part and the fraction part in a decimal. We read the decimal point as "and." We say 3.2 as "three **and** two-tenths."

Decimetre: A unit to measure length. We write one decimetre as 1 dm.
1 dm = 0.1 m and 1 dm = 10 cm

Degree: 1. A unit to measure the size of an angle. The symbol for degrees is °.

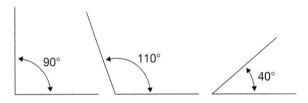

2. A unit to measure temperature. We write one degree Celsius as 1°C.

Denominator: The part of a fraction that tells how many equal parts are in one whole. The denominator is the bottom number in a fraction.

Diagonal: A line that joins opposite corners or vertices of a figure.

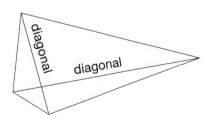

Difference: The result of a subtraction. The difference of 5 and 2 is 3; or 5 – 2 = 3.

Edge: See Cube.

Elapsed time: The amount of time that passes from the start to the end of an event. The elapsed time between when you eat lunch and the end of school is about 3 hours.

Equally probable: The outcomes of an event that are equally likely. For example, if you toss a coin, it is equally probable that the coin will land heads up as tails up.

Equation: Uses the = symbol to show two things that represent the same amount. 5 + 2 = 7 is an equation.

Estimate: Close to an amount or value, but not exact.

Face: See Cube.

Factor: Numbers that are multiplied to get a product. In the multiplication sentence, 3 × 7 = 21, the factors of 21 are 3 and 7.

Gram: A unit to measure mass. We write one gram as 1 g. 1000 g = 1 kg

Grid: See Coordinates.

Growing pattern: A number pattern where we add a number to a term or multiply a term by a number to get the next term.

Hexagon: A polygon with 6 sides.

Hundredth: A fraction that is one part of a whole when it is divided into 100 equal parts. We write one hundredth as $\frac{1}{100}$ or 0.01.

Image: The figure that is the result of a transformation. This is a rectangle and its image after a translation of 6 right and 1 up.

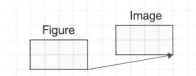

Improbable: An event that is unlikely to happen but not impossible.

Improper fraction: A fraction that shows an amount greater than one whole. The numerator is greater than the denominator. $\frac{3}{2}$ is an improper fraction.

Key: See Pictograph.

Kilogram: A unit to measure mass. We write one kilogram as 1 kg. 1 kg = 1000 g

Kilometre: A unit to measure long distances. We write one kilometre as 1 km. 1 km = 1000 m

Kite: A figure with 4 sides where two pairs of adjacent sides are equal.

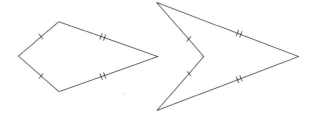

Line of symmetry: Divides a figure into two congruent parts. If we fold the figure along its line of symmetry, the parts match.

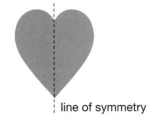

line of symmetry

Linear dimension: Length, width, depth, height, and thickness.

Litre: A unit to measure the capacity of a container. We write one litre as 1 L. 1 L = 1000 mL

Mass: Measures how much matter is in an object. We measure mass in grams or kilograms.

Metre: A unit to measure length. We write one metre as 1 m. 1 m = 100 cm

Millennium: A unit of time equal to 1000 years.

Millilitre: A unit to measure the capacity of a container. We write one millilitre as 1 mL. 1000 mL = 1 L

Millimetre: A unit to measure length. We write one millimetre as 1 mm. One millimetre is one-tenth of a centimetre; 1 mm = 0.1 cm. 10 mm = 1 cm

Mixed number: Has a whole number part and a fraction part. $3\frac{1}{2}$ is a mixed number.

Multiple: Start at a number then count on by that number to get the multiples of that number. Start at 3 and count on by 3 to get the multiples of 3: 3, 6, 9, 12, 15, …

Multiplication fact: A sentence that relates factors to a product. $3 \times 7 = 21$ is a multiplication fact.

Number line: Has evenly-spaced numbers marked in order.

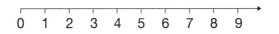

Numerator: The part of a fraction that tells how many equal parts to count. The numerator is the top number in a fraction. In the fraction $\frac{2}{3}$, the numerator is 2, and we count 2 thirds of the whole.

Octagon: A polygon with 8 sides.

Outcome: One result of an event or experiment. Tossing a coin has two possible outcomes. The coin could land heads up or tails up.

p.m.: A time between noon and just before midnight.

Parallel: Two lines that are always the same distance apart are parallel.

Parallelogram: A figure with 4 sides, where 2 pairs of opposite sides are parallel.

Pattern rule: Describes a pattern or how to make a pattern. To make the pattern 1, 2, 4, 8, 16, …, use the pattern rule: Start with 1, then multiply by 2 each time.

Perimeter: The distance around a figure or object. We can find perimeter by measuring and adding side lengths. The perimeter of this rectangle is: 2 cm + 4 cm + 2 cm + 4 cm = 12 cm.

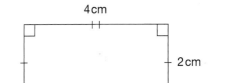

Pictograph: Uses pictures and symbols to display data. Each picture or symbol can represent more than one object. A key tells what each picture represents.

Polygon: A closed figure with three or more straight sides. We name a polygon by the number of its sides. For example, a five-sided polygon is a pentagon.

Prediction: You make a prediction when you decide how likely or unlikely it is that an event will happen.

Prism: A solid with 2 bases.

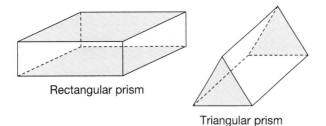

Rectangular prism

Triangular prism

Probability: Tells how likely it is that an event will turn out a certain way. Rolling a 6-faced number cube has 6 equally probable results. The probability that you will roll a 2 is $\frac{1}{6}$.

Probable: An event that is likely but not certain to happen.

Product: The result of a multiplication. The product of 5 and 2 is 10; or $5 \times 2 = 10$.

Proper fraction: Describes an amount less than one. A proper fraction has a numerator that is less than its denominator. $\frac{5}{7}$ is a proper fraction.

Protractor: An instrument that measures the number of degrees in an angle.

Pyramid: A solid with 1 base and triangular faces.

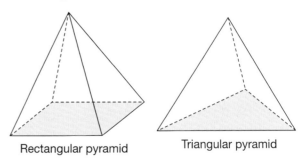

Rectangular pyramid   Triangular pyramid

Quadrilateral: A figure with 4 sides.

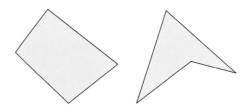

Range: Tells how spread out the numbers in a set of data are. We find the range by subtracting the least value from the greatest value. The range in the heights of the children is 122 cm – 100 cm = 22 cm.

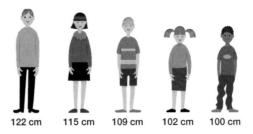

122 cm   115 cm   109 cm   102 cm   100 cm

Rectangle: A figure with 4 sides, where 2 pairs of opposite sides are equal and each angle is a right angle, or 90°.

Rectangular prism: See Prism.

Reflection: Reflects a figure in a mirror line to create a congruent image. This is a triangle and its reflection image.

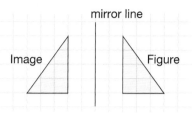

Regular figure: A polygon with all sides equal and all angles equal. Here is a regular triangle.

Related facts: Addition and subtraction have related facts. 2 + 3 = 5 is related to 5 − 3 = 2. Multiplication and division have related facts. 5 × 6 = 30 is related to 30 ÷ 5 = 6.

Remainder: What is left over when one number does not divide exactly into another number. For example, 12 ÷ 5 = 2 R2

Repeating pattern: A pattern with a core that repeats. The core is the smallest part of a repeating pattern. The repeating number pattern: 1, 8, 2, 1, 8, 2, 1, 8, 2,…has a core of 1, 8, 2.

Rhombus: A figure with 4 equal sides, where 2 pairs of opposite sides are parallel.

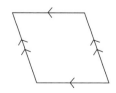

Right angle: Two lines that meet in a square corner make a right angle. A right angle measures 90°.

Rotation: Turns a figure around a turn centre. This is a triangle and its image after a rotation of a $\frac{1}{4}$ turn about one vertex:

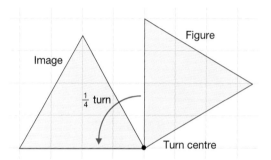

Same-step growing pattern: A number pattern where the same number is added each time.

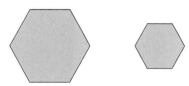

Similar figures: Two figures are similar when they have the same shape. Two similar figures do not have to be the same size. These hexagons are similar.

Skeleton: The frame of a solid that shows the edges and vertices of the solid. This is the skeleton of a pentagonal prism:

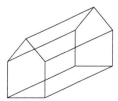

431

Solid: Has length, width, and height. Solids have faces, edges, vertices, and bases. We name some solids by the number and shape of their bases.

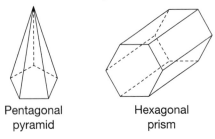

Pentagonal pyramid   Hexagonal prism

Sphere: A solid shaped like a ball.

Square: A figure with 4 equal sides and each angle is a right angle or 90°.

Square centimetre: A unit of area that is a square with 1-cm sides. We write one square centimetre as 1 cm^2.

Square metre: A unit of area that is a square with 1-m sides. We write one square metre as 1 m^2.

Sum: The result of an addition. The sum of 5 and 2 is 7; or 5 + 2 = 7.

Survey: Used to collect data. You can survey your classmates by asking them which is their favourite ice cream flavour.

Tenth: A fraction that is one part of a whole when it is divided into ten equal parts. We write one-tenth as $\frac{1}{10}$ or as 0.1.

Term: One number in a number pattern. For example, the number 4 is the third term in the pattern 1, 2, 4, 8, 16, …

Transformation: A translation (slide), a reflection (flip), and a rotation (turn) are transformations.

Translation: Slides a figure from one location to another. A translation arrow joins matching points on the figure and its image. This figure has been translated 6 squares left and 2 squares up.

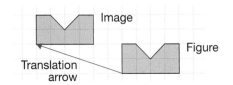

Translation arrow: See Translation.

Trapezoid: A figure with 4 sides, where 1 pair of sides is parallel.

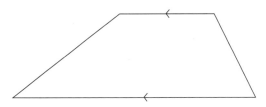

Tree diagram: A picture that shows the different ways to arrange objects.

Triangular prism: See Prism.

Triangular pyramid: See Pyramid.

Turn centre: See Rotation.

Vertex (plural: vertices): 1. A point where two sides of a figure meet.

2. A point where two or more edges of a solid meet.

Volume: The number of congruent cubes that make up a solid.

Index

Acknowledgments

The publisher wishes to thank the following sources for photographs, illustrations, and other materials used in this book. Care has been taken to determine and locate ownership of copyright material in this text. We will gladly receive information enabling us to rectify any errors or omissions in credits.

Photography

Cover Mark Hamblin/age fotostock; pp. 2-3 Ray Boudreau; p. 4 (left) Image State/firstlight.ca; p. 4. (right) Stone/Frank Siteman; p. 5 (left) Stone/Rick Rusing; p. 5 (right) Taxi/Hans Neleman; pp. 14-15 Ray Boudreau; p. 17 Ray Boudreau; p. 19 Ray Boudreau; p. 20 Ray Boudreau; p. 24 Ray Boudreau; pp. 26-27 Ray Boudreau; p. 28 Tom Bean/Corbis/Magma; p. 30 (top) A. Ramey/PhotoEdit Inc.; p. 30 (bottom) Ray Boudreau; p. 36 Ray Boudreau; p. 48 Used by permission of Scott Suko; p. 58 (top) Corel; p. 58 (bottom) Stockbyte; p. 59 Richard Lord/PhotoEdit Inc.; p. 62 Ray Boudreau; p. 64 The Image Bank/Cousteau Society; p. 67 Ray Boudreau; pp. 70-71 Ray Boudreau; p. 75 Image State/firstlight.ca; p. 80 Ray Boudreau; p. 85 Ray Boudreau; p. 88 Henry Horenstein/Index Stock Imagery, Inc.; p. 89 Ray Boudreau; p. 93 Ray Boudreau; pp. 98-99 Ray Boudreau; p. 100 Ray Boudreau; p. (top) Corel; p. 103 (centre and bottom) Ray Boudreau; p. 105 (top left and right) Ray Boudreau; p. 105 (centre left) Photodisc Green/C Squared Studios; p. 105 (centre right) Corel; p. 105 (bottom left) Tom Stillo/Index Stock Imagery, Inc.; p. 106 Ray Boudreau; p. 107 (top) Photodisc Green/David Buffington; p. 107 (bottom) Ray Boudreau; p. 110 Ray Boudreau; pp. 116-117 Ray Boudreau; p. 118 Jeff Greenberg/PhotoEdit Inc.; p. 122 Ray Boudreau; p. 126 Michael Newman/PhotoEdit Inc.; p. 127 Ray Boudreau; p. 131 Ray Boudreau; p. 135 Used by permission of Bombardier; p. 137 Ray Boudreau; p. 139 Ray Boudreau; p. 140 Ray Boudreau; p. 142 Taxi/Jeff Kaufman; p. 148 Corel; p. 151 Ray Boudreau; p. 154 Dave Reede/firstlight.ca; p. 157 Ray Boudreau; p. 161 Rubberball Images; p. 164 Mary Kate Denny/PhotoEdit Inc.; p. 167 Ray Boudreau; p. 169 Corel; p. 172 Reuters NewMedia Inc./Corbis; p. 173 Jeff Greenberg/PhotoEdit Inc.; p. 175 Corel; pp. 176-177 Ray Boudreau; p. 178 Ray Boudreau; p. 181 Eyewire; p. 191 Ray Boudreau; p. 196 Stone/Kathi Lam; p. 196 (top and bottom left inset) Corel; p. 196 (top and bottom right inset) Corel; p. 197 Kit Houghton/Corbis/Magma; p. 200 (top) Corel; p. 200 (bottom) Ray Boudreau; p. 203 Ray Boudreau; p. 205 Ray Boudreau; p. 206 Ray Boudreau; p. 207 (top left) Digital Vision; p. 207 (top centre) Corel; p. 207 (top right) The Image Bank/AJA Productions; pp. 212-213 Ray Boudreau; p. 220 Ray Boudreau; pp. 222-223 Ray Boudreau; p. 226 (top left) Robert A. Tyrrell Photography; p. 226 (top right) Corel; p. 229 (top right) Dwayne Newton/PhotoEdit Inc.; p. 229 (centre left) Photo Researchers Inc.; p. 229 (centre inner left) Stockbyte; p. 229 (centre inner right) Photo Researchers Inc.; p. 229 (centre right) Runk/Schoenberger/Grant Heilman Photography; p. 229 (bottom) Image Source; p. 235 Chip Henderson/Index Stock Imagery Inc.; p. 237 Miles Ertman/Masterfile; p. 240 Ray Boudreau; p. 244 Corel; p. 250 Ray Boudreau; p. 251 Ray Boudreau; p. 252 Ray Boudreau; p. 255 David Young-Wolff/PhotoEdit Inc.; p. 258 Ray Boudreau; pp. 266-267 (left) Tom Bean/Corbis/Magma; pp. 266-267 (centre) Michael Newman/PhotoEdit Inc.; pp. 266-267 (right) Tony Freeman/PhotoEdit Inc.; pp. 268-269 Ray Boudreau; p. 272 Ray Boudreau; p. 277 Ray Boudreau; p. 280 Ray Boudreau; p. 282 Ray Boudreau; p. 285 Ray Boudreau; p. 287 Myrleen Ferguson Cate/PhotoEdit Inc.; p. 288 Ray Boudreau; pp. 290-291; Ray Boudreau; p. 294-295 Ray Boudreau; p. 297 Ray Boudreau; p. 301 The Image Bank/Yellow Dog Productions; p. 304 Ray Boudreau; p. 305 Tony Freeman/PhotoEdit Inc.; p. 320 Ray Boudreau; p. 323 Ray Boudreau; p. 324 Ray Boudreau; p. 327 Ray Boudreau; p. 329 (top) Darrell Gulin/Corbis; p. 329 (bottom) Ray Boudreau; p. 330 Tony Freeman/PhotoEdit Inc.; p. 332 Ray Boudreau; p. 335 Ray Boudreau; p. 339 (bottom) The Image Bank/Etienne Follet; p. 342 Ray Boudreau; p. 345 Ray Boudreau; p. 351 Ray Boudreau; p. 360 (inset) Omni Photo; p. 360 (bottom) Ray Boudreau; p. 361 (bottom left) Rob Melnychuk/Photodisc; p. 361 (bottom centre) Patrick Bennett/Corbis; p. 361 (bottom right) Susan Van Etten/PhotoEdit Inc.; p. 363 (bottom right) Laura Dwight/PhotoEdit Inc.; pp. 362-363 Ray Boudreau; p. 364 Ray Boudreau; p. 369 Ray Boudreau; p. 372 Ray Boudreau; pp. 382-383 Ray Boudreau; p. 385 Ray Boudreau; p. 387 Ray Boudreau; p. 388 (top left) Photodisc Green/Hisham F. Ibrahim; p. 388 (top right) Steve Gorton/Dorling Kindersley Media Library; p. 388 (bottom left) Used by permission of Georgia Mills Direct; p. 388 (bottom right) Michelle D. Bridwell/PhotoEdit Inc.; p. 389 Ray Boudreau; p. 390 David Young-Wolff/PhotoEdit Inc.; p. 393 John Burnett; pp. 396-397 Ray Boudreau; p. 402 Corbis; p. 403 Ray Boudreau; p. 404 Ray Boudreau; p. 410 Ray Boudreau; p. 413 Ray Boudreau; pp. 418-419 Ray Boudreau; p. 418 (top inset) Tom Prettyman/PhotoEdit Inc.; p. 418 (bottom inset) Taxi/West Rock; p. 419 (right inset) Tom Prettyman/PhotoEdit Inc.; pp. 420-421 Ray Boudreau

Illustrations

Kasia Charko, Leanne Franson, Linda Hendry, Paul McCusker, Grant Miehm, Suzanne Mogensen, Allan Moon, NSV Productions, Dusan Petricic, Michel Rabagliati, Bill Slavin, Craig Terlson